UI5 User Guide

How to develop responsive data-centric client web applications

Carsten Heinrigs

UI5 User Guide: How to develop responsive data-centric client web applications

Carsten Heinrigs

Copy Editor: John T. H. Dobson
Cover Designer: Rainer Roland

1. Edition
Copyright © 2018 Carsten Heinrigs

ISBN 978-3-9819591-1-6 (EPub)
ISBN 978-3-9819591-0-9 (Paperback)
ISBN 978-3-9819591-2-3 (PDF)

Table of Contents

List of Figures

Code Listings

Preface

Back in the late 1990s, when I first began to professionally develop web applications, we usually developed page by page. Every page was complete, which means self-contained and separated. There was little shared code, maybe only for the connections to data sources and some default application settings. Modifying such an application often meant repetitive changes to all affected pages. For small applications and simple services, this was fine and may still be the cheapest way. Why use an elaborate approach and extensive frameworks, if a simple CGI-script is sufficient to fulfill the requirements?

In time, when web applications grew in size and complexity, this approach was no longer feasible. With growing size of an application, repetitive code is difficult to maintain consistently, and changes become increasingly troublesome and expensive. Developing teams also grew and developers specialized. We began using more and more templates to separate programming logic and view generation. And with improved browser compliance Cascading Style Sheets (CSS) were used to separate layout and design issues from HTML.

Various servers and server-side frameworks competed to provide solutions for common aspects of web development, like routing, authentication and authorization, connection pooling of data sources, templating and reusability of parts of the user interface, and user input sanitation. Applying the Model-View-Controller (MVC) pattern emerged as the new standard. Still, at that time, web application HTTP requests were usually responded to by full HTML pages generated on the server. Caching was the big thing to improve response times and take load of the involved servers.

Client-side JavaScript is a language, which has been part of web development since the early browser versions. It has mostly been used to add dynamic features to otherwise static webpages and to give instant feedback to user input and actions. Long before the XMLHttpRequest and AJAX, data were loaded in a so called hidden HTML frame of 1 pixel height and processed with JavaScript to avoid the repeated loading of full web pages to respond to user interaction. In time, when PCs got faster CPUs and more memory, it became reasonable to have the client hold more data and do some serious work. Faster JavaScript engines and the hype surrounding AJAX brought another push for client-side JavaScript.

More recently, generating and modifying user interfaces completely with client-side JavaScript has become fashionable. Web servers are no longer responsible for generating HTML pages, but mainly for securely and speedily delivering assets and data following authorized requests. The view and controller parts of the application are separated from the server-side and moved to the client. In this setup, the model part has both server and client-side aspects.

Having developed client-side JavaScript features and applications for years, mostly with only rudimentary external library support, I joined a team of developers working with UI5 to build custom shop floor applications. None of us had done much work with UI5 and so we had no experienced lead developer to guide us. The motivation to write this book stems from the experiences gained in these projects, especially the process of finding common ways of handling typical issues. Exploring the depths of UI5 ourselves, we repeatedly found the need to refactor the whole code even at an early stage after discovering how to proceed on a better path than we previously thought.

1. Why this book?

There are only few books about UI5 on the market. I can recommend the "SAPUI5: The Comprehensive Guide to UI5" for a detailed overview and to understand the general structure of UI5. But it is of limited help to quickly find a good way to solve whatever task is at hand.

Working with UI5, the API Reference is an indispensable source of information, but it is just a reference for the hundreds of objects and their numerous functions. The general documentation included in the UI5 SDK is helpful to get started, but lacks practical details and examples. On the other hand, the code samples lack explanation.

UI5 provides a vast number of namespaces and objects with numerous functions. This is confusing and does not help developers beginning to use the toolkit to learn what is relevant to solve the task at hand. Also, as there are many ways to get something done, it is easy to get things wrong and end up with an inflexible code base, difficult to change and test. When developers become hesitant to touch working code and customers get nervous that modifications take too long and cause seemingly unrelated errors to pop up, we know that we are in serious trouble.

I decided to write this book after realizing that UI5 can actually be very convenient to build data-centric web user interfaces. The main goal is to teach you, the reader, how to use UI5 efficiently to build high quality user interfaces. The book does not cover all of UI5, or even most of it. Instead the focus is on practical solutions for specific tasks, more like a user guide than a technical documentation.

2. Who this book is for

This book is mainly for web application developers. To follow the examples in the book requires some familiarity with JavaScript. Certain parts of the book will be difficult to follow without some understanding of asynchronous HTTP requests. Deep knowledge of the Hypertext Markup Language (HTML) and Cascading Style Sheets (CSS) is not required, however.

If you are interested in finding out how UI5 works, or if you have to use UI5 in your project, this book is for you. No prior knowledge of UI5 is required, but I would like to think that even developers familiar with UI5 will find plenty of interesting approaches to common problems.

3. Structure of the book

Chapter 1, *Introduction* lets the reader get started with UI5 development. It introduces basic conventions and terminology of UI5 and also explains the conventions followed throughout the book.

In Chapter 2, *Building a basic responsive Web Application*, we build the template application to be used as basis for all further examples in the book. This chapter is demanding because many aspects are introduced, but only briefly explained. It is designed to allow the reader to reproduce the steps and get into the process of developing with UI5.

The next chapters are divided into parts. The first part covers the basic tools and user interface elements provided by UI5. It begins with Chapter 3, *Views and Pages*, giving an overview of the available page layouts and explaining their main features. Then we move on to Chapter 4, *Navigation and Routing* and present ways to restrict access for unauthorized users in Chapter 5, *User Permissions*. Handling user actions and giving feedback are the main topics of Chapter 6, *Events and Messages*. The following chapters are concerned with data and how to present and edit them. Chapter 7, *Models* shows how to bind data to user interface elements. How to present, sort and filter lists of data is covered by Chapter 8, *Lists and Tables*. Chapter 9, *Forms and Input Validation* completes this part.

The second part is about solutions to common problems of UI5 development and particularly how to separate domain or business logic from the user interface. It begins with Chapter 10, *Entity specifications: Mapping*, showing a way to organize and provide domain metadata. Then we look at the handling of requests to get the domain data in Chapter 11, *Request Handling*, followed by the presentation of basic objects for these data in Chapter 12, *Custom data objects*. Chapter 13, *Validation* is about validating user input and form data. After this excursion, we finally return to the user interface in Chapter 14, *Form Control Generation*.

The third part is about building an example application. We are building an example order application throughout Chapter 15, *Beginning application development*, Chapter 16, *Edit Order page* and Chapter 17, *Edit Address view*. After that, we look into One Page Acceptance testing in Chapter 18, *Write user interface tests*. We conclude this part with an introduction of how to automate necessary project related tasks, like building a distribution package, generating documentation and maintaining a coding standard in Chapter 19, *Automate development tasks with Grunt*.

4. Online resources for the book

You can download zip archives containing all of the source code listed in the book from the author's website [https://cahein.de/ui5guide/]. The example code is also available at GitHub [https://github.com/cahein/ui5guide/tree/edition_1].

On the website you can also post whatever feedback you have regarding the book. Likewise, if you find errata or other problems with the book, please let me know.

5. Notes on the e-book version

A big problem for anyone creating an e-book are the numerous ways to view them. Many readers use dedicated e-reader devices of different brands and models, while many also use a tablet or desktop computer. The variety of reader/viewer applications further complicates the task. Instead of creating versions for particular devices and distribution channels, this e-book complies with the EPUB® 3.1 specification [https://www.idpf.org/epub/31/spec/epub-spec.html] by the International Digital Publishing Forum.

The code listings in the book are preformatted text displayed in a monospace font. Furthermore, to make the code easier to follow, comments have been added to some of the lines. The drawback of this is that the lines have a fixed width. To minimize the required width, we use a narrow monospace font, which has been embedded in the e-book. If you, nonetheless, find lines being cut off, you have to either decrease the font size or, if possible, increase the visible width of the application window.

About the Author

Carsten Heinrigs began to program HTTP requests, and to parse and transform HTML and SGML documents, in the early 1990s. This became the basis to get a full-time employment at Ocean-7 Development, Inc in New York City in the year 1999. Mostly, the Ocean-7 team was building custom web applications. Learning by doing was the way, always using various languages, new libraries and approaches to get the projects done. On top of that, the author was responsible for the Linux servers of the company. After returning to Germany in 2006, Carsten began to work as a freelancer. He currently lives in Bremen, Germany.

The author initially learned to program with Perl, and wrote DSSSL to transform SGML-documents. Later applications were often developed in Java. HTML, CSS and JavaScript were daily bread. XML was widely used and with it came XSLT, XPath and XQuery. Most projects used SQL databases, either directly of through object/relational mapping frameworks. As the language for various system tasks and rapid web development Ruby gradually replaced Perl.

As a programmer, Carsten was influenced by concepts coming from the Literate programming paradigm and the eXtreme Programming (XP) methodology. He places strong emphasis on the readability of code, on iterative and incremental development and constant refactoring. He enjoys opportunities for pair programming as a way to improve both the quality of code and the knowledge of the programmers.

Carsten regards custom software development, in general, and user interface development in particular, primarily as a communicative process, bringing together all concerned stakeholders.

Chapter 1. Introduction

1.1. Why UI5?

I am and have always been an open source developer, used to downloading, exploring and using whatever tools, libraries and applications are available. Throughout the years I have become increasingly sceptical towards adding dependencies to extended external libraries to projects. How much time for coding needs to be saved to justify introducing a new dependency? How invasive is a library? Does it reduce complexity and simplify development? Does it receive timely security fixes? Which dependencies does it carry and how complex is updating and upgrading? How much effort does it take to replace it at a later stage? The way I see it, these questions require good answers. Otherwise, it is much better to use the common languages and standards.

SAP is not very popular in the open source community. This has some valid reasons if we think about their expensive certification schemes and license policies leading to inflexibility and closed developer circles. But OpenUI5 is open source and I don't see any reason, why we should treat it differently from other "toolkits" in the field, which come from Google or Facebook. Likewise, we should evaluate open standards, like OData, for their usefulness, and not push them aside because we don't like the companies behind them.

UI5 is a JavaScript library of SAP to build browser user interfaces. They call it "UI Development Toolkit for HTML5". This slogan is misleading, because with UI5 we usually don't write any HTML at all. Instead we write JavaScript and maybe XML. But UI5 generates HTML and uses features defined in the W3C HTML5 Recommendation. The toolkit is built upon functionality provided by third party JavaScript libraries like jQuery, D3, DataJS, LESS, among others.

Is UI5 a library, a toolkit, a framework or something else? These are just terms not worth being too opinionated about. SAP calls it a toolkit, so I use that term to avoid any unnecessary confusion.

UI5 is an imposing toolkit. We ought not to touch the UI5 generated part of the HTML Document Object Model (DOM) directly and use custom styles sparingly. This is rather unconventional but quite a relief for someone like me who, over the years, has had to generate, transform and style SGML, HTML and XML. With UI5 it's all JavaScript.

The main strength of UI5 is that we can build user interfaces which adjust nicely to different devices, without much need for device-specific coding or extensive *Cascading Style Sheets (CSS)* media queries. User interaction triggers the expected events, which can be handled with an attached function. Multi-lingual support is easily implemented and convenient to use, including region-specific formatting of values, often called locale (date and number formats, currency). Even accessibiliy features are well prepared and only require little additional effort to make it work. Much of the hard work of building browser user interfaces is hidden in the toolkit.

On the other hand, don't use UI5 if you have to build some artistic page with a unique look and feel or a quickly loading page for high traffic sites. UI5 is best for workplace applications and administrative user interface parts which require little custom styling. It may also be used to provide just a part of the user interface, for example the cart and checkout forms of an online shop.

To present data as responsive lists, tables and forms and to provide elements for navigating, sorting, filtering, searching and grouping, we don't need more than functional styles and the elements should consistently look and behave the same. In a predictable interface, users feel more comfortable and produce better results.

As a general rule, if we want to build a client JavaScript application to present and edit whichever domain data, you should give UI5 a closer look.

1.2. Getting started

There are two versions of UI5. SAPUI5 is integrated in assorted SAP products. OpenUI5 is open source with an Apache License Version 2.0. SAPUI5 provides some additional namespaces, most notably those helping with data visualization. Apart from that, both OpenUI5 and SAPUI5 are identical.

To get going, download the OpenUI5 SDK [http://openui5.org/download.html] and save it somewhere. I recommend creating a folder for multiple versions of UI5 to be able to easily test our work with different UI5 versions. Before you extract the archive, be aware that it doesn't have a common subfolder for all the containing files and folders. Better extract it into an empty folder.

OpenUI5 package listing

```
cahein@nobux:~/progs/javascript/openui5$ ls
1.38  1.44  1.52  1.56
cahein@nobux:~/progs/javascript/openui5$ cd 1.56
cahein@nobux:~/progs/javascript/openui5/1.56$ tree --noreport --dirsfirst -L 1
.
├── content
├── discovery
├── docs
├── downloads
├── js
├── resources
├── test-resources
├── theme
├── versioninfo
├── demoapps.html
├── explored.html
├── explored_v1.html
├── favicon.ico
├── iconExplorer.html
├── index.html
├── index_v1.html
├── legal_agreement_with_privacy.html
├── LICENSE.txt
├── NOTICE.txt
├── patchinfo.html
├── README.txt
├── releasenotes.html
├── search.html
└── versioninfo.html
```

 We only need the `resources` folder of the SDK to develop and run UI5 applications.

We find both an `index.html` and `index_v1.html` in the OpenUI5 SDK folder, both starting a UI5 application. While the Firefox browser allows us to load the application from the file system, the Chrome browser fails with "Cross origin requests" errors unless we start the browser with the `--allow-file-access-from-files` option to allow requests using the file protocol.

Below you see Version 1 of the documentation (`index_v1.html`), which I prefer to the current version. It is faster to navigate and the API section provides a more compact overview.

OpenUI5 index page (Version 1)

1.3. Notes on UI5

UI5 is very large and under constant development. New versions come out frequently and the lists of new and deprecated features are usually long. But the core code base is stable and well tested.

 The maintenance status of UI5 versions is inconsistent. For example, at the time of writing, version 1.38 is the latest version scheduled to receive fixes throughout 2018. 1.44 will receive maintenance throughout 2019 and the latest version 1.52 until the end of 2020. Intermediate versions 1.40, 1.42, 1.46, 1.48, 1.50 and 1.54 are already out of maintenance. The latest stable version at the time of writing was 1.56. It will not receive long-term maintenance. For more information, visit OpenUI5 Versions Maintenance Status [https://openui5.hana.ondemand.com/versionoverview.html].

Because UI5 is a toolkit to build user interfaces, the book is mainly about building an application with a user interface (UI). To begin with UI5 speak, such an application is called a `UIComponent`. A UI5 application can use multiple components from different locations, only restricted by the *Cross-Origin Resource Sharing (CORS)* mechanism.

A Component has a *Web App Manifest*, which is using the JSON format. The manifest can be used to configure numerous things, like dependencies, data sources and cross-navigation scopes, but we mainly use it to configure the application `routes` and `targets`. A route has a `pattern` to match a hash value appended to the URL, a unique `name` allowing the `Router` to identify the route, and a `target` pointing to an object in the manifest `targets` section. A target specifies a view name and a place, where the content created by the `View` is to be added to the HTML.

Technically, a `View` is an object which provides functions to manage an array of `Control` objects and can connect to a `Controller` to handle the user input and actions. The `Control` objects may use `Element` objects to construct their content. We speak about content controls to summarize all objects generating some kind of HTML for the page.

A `Fragment` is meant to be a reusable UI part without "any controller or other behavior code involved" (UI5 documentation "Reusing UI Parts: Fragments"). I don't see, why this is always wise. When a fragment has clearly defined behavior, which can be coded independent from the view they are used for, we may want to include the code in the fragment. This will both improve readability and reduce complexity. Instead of treating this as a dogma, we had better look at each fragment and decide on a case to case basis where to put related 'controller' code.

Because classical desktop-only browser applications are increasingly replaced by *responsive applications*, the book only introduces content controls with responsive capabilities, and primarily those required for most common tasks. To explore all available controls, look into the UI5 API Reference and Samples.

UI5 allows views to be constructed in various formats (XML, JS, JSON, HTML). SAP seems to favor XML views and fragments. All sample views and fragments of the UI5 documentation are XML. On the other hand, the API Reference is all JavaScript.

XML appears somehow to be more readable, but JavaScript can be written quite readably, as well. After all, we see the same control names, like Page, Toolbar, Button, Table, Column, List, Item, and their aggregation names and properties, too. The major difference is that XML is hierarchical and nesting is inherit, while in JavaScript we have variables holding controls, which may be used anywhere in the code.

As a rule, I prefer to use JavaScript for both views and fragments. Yet, the separation of view and controller aspects is observed throughout the book and it should be simple enough to rewrite the views in XML if needed.

1.3.1. Extended objects: common functionality

UI5 objects are not really classes in the sense of ECMAScript 6, but are called classes nonetheless. Regardless of this rather academic observation UI5 provides common functionality by extending objects.

The base class of all UI5 objects is the `sap.ui.base.Object`. It provides access to the object metadata through its `getMetadata` function.

The main class of UI5 is the `sap.ui.core.Core`, which boots the framework and can create a `sap.ui.core.Component` or `sap.ui.core.UIComponent`.

All user interface elements extend the `sap.ui.base.EventProvider`, which provides functions to deal with events. In general, we find an `attach` and `detach` function for every control event. For example, the `Button` press event has `attachPress` and `detachPress` functions.

The `sap.ui.base.ManagedObject` extends the `EventProvider`. It provides the functionality for data binding and for handling object properties, aggregations, associations and events, all of which are identified by a name.

In UI5 data binding means to connect data held by a `Model` (provider) with an object extending the `ManagedObject` (consumer). Model data are accessed by a property path. To be accessible, the Model must be within the scope of the ManagedObject, that means it must be set either to the object we want to bind data to, or to one of its parents. We can set a Model to any ManagedObject with the setModel function and get it with the getModel function.

All objects extending the ManagedObject can be constructed with two optional parameters. The first is an ID string, the second a settings object for the various properties, associations, aggregations and events, of which are inherited and others specific to the particular object.

- *Property* values must be primitives. Only the JavaScript data types String, Number and Boolean are used. All have default values. If property values are limited, UI5 uses enumeration objects to define allowed values. In this book, strings are used as values, but a reference to the enumeration object is generally mentioned. For each property the object provides getter and setter functions. We can bind properties to a model property.
- *Aggregations* hold references to other objects somehow extending the ManagedObject. They must be of a certain type and may either be a single object or an array of objects. We can bind an aggregation to a model property. An array of data objects is bound to aggregations with the help of template controls of the required type.
- *Associations* must also be of a specific type. Associated is either a single object ID or an array of IDs. An association may be the ID of a selected item or row, a legend for the calendar, or some invisible text control used by screen readers.
- *Events* need a handler function attached to it, which is given a related event object. The event object always has a source and often additional parameters. The UI5 API Reference lists available parameters.

In UI5 all content controls are subclasses of the sap.ui.core.Element, which extends both the sap.ui.base.EventProvider and the sap.ui.base.ManagedObject.

The Element object provides the tooltip expecting a string and the layoutData expecting a single object of type sap.ui.core.LayoutData, while the customData and dependents aggregations expect an array of objects.

The related functions always follow the same pattern. For example, to handle the tooltip property we have the destroyTooltip, getTooltip and setTooltip functions. And to handle the array of custom-Data we have the addCustomData, destroyCustomData, getCustomData, indexOfCustomData, insertCustomData, removeAllCustomData and removeCustomData functions.

All sap.ui.core.Control objects extend the Element. It adds the visible, busy and busyIndicatorDelay properties and the related getter and setter functions (getVisible/ setVisible, getBusy/ setBusy). The Control also provides functions to handle style classes (addStyleClass, hasStyleClass, removeStyleClass and toggleStyleClass). These functions give us a way to apply custom style directives. Note that only custom styles, which were previously added, can be removed. But beware, UI5 styles are complex and often difficult to overwrite.

A special category of controls are the so-called layout controls, which represent a web page layout. These controls generate HTML containers representing aggregations to which controls are added.

1.3.2. Dependency handling

UI5 offers two different sets of functions to handle dependency loading:

- The functions sap.ui.require and sap.ui.define are designed to support *Asynchronous Module Definitions (AMD)*. Currently the modules/ dependencies are still loaded synchronously but this is going to be changed in upcoming releases.

- The jQuery.sap.require function loads and executes the given modules/ dependencies synchronously and will continue to do so. The corresponding jQuery.sap.declare function registers a module as existing. Both functions are deprecated with version 1.52, but still being used internally by the sap-ui-core and library files.

Making dependencies transparent is an important improvement. An unfortunate effect of using the AMD approach is that all dependent code needs to be AMD compliant as well. Due to the generally asynchronous loading of resources, dependencies are managed by a loader.

There are a few AMD compliant loaders available today. I prefer RequireJS [http://requirejs.org/] because it is small (version 2.3.5 minified has only 17738 bytes) and only concerned with loading files/ modules and handling dependencies. UI5 includes version 2.1.8 as a third party resource, but uses the above mentioned custom functions instead.

Throughout the book we use the above-mentioned sap.ui.require and sap.ui.define functions for UI5 objects and dependencies. For our custom library we refrain from using any dependency handler and simply load the files in the required order.

1.3.3. OData

OData is an OASIS Standard technically named "OASIS Open Data Protocol". The committee is presided over by SAP and Microsoft with several other major companies involved. The current version is OData 4. It specifies a standard way of defining REST services and how to provide metadata about the defined entities and collections. It also includes specifications about parameters concerning paging, sorting, filtering and searching.

It is no coincidence, that the major companies selling large monolithic applications are pushing this standard. It helps them define REST services for their data. If well defined and stable OData services are available, they can be convenient to use and avoid significant work.

Because the OData implementation provided by UI5 is good and stable, there is no reason not to use it. But REST services implementing the OData protocol are not always well adapted to the specific user interface requirements. Rather than spreading such problems throughout the application code, it will be best to clearly address them in one place through custom UI5 ODataModel objects.

Having said that I must clarify that in this book we are not going to cover OData services. Please do not interpret this as a statement against OData. The simple truth is that while I have worked with OData services, I did not have enough professional exposure to feel comfortable offering you best practices and good advice on the subject, that's all.

1.4. JSON and types

> JSON is a lightweight, text-based, language-independent data interchange format. It was derived from the ECMAScript programming language, but is programming language independent. JSON defines a small set of structuring rules for the portable representation of structured data.
> —The JSON Data Interchange Format

All HTTP requests in this book expect the response to be MIME type application/json. Also, the application manifest and other configuration data are formatted in JSON.

JSON has two basic data structures: array and object. An array is surrounded by square brackets '[]' and an object by curly brackets '{}'. Objects contain name/value pairs. The name and value are separated by a colon ':'. Each object, array and name/value pair is separated by a comma ','. Whitespace is ignored unless it is part of a value.

Values may be of type number or string. Additionally, the JSON standard defines three literal name tokens: boolean values `true` and `false`, and a `null` value. JavaScript has only two additional primitive types: `undefined` and `Symbol`.

Incoming data usually come from a source with a different set of data types. The information contained in the type definition is lost along the way and therefore needs to be provided in some way. The OData standard defines a JSON dialect to make metadata available. Anyway, incoming data often need to be processed to do some initial re-formatting and type conversion, for example to convert a date string to a JavaScript Date instance.

Throughout the book, you can find many types which, depending upon the context, refer to something else. This can be confusing, but seems unavoidable. For example, the UI5 `Input` control has a `type` property which sets the `type` attribute of the HTML `input` element. And for the `value` property we can set a `type` which is used to format and validate the value of the `Input` control.

There are some relevant sets of types to consider:
- JavaScript types and data structures [https://developer.mozilla.org/en-US/docs/Web/JavaScript/Data_structures].
- UI5 defined general data types under the namespace `sap.ui.model.type`.
- OData uses EDM Primitive Data Types [https://docs.microsoft.com/en-us/dotnet/framework/data/adonet/entity-data-model-primitive-data-types]. These correspond to the types of UI5 namespace `sap.ui.model.odata.type`.
- Types like date, email address, phone number and whatever custom types.
- Allowed values for UI5 `type` properties are often specified as enumerations of strings.

1.5. Some words about JavaScript

JavaScript was first announced at the end of 1995. It had a common specification standardized by the ECMA International organization since June 1997 named ECMA-262. This is why JavaScript is also called ECMAScript®. There have always been different implementations. And browser inconsistencies have always been part of JavaScript client-side development. While standard compliance has increased in recent years, the diversity of devices and their capabilities has also increased. Our testing requirements need to take that into account.

For many years, the ECMA-262 standard remained stable. But since 2015 the standard has been continuously worked on and a new edition has been published every year. There are many interesting new features and the major browser vendors are striving to implement most of it for their newer versions. But browsers not supporting these features are still being used on too many systems to just ignore them. Most developers promote the use of the most current standard and best practises. Nevertheless, the handling of old browsers is an additional task to take care of and professional programming is not just a fun activity. We simply have to look at the costs and benefits of using whichever feature. Anyway, always bear in mind that good coding does not depend upon using the latest features!

JavaScript has only few data types, but the type of any property and variable can be anything from a string to a function. This feature offers a lot of possibilities and flexibility, but may lead to unexpected behaviour difficult to debug. It helps to test function parameters with `typeof` and `instanceof` to get more robust code.

For example, to make sure that a certain required function is available we use the `typeof` operator. The `indexOf` function is available for types Array and String. To ensure the function is available we test it like this:

```
function funcName(arrayOrString) {
    if (typeof arrayOrString.indexOf !== "function") {
        throw TypeError("Cannot continue without indexOf");
    }
    // do something using the indexOf function
}
```

If a function requires an instance of a particular object, we had better test it. Here we make sure that the given parameter is an Array:

```
function funcName(a) {
    if (!(a instanceof Array)) {
        throw TypeError("We need an Array here");
    }
    // do something with the array
}
```

And it won't hurt to use the corresponding `try { } catch(e) { }` to make use of the error messages thrown. Otherwise, the code execution may come to a halt.

A variable which hasn't been declared is not `undefined` (primitive type), but its type is undefined. This is why it is safer to write (`typeof somevar === "undefined"`) instead of (`somevar === undefined`), which will throw a `ReferenceError` if the variable is not declared.

Owing to the popularity of object oriented languages, many developers are used to constructors, classes and inheritance and try to emulate these concepts in JavaScript. The ECMAScript standard introduced classes in edition 6 of June 2015. Apart from that, JavaScript is very flexible and offers a wealth of possibilities to implement functionality.

JavaScript allows constructs to implement internal scope for variables and functions. Only selected variables and functions are made accessible to the outside. This is known as module pattern. The basic language feature making this possible is known as anonymous closure or immediately-invoked function expressions (IIFE). Here is the most simple example:

```
(function() {
}());
```

We can easily add parameters to it:

```
const someObject = {};

(function(someObject) {
}(someObject));
```

Only those variables and functions which are either added to a defined object or returned by the function as object property are being made accessible. This helps us to control the scope and also to choose public function names which are different from those used within the function expression. It is a simple and straightforward way to organize functionality and design an API.

The following example code adds the sayHi function as saySomething property to the ans object:

```
const ans = {};
(function() {
   let _counter = 0;
   function countGreetings() {
      _counter++;
   }
   function sayHi() {
      countGreetings();
      console.log("Moin " + _counter);
   }
   ans.saySomething = sayHi;
}());
```

The same result can be achieved like this:

```
const ans = (function() {
   function sayHi() {
      console.log("Moin");
   }
   return {
      saySomething: sayHi
   }
}());
```

JavaScript as a language doesn't have namespaces. But because any variable and object property can hold any type, a namespace can be easily created:

```
const ans = {};
ans.to = {
   add: {}
};
ans.to.add = function(str) {
   alert(str);
};
ans.to.add("this is just a silly example");
```

Namespaces are just object property paths with objects along the path levels. They provide a convenient way to group functionality.

Another unusual and therefore often confusing feature of JavaScript is the change of this. In programming languages it is usually the receiving context, which determines 'this'. In JavaScript it is the calling context. Thus 'this' depends on how the function is called. This feature frequently leads to problems and errors difficult to debug. We just have to be aware of it when we write and call functions.

To set the context explicitly, the bind, call and apply functions can be used. Here is another example adding the saySomething function to the ans object by explicitly setting the this context:

```
const ans = {};
(function() {
   function sayHi() {
      console.log("Moin");
   }
   this.saySomething = sayHi;
}).apply(ans));
```

1.5.1. Synchronous Requests

> Synchronous XMLHttpRequest outside of workers is in the process of being removed from the web
> platform as it has detrimental effects to the end user's experience. (This is a long process that takes
> many years.) Developers must not pass false for the async argument when current global object is a
> Window object. User agents are strongly encouraged to warn about such usage in developer tools and
> may experiment with throwing an "InvalidAccessError" DOMException when it occurs.
> —XMLHttpRequest - Living Standard — Last Updated 15 June 2018

When we request some URL synchronously, the code stops execution while waiting for the response.
Meanwhile, the application freezes and the user doesn't know what is going on. This is why synchro-
nous request have a bad reputation and browser vendors have deprecated the use of synchronous
XMLHttpRequest.

To standardize the handling of asynchronous operations, the ECMAScript 2015 specification includes a Promise object. A Promise has three states. Initially it is 'pending', then it may settle to either
'fulfilled' (success) or 'rejected' (failure). For this, it provides the related methods then and catch. Both
functions return a Promise object for chaining. Recently, these efforts have been supplemented by the
introduction of asynchronous functions using the async operator and a related await operator to wait
for a Promise to be fulfilled.

All this doesn't change the fundamental problem. With asynchronous requests, it is unknown, if and
when a response will come in, or an asset becomes available. This opens up many possible scenarios
to be dealt with. We neither know the sequence of responses nor their outcome. In effect, all code
which depends upon some request somewhere in the code now needs to handle the request state.
Asynchronous operations require additional coding and sometimes introduce unnecessary complexity to otherwise trivial issues.

The efforts to handle asychronous requests are convincing because they reflect the complexity of
servers and services we have to deal with. But there are also cases where asynchronous requests are
merely annoying and do more harm than good. On the one hand, these are cases where the failure of
an asynchronous operation is fundamental and the application just can't function, on the other hand
cases where a failure is highly unlikely and doesn't justify coding against it.

Keeping things simple and code readable are important aspects not to be pushed aside too easily just
to handle unlikely cases of request failure. On the other hand, when we use services whose condition
is essentially unpredictable, we had better prepare the application to handle all reasonable scenarios.

Think about a JSON file required to initialize a configuration object. A synchronous request simply
waits for the file to be loaded and then our object is ready. The code is straightforward, because
success and failure can be instantly assessed and handled. Turning this into a asynchronous request
we have to handle the event that the file has been successfully loaded and then call the object waiting
for the response. All other objects down the line depending upon the configuration being loaded also
have to be prepared to deal with the request state.

Instead of making this a principal issue, it is better to look at the likelihood of blocking scenarios
and the efforts required to handle asynchronous requests. If necessary resources are not available,
the application will simply not run. In such a scenario, the only benefit we get from asynchronous
requests is that we can show the user a polite message, telling him or her that the application won't
run. But if crucial files of the application can't be successfully requested within a reasonable time,
we have a serious problem beyond the scope of the web application. Still, we have to consider the

importance of the negative user experience not getting the message telling them that the application doesn't work. In this regard, the visitor of a public website is different from an employee using workplace applications. While courting the visitor might make sense, the worker will probably not care much about the message but mainly be concerned about not getting his work done.

Unfortunately, the major forces behind the JavaScript standard seem dedicated to imposing their perspective upon all. We see that implemented in the Fetch API, which doesn't allow any synchronous request. We therefore cannot replace the XMLHttpRequest with the better designed Fetch API without losing an important ability. Alternatively, we would have to program an essentially identical thing twice.

From my point of view, there are and continue to be valid reasons for using synchronous requests in particular cases. There is no reason to generally refrain from using the `async` parameter of the `XMLHttpRequest.open` function. As long as enough developers are using it, the major browser vendors will be forced to keep it for the forseeable future - despite all their scaremongering warnings.

1.6. Custom code

Learning to use UI5 was, in part, a process of separating code into custom namespaces. One is for application specific functions and another for more generally useful functions. In this book, we use the application namespace `oum` ("OpenUI5 User Manual") and the common library namespace `oui5lib` ("OpenUI5 Library"). To each of the namespace objects, we add a `namespace` function to easily handle further levels of the namespace. It will always return a defined object, either the already existing namespace or a newly created one.

The `oui5lib` is an open source GitHub project [https://github.com/cahein/oui5lib]. Basically, it is a collection of functions, fragments and controllers to speed up development with UI5. It came out of the processes of building applications with UI5. Most of the functions are just a way to avoid duplicating code. The library can be added to any UI5 application with little effort.

1.7. Conventions of example listings in the book

Generally speaking, coding conventions in JavaScript are extremely diverse. The so-called JavaScript coding "standard" is so different from other recommendations, that it still reads weird to many senior JavaScript developers. In reality, there is no accepted coding standard and therefore each project needs to specify its own.

For example, the UI5 "General Guidelines" recommend using tabs instead of spaces and have no maximum line length. I will not follow these. And the "Naming Conventions" for variables and object field names are strongly recommending to follow a flavor of Hungarian Notation, where the variable name is prefixed with a string indicating the variable type. I use it for some UI5 objects, for example 'oController' or 'oEvent'. The UI5 conventions regarding folder names are being followed.

Except for Chapter 2, *Building a basic responsive Web Application*, the basic view and controller setup code is always the same and is therefore usually omitted in the book examples. Likewise, the code to add controls to a layout control is generally left out, but is explained in Chapter 3, *Views and Pages*. As default layout we use the `sap.m.Page`.

In the views, `oController` is used to refer to the related controller. Unless otherwise mentioned, controllers are named the same as the views. Likewise, throughout the book, `oEvent` is used as name for event objects.

Controllers generally extend a `BaseController`, which provides convenience functions to get the `Router`, the `EventBus`, the i18n `ResourceBundle`, and for logging. In the controllers, `this` may refer to these functions.

Controller functions are written as properties:

```
functName: function(oEvent) {
}
```

1.8. Development Environment

UI5 development means writing JavaScript and XML. Additionally, we work with JSON formatted files. Nothing special. Simply use whatever programming environment you are comfortable with.

While it is possible to run UI5 applications from the file system, for development it is often better to have a webserver running. I use a simple ruby command for that:

```
ruby -run -e httpd /path/to/webapp/ -p 8801          Listen on port 8801
```

A helpful tool for UI5 development is the *UI5 Inspector extension* for the Chrome browser. It lets you navigate the UI5 object tree representation of the HTML page and also shows the properties and bindings of any object.

Chrome - UI5 Inspector Extension

For both Firefox and Chrome, there is an excellent tool to find accessibility defects, the aXe Developer Tools [https://axe-core.org/]. I strongly recommend using it, if only to learn about the accessibility guidelines.

Testing our applications with a screen-reading software and keyboard navigation is quite instructive because it helps us to find structural/navigational deficits of pages and spots where we have to add informative text. For the Linux operating system you can install the Orca [https://wiki.gnome.org/Projects/Orca] screen reader. Unfortunately, neither the Chrome nor the Opera browser support Orca. For Windows there are several screen readers of which NonVisual Desktop Access (NVDA) [https://www.nvaccess.org/] is open source and free of charge.

Node.js packages are used for various project related tasks, like testing, generating documentation, building and packaging. You can download NodeJS™ [http://nodejs.org/en/download/] and install it. Part of the installation is the Node Package Manager (**npm**). For information on how to use it, please look into the npm documentation [https://docs.npmjs.com/].

To help the team implement a common coding style and do some code quality verification, a so called linter or linting-tool can be used. Especially for JavaScript, which allows so much, such a tool can only be recommended. There are several libraries out there. I prefer ESLint [https://eslint.org/] mainly because it is highly configurable and generates helpful messages.

Do yourself a favor and install a command line JSON syntax validator. It will be much more convenient than using an online validator. Instead of pasting JSON into the text input area of an internet page, we can quickly validate a bunch of JSON files with one command. I prefer the Python demjson [https://deron.meranda.us/python/demjson/] package because it prints the most informative messages.

Output of JSON validation tool

```
cahein@nobux:~/projects/book/assets/mockdata$ jsonlint-py *.json
addresses.json: ok
order.json: ok
orders.json:16:16: Warning: Strict JSON does not allow a final comma in an object
 (dictionary) literal
    |  At line 16, column 16, offset 430
    |  Object started at line 12, column 16, offset 291
orders.json: ok, with warnings
products.json: ok
statuses.json: ok
cahein@nobux:~/projects/book/assets/mockdata$ █
```

On the other hand, if you don't have Python installed, consider the node package named "jsonlint-cli".

1.8.1. Testing

I have always liked writing tests, mainly because tests increase my confidence that the code actually does what it is supposed to. Additionally, having to write tests improves my coding and well-written tests best explain the use and purpose of functions under test. Unfortunately, despite all the talk about automated testing, even today customers don't like to pay for the initially required additional work because the return value is difficult to quantify.

So, if you find yourself in a situation, where you need to prioritise tests, the following thoughts might come in handy: In my opinion, writing tests for the user interface is least critical because the visual parts are usually the best tested ones of an application. By using the application, users tend to find errors and unexpected behavior quickly. The most critical tests concern the domain logic and conventions. These tests are not just a great source of information but are invaluable to gain user confidence. We must get the data right or we lose!

As JavaScript developers, we have to choose among a number of testing frameworks. Most of these are in-browsers test runners, which means we load a HTML file into a browser loading the testing framework itself and all other required code for the tests to be executed and the results shown. There are also headless testing frameworks which can run tests without a browser. To do that we can use a browser-independent JavaScript engine like Rhino [https://developer.mozilla.org/en-US/docs/Mozilla/Projects/Rhino]. The major advantage is that we can better integrate our tests into the development workflow, for example as part of our distribution building process. The major disadvantage is that our code should really be tested in the actual environment it is written for. But with some additional setup we can also do both.

UI5 comes bundled with third-party libraries for unit testing (QUnit [https://qunitjs.com/] and Sinon [https://sinonjs.org/]). Mainly for reasons of personal preference I use the Jasmine Testing Framework instead. Some of the tests presented in the book use the Jasmine Standalone package. You will have to download it to run the tests for yourself.

The Jasmine Standalone [https://github.com/jasmine/jasmine/releases] package is another zipped archive without a common top level folder. Beware to extract it into a separate folder. The archive contains a `lib` folder which contains the folder with all the Jasmine code we need.

Chapter 2. Building a basic responsive Web Application

You may expect to find some introductory "Hello World" example here, but there is already one in the UI5 Developer Guide "Get Started" section. The point is that any serious UI5 application needs preliminary work for setup and objects which we don't always want to repeat.

In this chapter, we will therefore build a basic web application without business logic. Step by step, the reader is introduced to concepts and flow of developing with UI5. The resulting application will be used as a template in the following chapters. Don't worry if questions remain open and you don't fully understand what is going on. As far as necessary, we will dive into the details of particular aspects in the following chapters.

The code presented in this chapter is nearly complete. If you are new to UI5, you will get the most out of it by reproducing the steps and using the browser console and UI5 Inspector to constantly inspect the state of the application along the way.

The following figure shows some basic objects composing a UI5 web application. The Core creates a UIComponent. The UIComponent creates content, which usually is a View providing a root element with aggregations for views. There are two such root elements for responsive applications. A full page root element is a sap.m.App with an aggregation named pages, while a sap.m.SplitApp provides two aggregations named masterPages and detailPages.

We use a Router to have View objects, mostly providing some kind of Page, placed into an aggregation specified by controlId and controlAggregation.

Figure 2.1. Basic structure of a UI5 Application

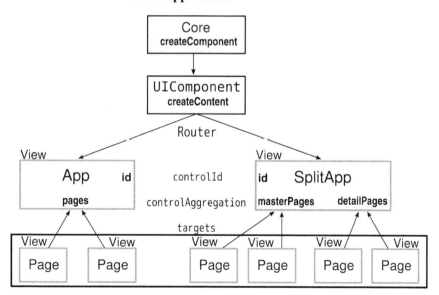

2.1. Bootstrap the Core

Final Class sap.ui.core.Core

Core Class of the SAP UI Library

This class boots the Core framework and makes it available for the application via method sap.ui.get-Core().

—openUI5 API

We begin our application by creating a project folder with a document root folder for a web server to serve files from. According to UI5 conventions, the document root folder is named webapp. Into that folder we either link or copy the UI5 SDK resources folder. All files and folders created in this chapter go into the webapp folder.

To use UI5, we first have to load the main file of the toolkit, which is called sap-ui-core.js. To do that, we create an index.html file with the bootstrap script element.

The sap-ui-core.js file is expected to be located in the resources subfolder relative to the index.html.

Listing 2.1. sap-ui-bootstrap

```
<!DOCTYPE HTML>
<html>
  <head>
    <title>UI5 User Guide</title>
    <meta http-equiv="content-type" content="text/html;charset=UTF-8"/>
    <script id="sap-ui-bootstrap"
            type="text/javascript"
            src="resources/sap-ui-core.js"
            data-sap-ui-theme="sap_belize"                    Stylesheet theme name
            data-sap-ui-libs="sap.m"
            data-sap-ui-preload="async"
            data-sap-ui-bindingSyntax="complex"></script>
  </head>
  <body>
  </body>
<html>
```

As a first step, we just need to ensure that the UI5 Core is loaded and ready. After loading the index.html into a browser, we should now be able to get the sap.ui.core.Core object using the browser console.

```
> core = sap.ui.getCore();
⟨·  ▶ I
      {addPrerenderingTask: f, applyChanges: f, applyTheme: f, attachControlEvent: f,
> configuration = core.getConfiguration();
⟨·  ▶ I
      {applySettings: f, getAccessibility: f, getAnimation: f, getAppCacheBuster: f,
> sLanguage = configuration.getLanguage();
⟨·  "en-US"
> locale = configuration.getLocale();
⟨·  ▶ I
      {getExtension: f, getExtensionSubtags: f, getLanguage: f, getPrivateUse: f, get
```

2.2. Application manifest

> This specification defines a JSON-based manifest file that provides developers with a centralized place to put metadata associated with a web application.
>
> —Web App Manifest - W3C Working Draft 22 September 2017

Our application needs a manifest. The general format of a web application manifest is specified as a W3C Working Draft [https://www.w3.org/TR/appmanifest/].

The specifics of the UI5 manifest are listed in the UI5 SDK "Developer Guide" section "Essentials > Structuring: Components and Descriptor > Descriptor for Applications, Components, and Libraries".

Now, let us create such a `manifest.json` file. We keep it minimal.

Listing 2.2. Descriptor Application Manifest

```
{
    "start_url": "index.html",                    The application start URL
    "sap.app": {
        "id": "ui5guide",                         Mandatory attribute
        "type": "application",                     Application type: application, component, library
        "title": "{{ui5guide.title}}", ❶
        "applicationVersion": {                    Mandatory attribute
            "version": "0.1"
        }
    },
    "sap.ui": {
        "deviceTypes": { ❷
            "desktop": true,
            "tablet": true,
            "phone": false
        },
        "supportedThemes": [
            "sap_belize",
            "sap_belize_hcb",                      High Contrast Themes
            "sap_belize_hcw"
        ]
    },
    "sap.ui5": {
        "minUI5Version": "1.38.37",
        "contentDensities": { ❸
            "compact": true,
            "cozy": true
        },
        "dependencies": {
            "libs": {
                "sap.m": {}
            },
            "components": { }
        }
    }
}
```

❶   Mandatory. The `sap.app.title` property, and likewise the `sap.app.subtitle` and `sap.app.description` properties are defined as i18n keys in double curly brackets. The i18n key for the title is ui5guide.title. We will keep that in mind for the time when we want to implement multi-lingual support.

❷   Mandatory. Specify, on which devices the application is expected to run. There are three categories of devices: "desktop", "tablet", and "phone". Our sample application does not claim to be suited for mobile phones, at least in portrait orientation.

❸   Mandatory. Specify, which content density modes are supported. Available options are "compact" and "cozy". Density mode 'compact' features reduced dimensions of controls. Density mode 'cozy' optimizes for touch devices.

2.3. Create a Component

You can use a ComponentContainer to wrap a UIComponent and reuse it at any place within the openUI5 control tree.

To render UI components, you must wrap them in a ComponentContainer. It is **not** possible to use the placeAt method to place UI components directly in a page.

—openUI5 Developer Guide

A component may be an application, a supporting component or a library. Here, we want to build an application. In UI5, an application is called a component. There are two types of components:

• faceless components extending sap.ui.core.Component,

• components with a user interface extending sap.ui.core.UIComponent.

A UIComponent can be understood as an engine to create visible content for a web page. Just a few more steps and we will have something to show.

With the Core loaded and the manifest.json in place, we are ready to create a Component.

To be able to add content to the HTML page, our sap.ui.core.UIComponent needs to be wrapped in a sap.ui.core.ComponentContainer. Therefore, in the head element of the index.html, after the sap-ui-bootstrap script, we add the following code:

Listing 2.3. Create a Component

```
 1 <script type="text/javascript">
 2
 3 sap.ui.getCore().attachInit(function () { ❶
 4     sap.ui.require([
 5        "sap/ui/core/ComponentContainer"
 6     ], function (ComponentContainer) {
 7        const oumComponent = sap.ui.getCore().createComponent({
 8           id: "oumComponent", ❷
 9           name: "oum"                          Namespace of our custom Component
10        });
11        new ComponentContainer({ ❸
12           component: oumComponent              Associate the component
13        }).placeAt("oumContent");               Insert the ComponentContainer into the HTML
14     });
15 });
16
17 </script>
```

❶ With asynchronous loading in mind, we want to make sure that the Core is ready, before we let it create a Component. For this, we use the attachInit function. The OpenUI5 API explains: "The given function will either be called as soon as the framework has been initialized or, if it has been initialized already, it will be called immediately."

❷ The component id is required to get the Component from the Core using sap.ui.getCore().getComponent(componentId);

❸ The Shell control can be used as a wrapper for an App or SplitApp, allowing to set a background style and also providing properties for an application title and logo, among others. It mostly affects the user interface of wide browser windows.

```
new sap.m.Shell({
    title: "OpenUI5 User Guide",
    app: new ComponentContainer({
            component: oumComponent
        })
}).placeAt("oumContent");
```

In lines 4 to 6, we see the sap.ui.require syntax, which is the same for sap.ui.define (see Listing 2.4, "Initialize the Component"). This is the UI5 way of handling the loading of dependencies. For now, it is sufficient to note the path syntax used to load the sap.ui.core.ComponentContainer (line 5), which we then add as parameter to the function (line 6). This is used to instantiate a new ComponentContainer (line 11 to 13).

In lines 7 to 10, we use the createComponent function of the Core to import the Component with id "oumComponent" and name "oum". This means, that UI5 will first request oum/Component-preload.js and next oum/Component.js. Where does UI5 look for these resources?

> By default, all files have to be located in a subfolder of the resources folder of the Web application. If this location is not appropriate, deviations can be configured ...
>
> —openUI5 Developer Guide

The default resource path is resources. But we want our Component.js file to be in the webapp folder along with the index.html and the manifest.json. For this situation, UI5 has the concept of a resource path mapping. We add such an entry to the Listing 2.1, "sap-ui-bootstrap":

```
data-sap-ui-resourceroots='{
    "oum": "."
}'
```

With the above resource root entry added, UI5 resolves "oum" to ".", so that oum/Component.js is expected to be found at ./Component.js.

We create such a file Component.js and define our oum.Component, which extends sap.ui.core.UIComponent. Next, we create an empty Component-preload.js (we show how to generate the 'real' file in Section 19.4, "Building the distribution package"). This will be requested before the Component is initialized. We get an HTTP 404 error, if it can't be found.

Listing 2.4. Initialize the Component

```
sap.ui.define([
  "sap/ui/core/UIComponent"
], function (UIComponent) {
  const Component = UIComponent.extend("oum.Component", {
    metadata: {
      manifest: "json"                        Read the metadata from the manifest.json
    }
  });

  oum.Component.prototype.init = function() {      The Component init function
    UIComponent.prototype.init.apply(this, arguments);
  };
  return Component;
});
```

In line 13 of our Listing 2.3, "Create a Component", we tell the ComponentContainer to be placed at "oumContent". We add this 'place' with a few lines of HTML into the body container of the index.html.

```
<section class="sapUiBody">
  <div id="oumContent"></div>
</section>
```

 While UI5 is often used to construct complete pages, we can place content from a UI5 UI-Component anywhere in the HTML DOM. This makes it possible to use UI5 just for some parts of an application or website.

At this stage, excluding the resources folder, we have the following files in our webapp folder:

```
├── Component.js
├── Component-preload.js
├── index.html
└── manifest.json
```

Let's take a break at this point and load the application in a browser. The HTML source looks like this:

```
<html class="sap-desktop  sapUiTheme-sap_belize sapUiMedia-Std-Tablet sapUiMedia-
StdExt-Tablet" dir="ltr" data-sap-ui-browser="cr61" data-sap-ui-os="linux" lang="en-US"
data-sap-ui-animation="on">
  ▶ <head>…</head>
  ▼ <body role="application">
    ▼ <section class="sapUiBody">
      ▼ <div id="oumContent" data-sap-ui-area="oumContent">
        ▶ <div id="__container0" data-sap-ui="__container0" class=
          "sapUiComponentContainer">…</div>
        </div>
      </section>
      <div aria-hidden="true" id="sap-ui-preserve" class="sapUiHidden
      sapUiForcedHidden" style="width: 0px; height: 0px; overflow: hidden;"></div>
    </body>
  </html>
```

UI5 generates and modifies the HTML. Different versions of UI5 do it differently. It should be clear that we don't want to directly manipulate the generated Document Object Model (DOM). That could only lead to trouble and debugging nightmares. Instead, we are going to use UI5 to do it for us.

Back in the browser console, we see some HTTP 404 errors, because the component tries to load language properties from the default URI i18n/i18n.properties. We can ignore them for now. But we should now be able to access the Component:

Figure 2.2. Browser console: Access Component

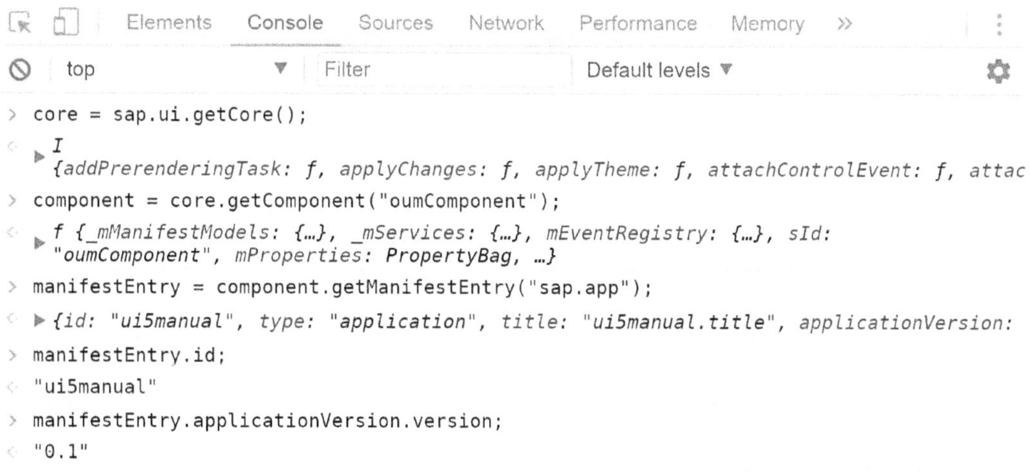

2.4. Router

So far, our component shows a blank screen. For now, we leave it at that and move on to prepare the routing instead. The routing configuration is part of the application manifest. We begin by adding a routing section to the Listing 2.2, "Descriptor Application Manifest":

Listing 2.5. Routing section of the manifest

```
1  "sap.ui5": {
2     ...
3     "routing": {
4        "config": { ❶
5           "routerClass": "oum.Router",
6           "viewType": "JS",
7           "viewPath": "oum.view",
8           "controlId": "oumApp",                  See Listing 2.7, "XML view with sap.m.App"
9           "controlAggregation": "pages"
10       },
11       "routes": [                                 The routes array
12          {
13             "pattern": "",
14             "name": "home",
15             "target": "entry"
16          }
17       ],
18       "targets": {                                The named targets
19          "app": {
20             "viewName": "app",                    ./view/app.view.xml
21             "viewType": "XML"
22          },
23          "entry": {
```

```
24              "viewName": "entry",              ./view/entry.view.js
25              "title": "{ui5guide.title}"
26          }
27        }
28      }
29 }
```

❶   The config section contains the global router configuration and default values that apply for all routes and targets.

In line 5, we specify a custom router class oum.Router. A custom Router is easily set up and gives us more flexibility during the development process. It extends the sap.m.routing.Router.

Listing 2.6. Initial custom Router

```
sap.ui.define([
    "sap/m/routing/Router"
], function (mRouter) {
    mRouter.extend("oum.Router", {
        constructor: function() {
            mRouter.apply(this, arguments);
        },
        destroy: function() {
            mRouter.prototype.destroy.apply(this, arguments);
        }
    });
});
```

To make it work, we have to make sure that the oum.Router is loaded before the UIComponent is constructed, which is why we add it to to the dependencies. Then we can initialize the oum.Router in the Component init function (see Listing 2.4, "Initialize the Component"):

```
sap.ui.define([
    "sap/ui/core/UIComponent",
    "oum/Router"
], function (UIComponent) {
    ...

    oum.Component.prototype.init = function() {
        UIComponent.prototype.init.apply(this, arguments);

        this.getRouter().initialize();
    };
    return Component;
});
```

Now, let's get back to Listing 2.5, "Routing section of the manifest". In the routes section (lines 11 to 17), we add a route with a pattern "" and a name "home", which will load the target "entry" (lines 23 to 26) into the controlAggregation "pages" (line 9) of the root control with controlId "oumApp" (line 8).

When we load the index.html without any pattern, our oum.Router is configured to navigate to the route named "home" with a target "entry".

In the targets section, we specify two targets, which we have to provide. We defined our viewPath as "oum.view" (line 7). Because we defined a resource root "oum" as ".", our views go into the folder ./view.

For the `App` view, we use XML, which is not the default `viewType` (line 6). The default values set in the `routing/config` section may be overwritten by each target entry. Therefore, we have to specify it explicitly in our target configuration (line 21).

2.5. First views

A view is a file in the `view` folder. The name is composed of the `viewName` and the `viewType`. According to the UI5 naming conventions the name of our "app" view of type XML is `app.view.xml`.

Listing 2.7. XML view with sap.m.App

```
<mvc:View xmlns="sap.m"
          xmlns:mvc="sap.ui.core.mvc"
          displayBlock="true">
  <App id="oumApp"
       defaultTransitionName="slide"
       />
</mvc:View>
```

 The `<App>` id attribute value "oumApp" is the `controlId` default value (Listing 2.5, "Routing section of the manifest" line 8).

To load the app view, we use the `createContent` function of the `UIComponent` by adding some lines to our `Component.js`:

```
oum.Component.prototype.createContent = function() {
    return sap.ui.view({
        viewName: "oum.view.app",
        type: "XML"
    });
};
```

So far, we still haven't created any visible content. It is about time for our first view to show at least something.

With the default `routing.config.viewPath` specified as "oum.view", "entry" is expected to resolve as "oum.view.entry" and requested as `./view/entry.view.js`. Therefore, we create a file `entry.view.js` in the `view` folder.

Listing 2.8. Basic JS View returning Page

```
sap.ui.jsview("oum.view.entry", {
    createContent: function(oController) {
        const entryPage = new sap.m.Page();
        return entryPage;
    }
});
```

 Since version 1.56, the `sap.ui.jsview` function has been marked as deprecated. Yet the API Reference for the OpenUI5 (v1.56) states, that there is no replacement for JavaScript views and the function still has to be used. This is not clever, but don't worry, because UI5 doesn't carelessly remove deprecated functions. Therefore, until things clear up, we leave this issue aside.

With our first two views in place, we have the following tree in our `webapp` folder:

```
├── view
│   ├── app.view.xml
│   └── entry.view.js
├── Component.js
├── Component-preload.js
├── index.html
├── manifest.json
└── Router.js
```

Let us load the `index.html` into the browser. We still see an empty page, but the Page header now has a background color. The Chrome web browser extension UI5 Inspector shows us more:

```
⌖  ⬚  │  Elements   Console   UI5   Sources   Network   Timeline   Profiles   Application

Control Inspector   Application Information

Search                        Filter results(0)   ✔ Show Namespace   ✔ Show Attributes

<!OpenUI5 v1.49.6>
▼<sap-ui-area id="sap-ui-static">
    <sap.ui.core.InvisibleText id="__text0">
▼<sap-ui-area id="oumContent">
  ▼<sap.ui.core.ComponentContainer id="__container0">
    ▼<sap.ui.core.mvc.XMLView id="__xmlview0">
      ▼<sap.m.App id="__xmlview0--oumApp">
        ▼<sap.ui.core.mvc.JSView id="__jsview0">
          ▼<sap.m.Page id="__page0">
              <sap.m.Bar id="__page0-intHeader">
```

 The `id` of our `<App>` is not "oumApp", like we specified in Listing 2.7, "XML view with sap.m.App". We don't get it from the `Core` either: `sap.ui.getCore().byId("oumApp")` returns `undefined`. Nevertheless, when we remove the id we get an error, because it is the default `controlId` configured in our manifest (see Listing 2.5, "Routing section of the manifest").

The generated HTML should not concern us too much, because we never want to directly manipulate the UI5-generated DOM. We are writing JavaScript and XML to build the application, not HTML.

2.6. Internationalization

In Listing 2.2, "Descriptor Application Manifest" we specified the `sap.app.title` of our application as `ui5guide.title`, but we haven't provided the related resources yet. UI5 uses property files as resource for the language specific texts, one for each language and an additional default language file.

By default, these property files go into the `i18n` folder. We begin with two languages, English and German ("en" and "de"), and need to create an `i18n_en.properties` and `i18n_de.properties` file. The default language properties file should further be copied to `i18n.properties`.

Initially, the language properties contain only the language specific string for key `ui5guide.title`.

```
ui5guide.title=UI5 User Guide
```

```
ui5guide.title=UI5 Benutzerhandbuch
```

To start with, UI5 determines the current language from the browser `window.navigator` object. Various language code formats are accepted. We don't want to deal with the complexities of language codes, so we can simplify the issue by just looking at the first two characters of the language code. In order to achieve this, we can add some code to our `Component init` function (see Listing 2.4, "Initialize the Component").

Listing 2.9. Loading the i18n Resource

```
 1 const configuration = sap.ui.getCore().getConfiguration();
 2 let languageCode = configuration.getLanguage();
 3 if (typeof languageCode === "string" && languageCode.length > 2) {
 4     languageCode = languageCode.substring(0, 2).toLowerCase();
 5 }
 6 const availableLanguages = ["en", "de"];                        Array of available languages
 7 if (availableLanguages.indexOf(languageCode) === -1) {
 8     languageCode = "en";                                        Default language
 9 }
10 configuration.setLanguage(languageCode);
11
12 const i18nModel - new sap.ui.model.resource.ResourceModel([
13     bundleUrl: "i18n/i18n.properties",
14     bundleLocale. languageCode
15 });
16 this.setModel(i18nModel, "i18n");                               Set the i18n model for the Component
```

First, we extract the current language string from the UI5 configuration (line 2). If it is longer than 2 characters, we cut off all characters after the second and change the remainder of the string to lower case (lines 3 to 5). If the language string is not one of the available languages, the default language is used (lines 6 to 9). To settle the issue, one of the available language strings is set as UI5 current language (line 10).

The resources are handled by a `ResourceModel`. To load the proper language file, the two parameters `bundleUrl` and `bundelLocale` have to be set (lines 12 to 15). The model is then set to the `Component` with the model name `i18n` (line 16).

After providing language properties and making them available for our component, we are now ready to add a title to our entry page (Listing 2.8, "Basic JS View returning Page"). We do that by setting the value for the `title` property of the `Page`.

Listing 2.10. Page with title

```
const entryPage = new sap.m.Page({
    title: "{i18n>ui5guide.title}"                               Model property notation: modelName>propertyPath
});
```

2.7. Adding a LanguageSwitcher

The language setting can be overwritten with a URL parameter `sap-language` (index.html?sap-language=de). That's good, but not enough. To allow the user to change the language derived from the `Navigator` object, the user interface needs a language switcher.

A language switcher requires an array of available languages, as well as a property to store the currently selected language. In Listing 2.9, "Loading the i18n Resource" we already specified available languages (line 6) and the default language (line 8).

At this point, the application will benefit from custom configuration data and custom library functions. Let us begin by creating a config.json in the webapp folder.

Listing 2.11. Custom configuration

```
{
    "componentId": "oumComponent",
    "availableLanguages": [ "en", "de" ],
    "defaultLanguage": "en"
}
```

As custom library namespace we use oui5lib. To prepare the namespace, create a folder oui5lib and in that folder a file init.js with the following code:

Listing 2.12. Initialize custom namespace

```
if (typeof oui5lib === "undefined") {
    var oui5lib = {};
}
oui5lib.namespace = function(string) {                    Function to get or create namespace
    let object = this;
    const levels = string.split(".");
    for (let i = 0, l = levels.length; i < l; i++) {
        if (typeof object[levels[i]] === "undefined") {
            object[levels[i]] = {};
        }
        object = object[levels[i]];
    }
    return object;
};

const xhr = new XMLHttpRequest();
xhr.open("GET", "config.json", false);                    Request config.json synchronously
xhr.onload = function() {
    if (xhr.status === 200 || xhr.status === 0) { ❶
        try {
            const configData = JSON.parse(xhr.responseText);    Parse incoming JSON
            oui5lib.config = configData;                        Store config data
        } catch (e) {
            throw new Error("Not valid JSON");
        }
    }
};
xhr.send();
```

❶   The HTTP response status 200 means 'OK'. A status 0 is not a valid HTTP status code and therefore can not come from a web-server. Instead, it is set by the XMLHttpRequest object and applies when the request URL uses the 'file' protocol. We add it here to be able to run the application from the file system, without a web-server.

We need to ensure that the oui5lib/init.js is loaded before the Component init function is executed. It could be done through a script tag in the index.html. But because the custom library belongs to the component, it is better to require it in the Component.js.

```
sap.ui.define([
  "sap/ui/core/UIComponent",
  "oum/Router",
  "oui5lib/init"
], function (UIComponent) {
  ...
});
```

Finally, in order for UI5 to find the resource, we also have to add another resource root to Listing 2.1, "sap-ui-bootstrap":

```
data-sap-ui-resourceroots='{
  "oum": ".",
  "oui5lib": "./oui5lib"
}'
```

On top of the configuration data, the language switcher will also need a function to set the current language and update the Component i18n `ResourceModel`. Let us use the namespace `oui5lib.configuration` and therefore create a file `configuration.js` in the `oui5lib` folder for this. The following code listing is quite long, but it merely consolidates the language-related code snippets we already looked at.

Listing 2.13. Custom namespace for configuration issues

```
(function () {
  const configuration = oui5lib.namespace("configuration");    Namespace oui5lib.configuration

  function getConfigData(key) {
    if (typeof oui5lib.config === "undefined" ||
        typeof oui5lib.config[key] === "undefined") {
      return undefined;
    }
    return oui5lib.config[key];
  }

  function getComponent() {                                      Function to get the Component
    const componentId = getConfigData("componentId");
    if (typeof componentId === "string") {
      return sap.ui.getCore().getComponent(componentId);
    }
    return null;
  }

  function setLanguageModel(languageCode) {
    const i18nModel = new sap.ui.model.resource.ResourceModel({
      bundleUrl: "i18n/i18n.properties",
      bundleLocale: languageCode
    });
    const component = getComponent();
    component.setModel(i18nModel, "i18n");                       Set i18n model for the Component
  }

  function getAvailableLanguages() {
    return getConfigData("availableLanguages");
  }

  function setCurrentLanguage(languageCode) {
    const availableLanguages = getAvailableLanguages();
```

```
    if (!(availableLanguages instanceof Array)) {                No available languages configured?
       return;
    }

    if (availableLanguages.indexOf(languageCode) === -1) {       Not one of the available languages?
       languageCode = getConfigData("defaultLanguage");          Use default language instead
    }
    const ui5configuration = sap.ui.getCore().getConfiguration();
    ui5configuration.setLanguage(languageCode);                  Set language of Core configuration
    setLanguageModel(languageCode);
    oui5lib.config.currentLanguage = languageCode;               Used by the following function
  }

  function getCurrentLanguage() {
    return getConfigData("currentLanguage");
  }


  configuration.getComponent = getComponent;                     Add functions to the namespace
  configuration.getAvailableLanguages = getAvailableLanguages;   Used by the LanguageSwitcher
  configuration.getCurrentLanguage = getCurrentLanguage;
  configuration.setCurrentLanguage = setCurrentLanguage;
}());
```

 Only the `getComponent`, `setCurrentLanguage`, `getCurrentLanguage` and `getAvailableLanguages` functions are added to the namespace. The `getConfigData` and `setLanguageModel` functions will be "private".

We use similar code in the `Component.js`. We should refactor it to avoid duplicating code for the same task. To be sure that the `setCurrentLanguage` function is loaded, we add it as a requirement to the `oui5lib/init.js` with

```
sap.ui.require([
    "oui5lib/configuration"                                      Loading happens synchronously
]);
```

Next, we replace the code from Listing 2.9, "Loading the i18n Resource" (lines 6 to 16) with

```
oui5lib.configuration.setCurrentLanguage(languageCode);
```

Everything needed for a language switcher is now ready and loaded. We will implement it as a fragment to be able to reuse it for different views. The name is `oum.fragment.LanguageSwitcher`, which resolves to path `./fragment/LanguageSwitcher.fragment.js`.

To define a fragment, the `sap.ui.jsfragment` function is used. The first parameter is the fragment name and the second an object with a `createContent` function returning a content control. Here, it is a `Select` control.

Listing 2.14. LanguageSwitcher fragment

```
sap.ui.jsfragment("oum.fragment.LanguageSwitcher", {
    createContent: function () {
        const languageSelect = new sap.m.Select({          Construct the Select control
            tooltip: "{i18n>language.select.tooltip}"        i18n
        });

        const availableLanguages = oui5lib.configuration.getAvailableLanguages();
        if (availableLanguages !== undefined) {
            let item;
            availableLanguages.forEach(function(languageKey) {
                item = new sap.ui.core.Item({                Construct Item for each language
                    text: "{i18n>language." + languageKey + "}",   i18n keys: language.de and language.en
                    key: languageKey
                });
                languageSelect.addItem(item);                Add the Item to the Select
            });
        }
        return languageSelect;                               Return the Select control
    }
});
```

We want to add the LanguageSwitcher to the header of the entry page. In the UI5 documentation we find the Bar control, which can be used in this case.

> The Bar control can be used as a header, sub-header and a footer in a page. It has the capability to center a content like a title, while having other controls on the left and right side.
>
> —openUI5 API

Let's change our entry view to use a sap.m.Bar control with the title in the middle and the LanguageSwitcher fragment to the right. To achieve this, the Page is modified to use the customHeader aggregation. We learn more about using this aggregation from the UI5 documentation.

> If this aggregation is set, the simple properties "title", "showNavButton", "NavButtonText" and "icon" are not used.
>
> —openUI5 API

By using a Bar for the page header the title property we use in Listing 2.10, "Page with title" is ignored. Instead, we now use the sap.m.Title control for the title. Its text comes from our i18n properties. The level is set for semantic purposes and the titleStyle to style the title text.

Listing 2.15. Add LanguageSwitcher fragment to Page

```
const headerTitle = new sap.m.Title({
    text: "{i18n>ui5guide.title}",                         i18n property
    level: "H2", titleStyle: "H2"                          Enumeration sap.ui.core.TitleLevel
});

const headerBar = new sap.m.Bar({
    design: "Header",                                      Enumeration sap.m.BarDesign
    contentMiddle: [ headerTitle ],
    contentRight: [
        sap.ui.jsfragment("oum.fragment.LanguageSwitcher")  Add fragment to the page header
    ]
```

```
});

const entryPage = new sap.m.Page({
    customHeader: headerBar                          Set customHeader aggregation
});
```

We introduced a few new i18n keys in Listing 2.14, "LanguageSwitcher fragment" ("language.se-lect.tooltip", "language.en" and "language.de"), which we have to add to the i18n properties. After reloading the application, we should see a title and a drop-down list in the header. Please note: You may have to clean the browser cache to see the i18n model refreshed.

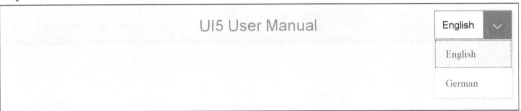

The language select control looks good, but unfortunately, it doesn't do anything yet. If the user selects a different language, we want our code to get busy. To achieve this we attach a function to the LanguageSwitcher Select change event. The UI5 API Reference explains when the event occurs:

This event is fired when the value in the selection field is changed in combination with one of the following actions:

- The focus leaves the selection field
- The Enter key is pressed
- The item is pressed

—openUI5 API

On top of handling a change of the selection, we would like to display the currently selected language. For this, we need to set our current language as the selectedKey of the control.

Listing 2.16. Attach handler to the change event of the language Select control

```
const languageSelect = new sap.m.Select({
    tooltip: "{i18n>language.select.tooltip}",
    selectedKey: oui5lib.configuration.getCurrentLanguage(),
    change: function (oEvent) {
        const selectedLanguage = oEvent.getParameter("selectedItem").getKey();
        if (oui5lib.configuration.getCurrentLanguage() !== selectedLanguage) {
            oui5lib.configuration.setCurrentLanguage(selectedLanguage);
        }
    }
});
```

Switching back to the browser, we clear the cache as a routine precaution, then reload the application and should now see the LanguageSwitcher switching the language.

```
                    UI5 Benutzerhandbuch                              Deutsch  ⌄
```

Let us look again at the filesystem tree at this stage:

```
├── fragment
│   └── LanguageSwitcher.fragment.js
├── i18n
│   ├── i18n_de.properties
│   └── i18n_en.properties
├── oui5lib
│   ├── configuration.js
│   └── init.js
├── view
│   ├── app.view.xml
│   └── entry.view.js
├── Component.js
├── Component-preload.js
├── config.json
├── index.html
├── manifest.json
└── Router.js
```

2.8. Logging

UI5 can be set into debugging mode by setting the URL parameter `sap-ui-debug` to `true` (index.html?sap-ui-debug=true). The generated console messages provide valuable insights about how UI5 works, but they are not really tailored to our needs. Let's change that.

Any serious logging implementation needs to output messages depending upon a logging level setting. It should be enough to use four logging levels: DEBUG, INFO, WARN, ERROR. Error messages will always be logged. To set an initial log level, we add a property to the `config.json`. During development we set `"logLevel": "DEBUG"`.

To get the log level, we add the related function to the `oui5lib.configuration` namespace:

```
function getLogLevel() {
    const logLevel = getConfigData("logLevel");
    if (logLevel === undefined) {
        return "WARN";                          Defaults to "WARN", if not configured
    }
    return logLevel;
}
configuration.getLogLevel = getLogLevel;        Add function to namespace
```

UI5 includes a Logging API under namespace `jQuery.sap.log`. It seems unnecessarily complex for our custom logger, which should simply log messages to the browser console. Therefore, let us next create a `logger.js` in our custom library folder (`webapp/oui5lib`).

Listing 2.17. Namespace oui5lib.logger

```
/* eslint no-console: "off" */                          Overwrite ESLint default configuration
/* eslint no-fallthrough: "off" */
(function () {
   const logger = oui5lib.namespace("logger");

   if (!window.console) {                               Without console object
      logger.debug = function(){};                      no logging
      logger.info = function(){};
      logger.warn = function(){};
      logger.error = function(){};
      return;
   }

   logger.debug = function(msg) {
      console.log("oui5lib - DEBUG " + msg);
   };
   logger.info = function(msg) {
      console.info("oui5lib - INFO " + msg);
   };
   logger.warn = function(msg) {
      console.warn("oui5lib - WARN " +  msg);
   };
   logger.error = function(msg) {
      console.error("oui5lib - ERROR " + msg);
   };

   const logLevel = oui5lib.configuration.getLogLevel();

   switch (logLevel) {                                  Disable logging depending upon the log level
   case "ERROR":
      logger.warn = function(){};
   case "WARN":
      logger.info = function(){};
   case "INFO":
      logger.debug = function(){};
   }
}());
```

We make loading mandatory by adding the logger as a dependency in the `oui5lib/init.js`:

```
sap.ui.require([
   "oui5lib/configuration",
   "oui5lib/logger"
], function() {
   oui5lib.logger.info("oui5lib successfully loaded");
});
```

To use the logger, let us add a logging entry in the LanguageSwitcher `change` event handler function of Listing 2.16, "Attach handler to the change event of the language Select control ".

```
const selectedLanguage = oEvent.getParameter("selectedItem").getKey();
oui5lib.logger.debug("selected language: " + selectedLanguage);
```

After clearing the browser cache and reloading the application, we should now see a log message in the console when we change the language selection.

```
oui5lib - selected language: de                            logger.js?eval:30
oui5lib - selected language: en                            logger.js?eval:30
>
```

2.9. More Routes and Pages

So far, we only have the entry view and don't fail gracefully, if a requested route doesn't exist. To change that, we add a `bypassed` property to the `routing.config` properties of Listing 2.5, "Routing section of the manifest".

Listing 2.18. Configuring target for non-existing routes

```
"bypassed": {
   "target": "noRoute"
}
```

The related target is added to the `routing.targets` section:

```
"noRoute": {
   "viewName": "noRoute",
   "viewType": "XML"
}
```

The view is of type XML.

Listing 2.19. No such route Page

```
<mvc:View xmlns="sap.m"
          xmlns:mvc="sap.ui.core.mvc">
  <MessagePage
      title="{i18n>http.404error}"
      text="{i18n>view.noRoute.text}"
      description="{i18n>view.noRoute.description}"/>
</mvc:View>
```

After adding the new i18n properties, we can see the page by requesting a non-existing route: `index.html#/help`.

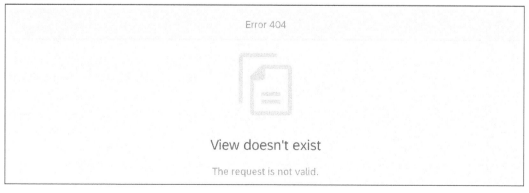

To assist the user with questions, our application should have a help section with a table of contents and the help content in two separate containers. This is the typical `SplitApp` scenario. The SplitApp has two aggregations named `masterPages` and `detailPages` to which we can add views.

Listing 2.20. XML view with SplitApp

```
<mvc:View xmlns="sap.m"
          xmlns:mvc="sap.ui.core.mvc"
          displayBlock="true">
  <SplitApp id="oumSplitApp"                                        ID of the SplitApp
           defaultTransitionNameDetail="slide"
           defaultTransitionNameMaster="slide"
           masterButtonTooltip="{i18n>help.master.button.tooltip}"
           />
</mvc:View>
```

We add a route to the `routes` section of the application manifest.

```
{
   "pattern": "help",
   "name": "help",
   "target": ["helpIndex", "helpIntro"]                            Two targets
}
```

And the related targets to the `targets`.

Listing 2.21. SplitApp target entries

```
"splitApp": {
   "viewName": "splitApp",
   "viewType": "XML"
},
"helpIndex": {
   "parent": "splitApp",                                           Parent target name
   "viewName": "help.index",
   "title": "{i18n>view.help.index.title}",
   "controlId": "oumSplitApp",                                     SplitApp ID
   "controlAggregation": "masterPages"                             SplitApp aggregation
},
"helpIntro": {
   "parent": "splitApp",
   "viewName": "help.intro",
   "title": "{i18n>view.help.intro.title}",
   "controlId": "oumSplitApp",
   "controlAggregation": "detailPages"
}
```

The target configuration tells the router to load the `View` "help.index" into the "splitApp" `parent` with `controlId` "oumSplitApp" into the `controlAggregation` "masterPages". Meanwhile, the "help.intro" is being loaded into the `controlAggregation` "detailPages".

If you have followed the excercises up to this point, you should now be able to create the help index and help intro views (see Listing 2.8, "Basic JS View returning Page"). If it should be an XML view (see Listing 2.7, "XML view with sap.m.App"), the `viewType` of the manifest targets would have to be specified, as the default is "JS". After that is done, the above request `index.html#/help` will now be serviceable.

To get to the help section, we want to add a button to the entry page right next to the language select. So far, our `oum.Router` (Listing 2.6, "Initial custom Router") hasn't been called directly to navigate. It extends the `navTo` function from the `sap.m.routing.Router`, which has a default behavior we want to change. We read about that in the documentation:

> IF the given route name can't be found, an error message is logged to the console and the hash will be changed to empty string.

> —openUI5 API

Instead of navigating to the home page, we want to navigate to the target named "noRoute". This is the same behavior we configured through the manifest `bypassed` property (see Listing 2.18, "Configuring target for non-existing routes").

Listing 2.22. Router function to navigate to a named target

```
vNavTo: function(routeName, routeParameters, replace) {
    const route = this.getRoute(routeName);
    if (typeof route === "undefined") {                         There is no route with the given name
        this.navTo("noRoute");
    } else {
        if (routeParameters === undefined || routeParameters === null) {
            routeParameters = {};
        }
        if (typeof replace !== "boolean") { ❶
            replace = false;
        }
        this.navTo(routeName, routeParameters, replace);         Navigate to the route
    }
}
```

❶ Parameter `replace` concerns the browser history. Here, the default is set to `false`, which means that browser history entries are set.

Now, we are ready to implement our help button. Because we want to be able to use the help button for other views as well, we implement it as a fragment with the path `fragment/HelpButton.fragment.js`. It will return a `sap.m.Button` with the `icon` and `tooltip` properties set and a handler function attached to the `press` event.

Fragments are not meant to do anything, but, in this case, it is clear what the help button is supposed to do, isn't it? Why put the function somewhere else?

Listing 2.23. HelpButton fragment

```
 1 sap.ui.jsfragment("oum.fragment.HelpButton", {
 2    createContent: function () {
 3       const btn = new sap.m.Button({
 4          icon: "sap-icon://sys-help",
 5          tooltip: "{i18n>button.help.tooltip}",
 6          press: function() {
 7             const component = sap.ui.getCore().getComponent("oumComponent");
 8             const router = component.getRouter();
 9             router.vNavTo("help");
10          }
11       });
12       return btn;
13    }
14 });
```

The icon URI (line 4) could also be specified with `sap.ui.core.IconPool.getIconURI("sys-help")`. The default `IconPool` of UI5 contains hundreds of names. Be aware, that these icons are no images but embedded font, which can be easily styled. The OpenUI5 SDK includes the Icon Explorer application to explore the icons. Start it by loading `test-resources/sap/m/demokit/icon-Explorer/webapp/index.html` into your browser. We can add or overwrite icons using the `IconPool.addIcon` function.

To add the button to the user interface, we add it as a fragment to the `contentRight` aggregation of the `Bar` control used for the `Page` `customHeader` aggregation (see Listing 2.15, "Add LanguageSwitcher fragment to Page").

```
const headerBar = new sap.m.Bar({
   design: "Header",
   contentMiddle: [ headerTitle ],
   contentRight: [
      sap.ui.jsfragment("oum.fragment.LanguageSwitcher"),
      sap.ui.jsfragment("oum.fragment.HelpButton")
   ]
});
```

Figure 2.3. Entry page with custom header

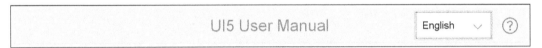

2.10. Adding Home and Back Buttons

When we navigate to the SplitApp with the two help views, there is no way back or home.

Figure 2.4. SplitApp Header

Nearly every application with a user interface needs 'back' and 'home' buttons. And because they are needed for most of the views, we need `BackButton` and `HomeButton` fragments.

But before we get to that, our router needs to be able to navigate back. In contrast to standard browser behavior, we don't ever want to navigate "away" from our application. If there is no prior application history, the back button will just navigate to "home".

Listing 2.24. Router function to navigate back

```
navBack: function() {
   const history = sap.ui.core.routing.History.getInstance();      Routing history singleton
   const previousHash = history.getPreviousHash();

   if (typeof previousHash === "undefined") {
      this.navTo("home", {}, true);
   } else {
      window.history.go(-1);
   }
}
```

Both the `BackButton` and `HomeButton` fragments need to get the `Router`, like the `HelpButton` (see Listing 2.23, "HelpButton fragment" lines 7 and 8). Instead of repeating the code, we move it into a utility namespace `oui5lib.util` and add it to the requirements in the `oui5lib/init.js`.

Listing 2.25. Setup custom utility namespace

```
(function (configuration) {
   const util = oui5lib.namespace("util");

   function getComponentRouter() {
      const component = configuration.getComponent()
      return component.getRouter();
   }

   util.getRouter = getComponentRouter;                    Add function getRouter to namespace
}(oui5lib.configuration));
```

After refactoring the HelpButton fragment, we get to the BackButton and HomeButton fragments. They are nearly identical, except for the `icon`, `tooltip` and routing target.

Listing 2.26. BackButton fragment

```
sap.ui.jsfragment("oum.fragment.BackButton", {
   createContent: function () {
      const btn = new sap.m.Button({                       Construct the button control
         icon: "sap-icon://nav-back",
         tooltip: "{i18n>button.back.tooltip}",
         press: function () {
            const router = oui5lib.util.getRouter();        Get the Router
            router.navBack();                               Navigate back in recorded history
         }
      });
      return btn;                                           Return the button control
   }
});
```

The only tasks left are to add new i18n entries and the new buttons to the help content page. We place the back button on the left side of the header and the home button on the right.

Listing 2.27. JavaScript view creating Page with custom header

```
sap.ui.jsview("oum.view.help.intro", {
   createContent: function(oController) {
      const pageTitle = new sap.m.Title({                  Construct the page title
         text: "{i18n>view.help.intro.title}",
         level: "H2",                                       Define the semantic level
         titleStyle: "H4"                                   Define the style
      });

      const page = new sap.m.Page({                         Construct the page layout
         customHeader: new sap.m.Bar({                       Use customHeader aggregation
            contentLeft: [
               sap.ui.jsfragment("oum.fragment.BackButton")   Add the 'back' button
            ],
            contentMiddle:[ pageTitle ],                      Add the page title
```

```
        contentRight: [
            sap.ui.jsfragment("oum.fragment.HomeButton")          Add the 'home' button
        ]
    }),
    content: [ ]
});
    return page;
  }
});
```

After reloading the application and navigating to the 'help' route, we will see the SplitApp detail view header with the 'back' and 'home' buttons.

Figure 2.5. Help view with navigation buttons

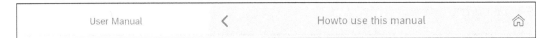

2.11. Adding tiles to the entry page

The typical UI5 entry page has tiles to navigate to the various sections of the application. The definition of these entry points should not be hidden in the view and controller code. Instead, we add it to our config.json.

```
{
    availableLanguages: [ "en", "de" ],
    defaultLanguage: "en",
    logLevel: "DEBUG",
    entryPoints: [                                    Array of entry point objects
        {
            "header": "{i18n>tiles.help.header}",
            "tooltip": "{i18n>tiles.help.tooltip}",
            "icon": "sap-icon://sys-help",
            "iconText": "{i18n>tiles.help.iconText}",
            "footer": "{i18n>tiles.help.footer}",
            "routeName": "help"
        }
    ]
};
```

To access the entry points definition, we add a function to the oui5lib.configuration namespace.

```
function getTilesDef() {
    const entryPoints = getConfigData("entryPoints");
    if (entryPoints !== undefined && entryPoints instanceof Array) {
        return entryPoints;
    }
    return false;
}
configuration.getEntryPoints = getTilesDef;                    Add function to namespace
```

After this, it is time to add the tiles to the entry view (view/entry.view.js). We will use a sap.m.GenericTile control to display each entry point.

Listing 2.28. Add Tiles to Page

```
 1 const tiles = [];
 2 const entryPoints = oui5lib.configuration.getEntryPoints();
 3 if (entryPoints) {
 4     let tile;
 5     entryPoints.forEach(function(tileDef) {
 6         tile = new sap.m.GenericTile({                    Construct a GenericTile
 7             header: tileDef.header,
 8             tooltip: tileDef.tooltip,
 9             tileContent: [
10                 new sap.m.TileContent({                   Construct TileContent
11                     content: new sap.m.ImageContent({
12                         src: tileDef.icon,
13                         description: tileDef.iconText
14                     }),
15                     footer: tileDef.footer
16                 })
17             ],
18             press: function(oEvent) {
19                 oController.routeTo(oEvent);              Attach function to 'press' event
20             }
21         });
22         tile.data("routeName", tileDef.routeName);        Add the routeName as custom data
23
24         tile.addStyleClass("sapUiTinyMarginBegin");
25         tile.addStyleClass("sapUiTinyMarginTop");
26         tile.addStyleClass("tileLayout");
27
28         tiles.push(tile);                                 Add GenericTile to tiles array
29     });
30 }
```

At this point, the entry Page is constructed like this:

```
const landmarks = new sap.m.PageAccessibleLandmarkInfo({
    headerRole: "Region",
    headerLabel: "{i18n>view.entry.headerLabel}",
    contentRole: "Main",
    contentLabel: "{i18n>view.entry.contentLabel}"
});
const entryPage = new sap.m.Page({
    landmarkInfo: landmarks,
    customHeader: headerBar,
    content: [ tiles ]
});
```

 The landmark labels inform the user about the purpose of the correspondent page section. An english example text for the headerLabel is "select language, navigate to help section" and for the contentLabel "application entry points".

If we reload the application and click on or touch the tile, nothing happens. Instead, we see an error in the browser console saying "Uncaught TypeError: oController.routeTo is not a function". To correct the error, we have to connect the view with a controller providing the attached routeTo function.

But before we come to the actual controller code, we introduce a custom controller implementation to be used as a base class for all our controllers. This will allow us to easily provide common functions for all controllers extending this base class.

2.11.1. Use a BaseController

The default `sap.ui.core.mvc.Controller` has some missing functions, which are needed for most controllers. Extending controllers is the best way to share controller functions used by multiple views. Common functions are imported, while view specific controller functions remain separated.

Listing 2.29. A custom BaseController

```
sap.ui.define([
   "sap/ui/core/mvc/Controller"
], function (oController) {
   "use strict";

   const BaseController = oController.extend("oui5lib.controller.BaseController", {
      getRouter: function () {                                    Get the component Router
         return sap.ui.core.UIComponent.getRouterFor(this);
      },
      getEventBus: function () {                                  Get the component EventBus
         return this.getOwnerComponent().getEventBus();
      },
      getResourceBundle: function () {                            Get the language ResourceBundle
         return this.getOwnerComponent().getModel("i18n").getResourceBundle();
      },

      debug: function (msg) {                                                Logging
         oui5lib.logger.debug(this.addControllerName(msg));
      },
      info: function (msg) {
         oui5lib.logger.info(this.addControllerName(msg));
      },
      warn: function (msg) {
         oui5lib.logger.warn(this.addControllerName(msg));
      },
      error: function (msg) {
         oui5lib.logger.error(this.addControllerName(msg));
      },

      addControllerName: function(msg) {
         const metadata = this.getMetadata();
         return metadata.getName() + " > " + msg;
      }
   });
   return BaseController;
});
```

If a controller extends the `BaseController`, logging can be both simplified and improved. Within these controllers, calling the logging functions is most convenient:

```
this.info("just an example");
```

Additionally, the log messages will now include the controller name for easier debugging.

2.11.2. Adding an entry controller

Now, let us return to the missing event handler function of Listing 2.28, "Add Tiles to Page". To connect a controller with a view, we add the function getControllerName to the entry view which returns the controller name to be connected to the view.

```
getControllerName: function() {
    return "oum.controller.entry";
}
```

According to the UI5 naming scheme and the sap-ui-resourceroots setting, the controller goes into the folder controller and has the filename entry.controller.js.

Listing 2.30. The entry controller extends the BaseController

```
1 sap.ui.define([
2     "oumlib/controller/BaseController"
3 ], function(BaseController) {
4     "use strict";
5
6     const entryController = BaseController.extend("oum.controller.entry", {
7         onInit: function () { ❶
8             this.getRouter().getRoute("home")
9                             .attachMatched(this._onRouteMatched, this);
10        },
11        _onRouteMatched: function(oEvent) {
12            this.debug("coming home");                    Use BaseController debug function
13        },
14
15        routeTo: function(oEvent) {
16            const tile = oEvent.getSource();
17            const routeName = tile.data("routeName"); ❷
18
19            this.info("navTo: " + routeName);             Use BaseController info function
20            this.getRouter().vNavTo(routeName);
21        }
22    });
23
24    return entryController;
25 });
```

❶   The onInit function (lines 7 to 10) is used for nearly every controller to set models required for the view. Additionally, the controller usually needs to do something when the route of the view was requested. First, we get the route with a given name ("home") from the Router (line 8) and then use the attachMatched function of the Route to attach a handler function to the matched event (line 9).

❷   The routeName was set in Listing 2.28, "Add Tiles to Page" line 21.

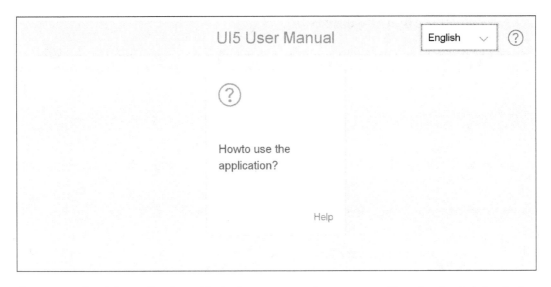

If we now reload the application with the browser console open, we will notice that it is beginning to give us feedback. This will be crucial for debugging our application. Having drawn near to the completion of the template component, we have created a lot of files:

```
├── controller
│   └── entry.controller.js
├── fragment
│   ├── BackButton.fragment.js
│   ├── HelpButton.fragment.js
│   ├── HomeButton.fragment.js
│   └── LanguageSwitcher.fragment.js
├── i18n
│   ├── i18n_de.properties
│   └── i18n_en.properties
├── oui5lib
│   ├── controller
│   │   └── BaseController.js
│   ├── configuration.js
│   ├── init.js
│   ├── logger.js
│   └── util.js
├── view
│   ├── help
│   │   ├── index.view.js
│   │   └── intro.view.js
│   ├── app.view.xml
│   ├── entry.view.js
│   ├── noRoute.view.xml
│   └── splitApp.view.xml
├── Component.js
├── Component-preload.js
├── config.json
├── index.html
├── manifest.json
└── Router.js
```

The template component doesn't do anything, but has everything in place to focus on content development. We will use it as starting point in the following chapters.

2.12. Adding a Footer

For most pages, a footer will hold various action controls. But the home page has no such actions. Instead, we want to show some basic information about the running application, like the application title and version.

The sap.m.Page has a footer aggregation accepting controls implementing sap.m.IBar. We have already used the sap.m.Bar for the header. For the footer we use the sap.m.Toolbar. This fragment is of type XML and its location fragment/AppInfoToolbar.fragment.xml.

Listing 2.31. XML Toolbar Fragment showing basic application information

```
<core:FragmentDefinition xmlns="sap.m"
                         xmlns:core="sap.ui.core">
   <Toolbar>
      <Text text="{i18n>application}"/>
      <Text text="{/appTitle}"/>
      <Text text="{i18n>version}"/>
      <Text text="{/appVersion}"/>
      <ToolbarSpacer/>
      <Text text="OpenUI5 Version: "/>
      <Text text="{/openui5Version}"/>
   </Toolbar>
</core:FragmentDefinition>
```

The fragment adds some i18n properties ("application", "version"). There are also data we need to get from the manifest ("appTitle", "appVersion") and UI5 ("openui5Version"). Implementing the Model-View-Controller (MVC) pattern, UI5 uses models to separate the data from the view. To provide the required model for the footer, we add a getAppInfoModel function to the oui5lib.configuration namespace.

```
function getAppModel() {
   const component = getComponent();
   const appConfig = component.getManifestEntry("sap.app");

   const appModel = new sap.ui.model.json.JSONModel({
      appTitle: appConfig.title,
      appVersion: appConfig.applicationVersion.version,
      openui5Version: sap.ui.version
   });
   return appModel;
}
configuration.getAppInfoModel = getAppModel;          Add function to namespace
```

Where do we set the model? As a general rule, it is best to choose the smallest scope possible. In our case, it is the Toolbar of the entry page footer aggregation. We, therefore, set the model in the controller/entry.controller.js onInit function.

```
const page = this.getView().getContent()[0]; ❶
page.getFooter().setModel(oui5lib.configuration.getAppInfoModel());
```

❶   Here, the sap.m.Page is the first and only item of the sap.ui.core.mvc.View content aggregation, which holds an array of content controls.

Finally, we add the fragment to the `footer` aggregation of the `Page` of our entry view.

```
const entryPage = new sap.m.Page({
    landmarkInfo: landmarks,
    customHeader: headerBar,
    content: [ tiles ],
    footer: sap.ui.xmlfragment("oum.fragment.AppInfoToolbar")
});
```

The `sap.m.Toolbar` will shrink its content with the available space. This causes a problem with mobile phones in portrait orientation. We can ignore this for now because our application manifest doesn't claim to be fully usable with mobile phones (see Listing 2.2, "Descriptor Application Manifest" under `sap.ui.deviceTypes`).

We will learn how to construct a more responsive toolbar in the following Chapter 3, *Views and Pages*.

Part I. Basics of UI5 development

In this part of the book, step by step, we will go through the basics of developing with UI5. We will begin with the various page implementations to help the reader to select the most fitting layout for a task or project (Chapter 3, *Views and Pages*). Next, we will cover the issues of navigation in general and routing in particular (Chapter 4, *Navigation and Routing*). This is being followed by a chapter exploring a client-side implementation of user access permissions (Chapter 5, *User Permissions*).

Having covered how to construct pages, how to navigate and limit access, we will move on to events and messages which are the core of user interaction (Chapter 6, *Events and Messages*). The following three chapters are concerned with page content. Beginning with models, which bind the data to the user interface controls (Chapter 7, *Models*), we will finally get to the main purpose of the whole effort, namely, the presentation and modification of the domain data as lists, tables (Chapter 8, *Lists and Tables*) and forms (Chapter 9, *Forms and Input Validation*).

Table of Contents

Chapter 3. Views and Pages

We have already seen some views and a controller in Chapter 2, *Building a basic responsive Web Application*. Without content, the view has nothing to show. The first level of content is a basic layout of visible areas and their relative positions. In this chapter, we will look at various page layouts offered by UI5.

A view instance of type JavaScript is defined using the function `sap.ui.jsview`. The function takes two parameters, a view name and a view object of type `sap.ui.core.mvc.JSView`. The only required function to be implemented is the `createContent` function, which must return an object extending `sap.ui.core.Control`, mostly some kind of page layout control.

Additionally, the view can be connected with a controller using the `getControllerName` function. The view will try to load and instantiate the controller by the returned name.

Listing 3.1. JSView example with controller

```
sap.ui.jsview("oum.view.mPageExample", {
    createContent: function(oController) {
        const page = new sap.m.Page();
        return page;
    },

    getControllerName: function() {
        return "oum.controller.pageExamples";
    }
});
```

The `sap.ui.core.mvc.JSView` extends `sap.ui.core.mvc.View`, which provides functions to access and change the `content` aggregation returned by the `createContent`. We can `getContent`, `addContent`, `insertContent`, `indexOfContent`, `removeContent`, `removeAllContent` or `destroyContent`. These functions allow us to programatically modify any view content.

To limit the visible space occupied by the `View`, the `width` and `height` properties of the `View` object can be set using the related `setWidth` and `setHeight` functions. Any valid `sap.ui.core.CSSSize` value is allowed. It appears as CSS style attributes of the generated HTML container.

A view is initialized, rendered and re-rendered, exited, and finally destroyed. In practice, the related events of the `View` are rarely used, because the corresponding functions for the controller are generally preferable.

3.1. Page layouts

UI5 has several implementations of layout controls representing a web page. A page layout provides areas for content. The layouts generally have a header and footer, which may or may not be shown. All have a main content area. The adaptability to different devices depends on the controls being used in the content aggregations.

Here, we just want to give an overview of available page implementations without diving too deeply into the details.

3.1.1. Basic responsive Page

The sap.m.Page is the most commonly used responsive layout control. It has a header with an optional sub-header, a content and a footer area.

Screenshot of example sap.m.Page

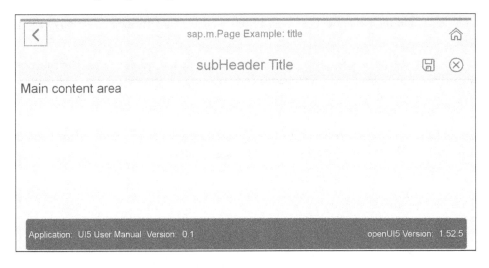

Figure 3.1. Sketch of sap.m.Page

customHeader showHeader	sap.m.IBar (Bar, OverflowToolbar, Toolbar) boolean	
	sap.m.Bar	
contentLeft	contentMiddle	contentRight
subHeader showSubHeader	sap.m.IBar (Bar, OverflowToolbar, Toolbar) boolean	
content enableScrolling	sap.ui.core.Control[] boolean	
footer showFooter floatingFooter	sap.m.IBar (Bar, OverflowToolbar, Toolbar) boolean boolean	

The customHeader, subHeader and footer aggregations require a control implementing sap.m.IBar (Bar, OverflowToolbar, Toolbar). All generate a horizontal container, but within the container the content is positioned differently.

> The sap.m.Bar control has three content areas: left, middle and right. If the available visible space is not sufficient for all content, the middle content will adjust. The sap.m.Toolbar will distribute content evenly among all shrinkable controls. This default behavior can be over-written by specifying sap.m.ToolbarLayoutData for the layoutData property of Toolbar elements. The sap.m.OverflowToolbar extends the Toolbar with an overflow area into which controls are moved in case the visible space is insufficient. We can control the overflow behavior by specifying sap.m.OverflowToolbarLayoutData.

The sap.m.Page has a landmarkInfo aggregation, which is important, as it allows screen readers to provide an overview of the page structure and to quickly navigate to the relevant content areas. The available roles are defined as part of the WAI-ARIA specifications under Landmark roles [https://www.w3.org/TR/wai-aria-1.1/#landmark_roles]. The corresponding UI5 enumeration is the sap.ui.core.AccessibleLandmarkRole with the following values: Banner, Complementary, Main, Navigation, None, Region, Search.

Defining landmark roles and labels can help all participants in the development process to communicate the structure of a page and clarify the functionality of page areas. Finding a short descriptive text for each page area gives the team a chance to find problems of confusing uses mixing different concerns. Here, we will use english text because they are more instructive than i18n properties we would normally use.

Listing 3.2. Define landmark roles and labels

```
const landmarkInfo = new sap.m.PageAccessibleLandmarkInfo({
    rootLabel: "example page constructed with sap.m.Page",
    headerRole: "Navigation",
    headerLabel: "back and home buttons besides main page title",
    subHeaderRole: "Complementary",
    subHeaderLabel: "save and cancel buttons",
    contentRole: "Main",
    contentLabel: "this is only an example without meaningful content",
    footerRole: "None"
});
```

The following listing constructs the related page with a header (lines 5 to 15), subHeader (lines 16 to 34), content (lines 35 to 41) and footer area (lines 42 to 44).

We will use the default header properties instead of the customHeader aggregation, which we only use in cases where the default header properties are insufficient. We already used the customHeader aggregation for Listing 2.15, "Add LanguageSwitcher fragment to Page".

The default header consists of a title text placed in the middle, a navigation back button on the left side, and some additional headerContent on the right side of the header container. The title properties are title and titleLevel (Enumeration sap.ui.core.TitleLevel). The relevant button properties are showNavButton and navButtonTooltip, and the related event navButtonPress.

Listing 3.3. Construct a sap.m.Page

```
1 sap.ui.jsview("oum.view.mPage", {
2    createContent: function(oController) {
3        const pageControl = new sap.m.Page({
4            landmarkInfo: landmarkInfo,
5            showHeader: true,                           Header settings
```

```
 6        title: "sap.m.Page Example: title",
 7        titleLevel: "H1",                                    Will add a title tag to the HTML
 8        showNavButton: true,
 9        navButtonTooltip: "{i18n>pageLayout.backButton.tooltip}",
10        navButtonPress: function() {
11            oController.navBack();                           Requires controller function
12        },
13        headerContent: [
14            sap.ui.jsfragment("oum.fragment.HomeButton")
15        ],
16        showSubHeader: true,                                 SubHeader settings
17        subHeader: new sap.m.Bar({
18            contentMiddle: [
19                new sap.m.Title({
20                    text: "subHeader Title",
21                    level: "H2", titleStyle: "H2"            Enumeration sap.ui.core.TitleLevel
22                })
23            ],
24            contentRight: [
25                new sap.m.Button({
26                    icon: "sap-icon://save",
27                    tooltip: "{i18n>button.save.tooltip}"
28                }),
29                new sap.m.Button({
30                    icon: "sap-icon://sys-cancel",
31                    tooltip: "{i18n>button.cancel.tooltip}"
32                })
33            ]
34        }),
35        enableScrolling: true,                               Content settings
36        content: [
37            new sap.m.Title({
38                text: "Main content area",
39                level: "H3", titleStyle: "H3"
40            }),
41        ],
42        showFooter: true,                                    Footer settings
43        floatingFooter: true,
44        footer: sap.ui.xmlfragment("oum.fragment.AppInfoToolbar") ❶
45    });
46    return pageControl;
47  }
48 });
```

❶   See Listing 2.31, "XML Toolbar Fragment showing basic application information"

3.1.2. Fiori DynamicPage

Use the DynamicPage if you need to have a title, that is always visible, and a header, that has configurable Expanding/Snapping functionality. If you don't need the Expanding/Snapping functionality it is better to use the sap.m.Page as a lighter control.

—openUI5 API

The namespace sap.f refers to SAP Fiori UX (User eXperience), which is basically a set of design guidelines to improve and standardize the user experience of web applications.

The sap.f.DynamicPage introduces a feature, where the top page area consists of two parts: a title and a header. The naming is confusing because the 'title' is really just the top header and both 'title' and 'header' generate HTML header elements. Anyway, the header area may or may not be displayed. The two states are called snapped and expanded. Depending upon the state of the header different content can be specified for the title area.

The user can toggle the header state manually by clicking either the title area or the provided collapse button. Both can be deactivated by setting the DynamicPage toggleHeaderOnTitleClick property to false. The header will be automatically snapped if the user scrolls below the page bottom. This behavior can be prevented by setting the preserveHeaderStateOnScroll property to true. The whole switching behavior can be deactivated by the user 'pinning' the header.

Screenshot of example sap.f.DynamicPage

The following screenshot has the footer hidden and the 'header' snapped/collapsed.

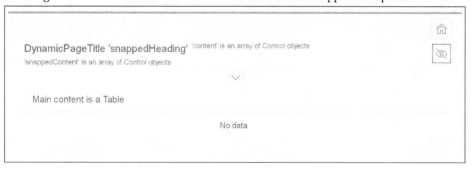

Figure 3.2. Sketch of sap.f.DynamicPage

title	sap.f.DynamicPageTitle	heading snappedHeading expandedHeading	sap.ui.core.Control sap.ui.core.Control sap.ui.core.Control
toggleHeaderOnTitleClick **preserveHeaderStateOnScroll**		content snappedContent expandedContent	sap.ui.core.Control[] sap.ui.core.Control[] sap.ui.core.Control[]
		navigationActions actions breadcrumbs	sap.m.Button[] sap.ui.core.Control[] sap.m.Breadcrumbs
header	sap.f.DynamicPageHeader	content	sap.ui.core.Control
headerExpanded		pinnable	
content	sap.ui.core.Control[]		
footer **showFooter**	sap.m.IBar (Bar, OverflowToolbar, Toolbar)		

Constructing a DynamicPage, we need to use a sap.f.DynamicPageTitle and sap.f.DynamicPageHeader.

The DynamicPageTitle has a heading aggregation, which usually will be some kind of title to be displayed on the left side of the 'title' header. Instead of a static heading we can also use the snappedHeading and expandedHeading aggregations, which display different content depending on the state of the DynamicPageHeader (expanded or snapped/collapsed).

The content aggregation is independent from the 'header' state. The content controls are positioned in the middle of the 'title' header area.

Positioned after the heading and content aggregations come the snappedContent and expandedContent aggregations. They can hold any array of content controls and work like the corresponding heading aggregations.

Placed on the right side of the 'title' header are the user actions. The navigationActions appear on top of the more general actions.

Listing 3.4. Construct a sap.f.DynamicPageTitle

```
const dynamicPageTitle = new sap.f.DynamicPageTitle({
    snappedHeading: new sap.m.Title({                        Shown when 'header' is collapsed
        text: "DynamicPageTitle 'snappedHeading'",
        level: "H2",
        titleStyle: "H2"
    }),

    snappedContent: [
        new sap.m.Text({
            text: "'snappedContent' is an array of Control objects"
        })
    ],
```

```
expandedHeading: new sap.m.Title({                    Shown when 'header' is expanded
   text: "DynamicPageTitle 'expandedHeading'",
   level: "H2",
   titleStyle: "H2"
}),

expandedContent: [
   new sap.m.Text({
      text: "'expandedContent' is an array of Control objects"
   })
],

content: [
   new sap.m.Text({
      text: "'content' is an array of Control objects"
   })
],
navigationActions: [
   sap.ui.jsfragment("oum.fragment.HomeButton")
],
actions: [
   new sap.m.OverflowToolbarButton({              Shows the text only when in the overflow area
      icon: "sap-icon://show",
      text: "{i18n>pageLayout.footer.hide}",
      tooltip: "{i18n>pageLayout.footer.hide.tooltip}",
      press: function(oEvent) {
         oController.toggleFooter(oEvent); ❶
      }
   })

]
});
```

❶ The `toggleFooter` function attached to the ObjectPageHeaderActionButton press event must be
    provided in the connected controller.

Listing 3.5. Controller function to toggle footer visibility

```
toggleFooter: function(oEvent) {
   const button = oEvent.getSource();

   const page = this.getView().getContent()[0];

   const footerShown = page.getShowFooter();
   if (footerShown) {
      button.setText("Show Footer");
      button.setTooltip("Show Footer");
      button.setIcon("sap-icon://hide");
   } else {
      button.setText("Hide Footer");
      button.setTooltip("Hide Footer");
      button.setIcon("sap-icon://show");
   }
   page.setShowFooter(!footerShown);
}
```

Below the `DynamicPageTitle` appears the `DynamicPageHeader`. It has a `content` aggregation holding an
array of content controls, which may either be displayed (expanded) or hidden (snapped/collapsed).

It further has a boolean property `pinnable`, which means that a button with a pushpin icon may or may not be shown allowing the user to disable the snapping/expanding feature and make the control sticky.

Listing 3.6. Construct a sap.f.DynamicPageHeader

```
const dynamicPageHeader = new sap.f.DynamicPageHeader({
    pinnable: true,
    content: [
        new sap.m.Text({ text: "DynamicPageHeader 'content'" }
    ]
});
```

Apart from the header parts, the `sap.f.DynamicPage` is similar to the `sap.m.Page`. An important difference is that for the DynamicPage the `content` aggregation is expected to be a single content control instead of an array of controls. Here, we use a `sap.m.Table`.

Listing 3.7. Construct a basic sap.f.DynamicPage

```
sap.ui.jsview("oum.view.dynamicPage", {
    createContent : function(oController) {
        ...
        const dynamicPage = new sap.f.DynamicPage({
            title: dynamicPageTitle,              The 'title' (top) header
            toggleHeaderOnTitleClick: true,

            header: dynamicPageHeader,            The 'header' (bottom) header
            headerExpanded: true,                 Set initial 'header' state

            content: new sap.m.Table({            Main content
                headerText: "Main content is a Table"
            }),

            showFooter: true,                     Footer settings
            footer: sap.ui.xmlfragment("oum.fragment.AppInfoToolbar")
        });
        return dynamicPage;
    }
});
```

3.1.3. Fiori SemanticPage

> Using the SemanticPage facilitates the implementation of the SAP Fiori 2.0 design guidelines.
> —openUI5 API

The `sap.f.semantic.SemanticPage` uses the title/header feature with the expanding/snapping functionality of the `sap.f.DynamicPage`, but the related aggregation and property names are different.

The `SemanticPage` is an effort to further standardize the organization and presentation of user actions. The concept is to have actions, which always look the same and appear in a particular order in a certain area of the view. The idea is to help users feel familiar and thereby reduce the rate of problems and errors. The `sap.f.semantic` namespace lists a number of such actions, all extending the `sap.f.semantic.SemanticButton`. Most come with a predefined text and icon.

- The navigation actions appear in the top right area of the page. These are the `fullScreenAction`, `exitFullScreenAction`, and `closeAction`.
- The header actions are grouped into title actions and icon actions. The title actions are `titleMain-Action`, `editAction`, `deleteAction`, `copyAction` and `addAction`. There are many so-called icon actions, some of them grouped in a `Share` menu. Examples are the `sendEmailAction`, `sendMessageAction` or `printAction`.
- The footer actions positioned on the right side of the footer are the `footerMainAction`, the `positive-Action`, and the `negativeAction`. The footer may also have a `messagesIndicator` and a `draftIndicator` appearing on the left side of the footer.

Screenshot of example sap.f.SemanticPage (theme sap_belize_hcw)

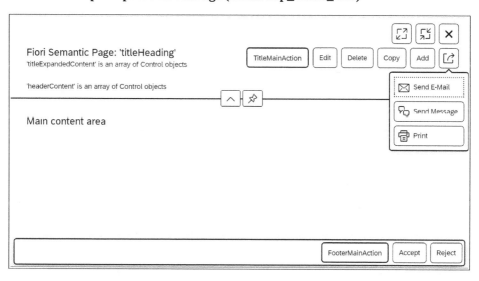

Figure 3.3. Sketch of sap.f.SemanticPage

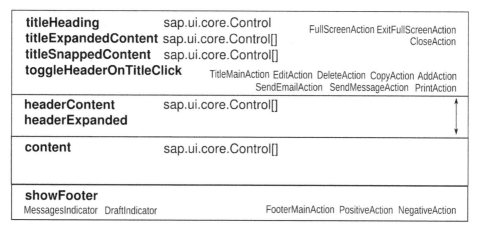

For extra functionality beyond the wealth of predefined common actions, there are custom properties for each button area (`titleCustomTextActions`, `titleCustomIconActions`, `customShareActions`, and `footer-CustomActions`, which all expect an array of `sap.m.Button` objects.

Listing 3.8. Construct a basic sap.f.semantic.SemanticPage

```
sap.ui.jsview("oum.view.semanticPage", {
   createContent : function(oController) {
      const semanticPage = new sap.f.semantic.SemanticPage({
         titleHeading: new sap.m.Title({
            text: "Fiori Semantic Page: 'titleHeading'"
         }),

         titleSnappedContent: [                    Shown when header is collapsed
            new sap.m.Text({ text: "'titleSnappedContent' is an array of Control objects" })
         ],
         titleExpandedContent: [                   Shown when header is expanded
            new sap.m.Text({ text: "'titleExpandedContent' is an array of Control objects" })
         ],

         headerContent: [
            new sap.m.Text({ text: "'headerContent' is an array of Control objects" })
         ],

         content: [                                Main content
            new sap.m.Title({
               text: "Main content area",
               level: "H2", titleStyle: "H3"
            })
         ],

         closeAction: new sap.f.semantic.CloseAction(),         Navigation actions
         fullScreenAction: new sap.f.semantic.FullScreenAction(),
         exitFullScreenAction: new sap.f.semantic.ExitFullScreenAction(),

         titleMainAction: new sap.f.semantic.TitleMainAction({   Header actions
            text: "TitleMainAction"
         }),
         editAction: new sap.f.semantic.EditAction(),
         deleteAction: new sap.f.semantic.DeleteAction(),
         copyAction: new sap.f.semantic.CopyAction(),
         addAction: new sap.f.semantic.AddAction(),

         printAction:  new sap.f.semantic.PrintAction(),         Icon actions
         sendEmailAction:  new sap.f.semantic.SendEmailAction(),
         sendMessageAction:  new sap.f.semantic.SendMessageAction(),

         showFooter: true, ❶
         footerMainAction: new sap.f.semantic.FooterMainAction({  Footer actions
            text: "FooterMainAction"
         }),
         positiveAction:  new sap.f.semantic.PositiveAction(),
         negativeAction:  new sap.f.semantic.NegativeAction(),
      });
      return semanticPage;
   }
});
```

❶   The footer area is reserved for semantic actions and therefore has no explicit content. Its visibility may be toggled by setting the showFooter property. By default, the footer is not shown (showFooter defaults to false).

To respond to the user pressing an action button, we have to attach an event handler function to the press event borrowed from the SemanticButton to each of the buttons.

3.1.4. Multi-section pages: ObjectPageLayout

> An ObjectPageLayout is the layout control, used to put together all parts of an Object page - Header, Navigation bar and Sections/Subsections.
>
> —openUI5 API

The sap.uxap.ObjectPageLayout is a flexible layout control with two header parts and a navigational menu to the page sections. It has numerous properties, which can be used to configure the layout and its behavior. For the full list of available properties and events, please look into the API Reference and the Samples/Explored section.

While the 'title' header (headerTitle) is always visible and shows critical information identifying the object, the 'content' header (headerContent) displays additional details, which can be flexibly presented because the aggregation accepts an array of controls.

Let us begin looking at the header, which has two parts, a headerTitle and a headerContent. Up to UI5 version 1.52 the headerTitle aggregation had to be a sap.uxap.ObjectPageHeader. Ever since, we have had an additional choice for the headerTitle using features from the sap.f.DynamicPage. This is an important step because it normalizes the header 'title' and 'content' expanded/snapped feature used for the sap.f.DynamicPage and the sap.f.semantic.SemanticPage, although still differently implemented.

The headerTitle aggregation now requires an implementation of sap.uxap.IHeaderTitle, which can either be a sap.uxap.ObjectPageHeader or the dynamic variant sap.uxap.ObjectPageDynamicHeaderTitle.

We begin with the old fashioned ObjectPageHeader. It is used to present the basic information about an object and provide common action buttons.

Screenshot of example sap.uxap.ObjectPageLayout with ObjectPageHeader

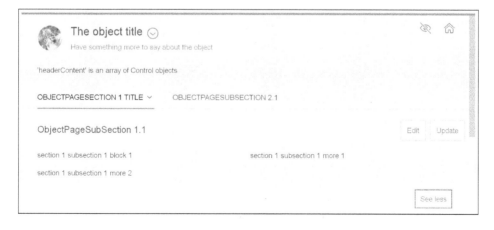

Figure 3.4. Sketch of sap.uxap.ObjectPageLayout

headerTitle sap.uxap.ObjectPageHeader sap.uxap.ObjectPageDynamicHeaderTitle **showTitleInHeaderContent** **showOnlyHighImportance**	

headerContent sap.ui.core.Control[] **showHeaderContent** **alwaysShowContentHeader**

showAnchorBar **showAnchorBarPopover** **upperCaseAnchorBar**

sections   sap.uxap.ObjectPageSection[]
                            title
                            titleLevel   Enum sap.ui.core.TitleLevel
                            importance   Enum sap.uxap.Importance
                            subSections sap.uxap.ObjectPageSubSection[]
                                                     blocks   sap.ui.core.Control[]
                                                     moreBlocks sap.ui.core.Control[]
                                                     actions   sap.ui.core.Control[]

footer   sap.m.IBar (Bar, OverflowToolbar, Toolbar) **showFooter**

Listing 3.9. Construct a sap.uxap.ObjectPageHeader

```
 1 const headerTitle = new sap.uxap.ObjectPageHeader({
 2    objectTitle: "The object title",
 3    objectSubtitle: "Have something more to say about the object",
 4
 5    objectImageURI: "image/objectImage.png",
 6    objectImageAlt: "A bee collecting pollen",
 7    objectImageShape: "Circle",              Enumeration sap.uxap.ObjectPageHeaderPictureShape
 8    isObjectIconAlwaysVisible: true,
 9
10    showTitleSelector: true,                 A selector arrow icon appears next to the title
11    titleSelectorPress: function() {
12       oController.handleTitleSelectorPress();
13    },
14    actions: [ ❶
15       sap.uxap.ObjectPageHeaderActionButton({
16          icon: "sap-icon://hide",
17          text: "{i18n>pageLayout.footer.show}",
18          tooltip: "{i18n>pageLayout.footer.show.tooltip}",
19          hideIcon: false,
20          hideText: true,
21          importance: "Low",                 Enumeration sap.uxap.Importance
22          press: function(oEvent) {
23             oController.toggleFooter(oEvent);
24          }
25       }),
26       sap.ui.jsfragment("oum.fragment.HomeButton")
27    ]
28 });
```

❶   The `actions` aggregation is displayed on the right side of the header. Like the name suggests, we generally use it for common buttons. UI5 provides a special button implementation `sap.uxap.ObjectPageHeaderActionButton`. Using its `importance` property, we can configure the order in which buttons are moved from the action bar into the action sheet (overflow menu). Furthermore, using the `hideIcon` and `hideText` properties, we can hide icon and text of a button when in the action bar, but both will show in the action sheet.

The `sap.uxap.ObjectPageDynamicPageTitle` extends the `sap.f.DynamicPageTitle` and is being constructed just like the above Listing 3.4, "Construct a sap.f.DynamicPageTitle". For the following example, instead of using the `snappedHeading` and `expandedHeading` properties, we use the `heading` property. We also add a few lines to show the use of the `breadcrumbs` aggregation.

Listing 3.10. Construct a sap.uxap.ObjectPageDynamicHeaderTitle

```
const headerTitle = new sap.uxap.ObjectPageDynamicHeaderTitle({
    heading: new sap.m.Title({
        text: "ObjectPageDynamicHeaderTitle 'heading' Title",
        level: "H2", titleStyle: "H2"
    }),
    breadcrumbs: new sap.m.Breadcrumbs({
        currentLocationText: "Example ObjectPageLayout",
        links: [
            new sap.m.Link({
                text: "Home",
                href: "index.html",
                press: function(oEvent) {
                    oController.handleBreadCrumb(oEvent);
                }
            })
        ]
    })
});
```

Screenshot of example sap.uxap.ObjectPageLayout with ObjectPageDynamicHeaderTitle

Below the header parts, we find the so-called anchor bar to navigate the constructed sections and subsections.

The `sap.uxap.ObjectPageLayout` has an aggregation `sections` containing an array of `sap.uxap.ObjectPageSection` objects. And each `ObjectPageSection` has an aggregation of `subSections`, which contain an array of `sap.uxap.ObjectPageSubSection` objects. The `ObjectPageSubSection` has three aggregations for content. There are `blocks`, which will always be visible when the subsection is visible. More blocks can be added to aggregation moreBlocks, which will only become visible upon clicking on a "See more" button. Any related buttons may be placed into aggregation actions.

All sections have a title used for the anchor bar. The anchor bar is positioned below the header areas and contains a navigational menu for the sections and subsections of the page. An optional titleLevel property may be used to semantically structure the hierarchy of section titles. Otherwise, UI5 will determine the title levels automatically. Using property importance we can determine which sections are visible or hidden when space is insufficient. Available values come from enumeration sap.uxap.Importance ("Low", "Medium", "High").

Listing 3.11. Construct a sap.uxap.ObjectPageSection

```
const firstPageSection = new sap.uxap.ObjectPageSection({          Construct page section 1
    title: "ObjectPageSection 1 title",
    subSections: [
        new sap.uxap.ObjectPageSubSection({                        Construct subsection 1.1
            title: "ObjectPageSubSection 1.1",
            blocks: [
                new sap.m.Text({ text: "section 1 subsection 1 block 1" })
            ],
            moreBlocks: [
                new sap.m.Text({ text: "section 1 subsection 1 more 1" }),
                new sap.m.Text({ text: "section 1 subsection 1 more 2" })
            ],
            actions: [
                new sap.m.Button({ text: "Edit", tooltip: "Describe edit" }),
                new sap.m.Button({ text: "Update", tooltip: "Describe update" })
            ]
        }),
        new sap.uxap.ObjectPageSubSection({                        Construct subsection 1.2
            title: "ObjectPageSubSection 1.2",
            blocks: [
                new sap.m.Text({ text: "section 1 subsection 2 block 1" })
            ]
        })
    ]
});

const secondPageSection = new sap.uxap.ObjectPageSection({        Construct page section 2
    title: "ObjectPageSection 2 title",
    subSections: [
        new sap.uxap.ObjectPageSubSection({                        Construct subsection 2.1
            title: "ObjectPageSubSection 2.1",
            blocks: [
                new sap.m.Text({ text: "section 2 subsection 1 block 1" })
            ]
        })
    ]
});
```

 The content blocks can be separated into XML views extending the sap.uxap.BlockBase. You can explore this feature in the Samples/Explored section of the UI5 documentation.

The ObjectPageLayout allows the flexible construction of complex pages with various hierarchically structured sections. It will be as responsive as the content of the blocks. That means, if the content of any block does not adjust to different devices and screens, the whole page will not adjust either.

Listing 3.12. Construct a sap.uxap.ObjectPageLayout

```
const pageLayout = new sap.uxap.ObjectPageLayout({
    headerTitle: headerTitle, ❶
    headerContent: [
        new sap.ui.layout.VerticalLayout({
            content: [
                new sap.m.Text({ text: "'headerContent' is an array of Control objects" })
            ]
        })
    ],
    sections: [
        firstPageSection, ❷
        secondPageSection
    ],
    showFooter: false,
    footer: sap.ui.xmlfragment("oum.fragment.Footer")
});
```

❶   Use either the object from Listing 3.9, "Construct a sap.uxap.ObjectPageHeader" or List-
     ing 3.10, "Construct a sap.uxap.ObjectPageDynamicHeaderTitle".
❷   See Listing 3.11, "Construct a sap.uxap.ObjectPageSection".

Instead of presenting content in sections of one page, we could also split the content into multiple
views.

3.1.5. Administrative applications: ToolPage

> The ToolPage is a layout control, used to put together the parts of a basic tools app - ToolHeader, Side-
> Navigation and contents area.
>
> —openUI5 API

If a more complex view with several menu items and submenus is needed, the ToolPage may be a
good choice.

Screenshot of example sap.tnt.ToolPage

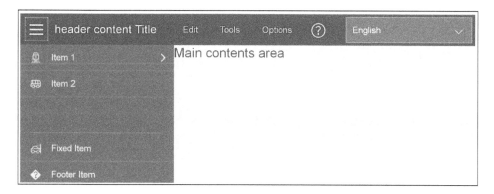

Figure 3.5. Sketch of sap.tnt.ToolPage

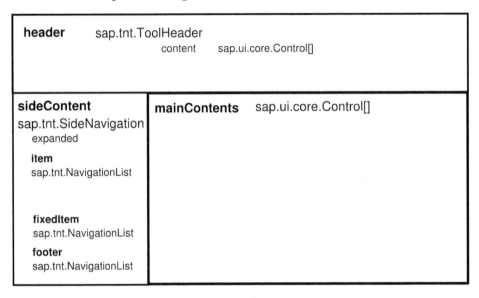

For the header aggregation, we need to construct a `sap.tnt.ToolHeader`, which extends the `sap.m.Over-flowToolbar`. The OverflowToolbar is a horizontal container which has an overflow area for toolbar content not fitting into the visible space. Other controls can, nevertheless, be added to the toolbar, but only the following controls can be moved into the overflow area:

- sap.m.Button
- sap.m.ToggleButton
- sap.m.OverflowToolbarButton
- sap.m.SegmentedButton
- sap.m.CheckBox
- sap.m.ComboBox
- sap.m.DatePicker
- sap.m.TimePicker
- sap.m.DateTimePicker
- sap.m.Input
- sap.m.SearchField
- sap.m.Select

Understanding the responsive behavior of the `OverflowToolbar` is critical in order to configure the content correctly.

The property `layoutData` can be set for every control extending `sap.ui.core.Element`. There are quite a few `sap.ui.core.LayoutData` implementations which mostly provide properties to style the element. In this case, where we have an extended `sap.m.OverflowToolbar`, we will use the `sap.m.OverflowToolbar-LayoutData`, which allows us to specify how the overflow should happen.

Using the `OverflowToolbarLayoutData`, we can set the `priority` referring to Enumeration `sap.m.Overflow-ToolbarPriority`. The default is `High`. The hierarchy of priorities is `AlwaysOverflow`, `Disappear`, `Low`, `High`, and `NeverOverflow`.

In addition to the `priority`, we can also assign content to a `group`, whose overall priority is determined as the highest priority of any content belonging to the group.

Listing 3.13. Construct a sap.tnt.ToolHeader

```
 1 const toolHeader = new sap.tnt.ToolHeader({
 2    content: [
 3       new sap.m.Button({                              Button to toggle side navigation
 4          icon: "sap-icon://menu2",
 5          type: "Transparent",
 6          tooltip: "Collapse Side Navigation",
 7          layoutData: new sap.m.OverflowToolbarLayoutData({   Specify LayoutData
 8             minWidth: "20px",
 9             priority: "NeverOverflow"
10          }),
11          press: function(oEvent) {                    Attach function to button press event
12             oController.toggleSideNavigation(oEvent);
13          }
14       }),
15       new sap.m.Title({
16          text: "header content Title",
17          level: "H1", titleStyle: "H4"
18       }),
19       new sap.m.ToolbarSpacer({ ❶
20          width: "20px",
21       }),
22       new sap.m.Button({                              Add further buttons
23          text: "Edit",
24          tooltip: "Describe edit",
25          type: "Transparent"
26       }),
27       new sap.m.ToolbarSeparator(), ❷
28       new sap.m.Button({
29          text: "Tools",
30          tooltip: "Describe tools",
31          type: "Transparent",
32          layoutData: new sap.m.OverflowToolbarLayoutData({   Specify LayoutData
33             group: 1,
34             priority: "Low"
35          })
36       }),
37       new sap.m.Button({
38          text: "Options",
39          tooltip: "Describe options",
40          type: "Transparent",
41          layoutData: new sap.m.OverflowToolbarLayoutData({   Specify LayoutData
42             group: 1,
43             priority: "Low"
44          })
45       }),
46       new sap.m.OverflowToolbarButton({ ❸
47          icon: "sap-icon://sys-help",
48          text: "{i18n>button.help.tooltip}",
49          type: "Transparent"
50       }),
51       new sap.m.ToolbarSpacer(), ❹
52       sap.ui.jsfragment("oum.fragment.LanguageSwitcher"),
53       sap.ui.jsfragment("oum.fragment.HomeButton")
```

```
54    ]
55 });
```

❷   The ToolbarSeparator adds a visual separator between content controls.
❶   The ToolbarSpacer adds space between content items in the toolbar. The space can be set with
        property width, which accepts any valid CSS size value.
❸   The OpenUI5 API explains, that the "OverflowToolbarButton is a version of Button that shows
        its text only when in the overflow area of a sap.m.OverflowToolbar. This control is intended
        to be used exclusively in the context of OverflowToolbar, when it is required to have buttons
        that show only an icon in the toolbar, but icon and text in the overflow menu."
❹   If the ToolbarSpacer is used without specifying a width, the space is calculated automatically.
        This feature can be used to dynamically position content within the toolbar. In this case, the
        LanguageSwitcher fragment is moved to the right side.

 The API Reference notes that the ToolbarSpacer should not be used with the ToolbarLayout-
        Data.

To expand or collapse the side navigation, we attached a function toggleSideNavigation to a button
press event (see Listing 3.13, "Construct a sap.tnt.ToolHeader" lines 12-14). The function uses the
view object to get the ToolPage to toggle between expanded and collapsed. Additionally, the event
object is used to get the source Button and reset its tooltip text.

Listing 3.14. ToolPage controller function: toggle side navigation

```
toggleSideNavigation: function(oEvent) {
   const button = oEvent.getSource();

   const view = this.getView();
   const page = view.getContent()[0];

   const sideExpanded = page.getSideExpanded();
   if (sideExpanded) {
      button.setTooltip("Expand Side Navigation");          Set tooltip text
   } else {
      button.setTooltip("Collapse Side Navigation");
   }
   page.setSideExpanded(!sideExpanded);                      Toggle sideExpanded property
}
```

After constructing the ToolHeader and providing the controller function to expand/collapse the side
navigation, we will now move on to implementing the side navigation as sap.tnt.SideNavigation,
which has three aggregations (item, fixedItem, and footer).

Each of the aggregations takes a sap.tnt.NavigationList, which has an items aggregation containing an
array of sap.tnt.NavigationListItem objects, which in its turn also has an items aggregation containing
another level of NavigationListItem objects. With these objects we can build multi-level menus.

Listing 3.15. Construct a sap.tnt.SideNavigation

```
 1 const sideNavigation = new sap.tnt.SideNavigation({
 2     expanded: true,
 3     itemSelect: function(oEvent) {                          Attach function to the itemSelect event
 4         oController.navigationItemSelect(oEvent);
 5     },
 6     item: new sap.tnt.NavigationList({
 7         items: [                                            NavigationList items array
 8             new sap.tnt.NavigationListItem({
 9                 key: "item1",
10                 text: "Item 1",
11                 icon: "sap-icon://cargo-train",             Top level items need an icon
12                 tooltip: "First top level item",
13                 expanded: false,                            Do not show the Subitems
14                 items: [                                    NavigationListItem items array
15                     new sap.tnt.NavigationListItem({
16                         key: "item11",
17                         text: "Item 1.1",
18                         tooltip: "First subitem of first top level item"
19                     }),
20                     new sap.tnt.NavigationListItem({
21                         key: "item12",
22                         text: "Item 1.2",
23                         tooltip: "Second subitem of first top level item"
24                     })
25                 ]
26             }),
27             new sap.tnt.NavigationListItem({
28                 key: "item2",
29                 text: "Item 2",
30                 icon: "sap-icon://bus-public-transport",
31                 tooltip: "Second top level item"
32             })
33         ]
34     }),
35
36     fixedItem: new sap.tnt.NavigationList({                  Fixed items
37         items: [
38             new sap.tnt.NavigationListItem({
39                 key: "fixed1",
40                 text: "Fixed Item",
41                 icon: "sap-icon://collision",
42                 tooltip: "Fixed items are positioned above the footer items"
43             })
44         ]
45     }),
46     footer: new sap.tnt.NavigationList({                    Footer items
47         items: [
48             new sap.tnt.NavigationListItem({
49                 key: "footer1",
50                 text: "Footer Item",
51                 icon: "sap-icon://incident",
52                 tooltip: "Footer items are always positioned at the bottom"
53             })
54         ]
55     })
56 });
```

It may be tedious to always provide a meaningful `tooltip`, but it definitely helps the users.

In Listing 3.15, "Construct a sap.tnt.SideNavigation" lines 3-5, we attached the `navigationItemSelect` function to the `itemSelect` event of the `SideNavigation`, which makes use of the event parameter `item` to get the item `key`. The key is the value of the `key` property of the `NavigationListItem`.

```
navigationItemSelect: function(oEvent) {
    const selectedItem = oEvent.getParameter("item");
    const selectedKey = selectedItem.getKey();
}
```

After constructing the `ToolHeader` and the `SideNavigation`, we can now construct the `sap.tnt.ToolPage`.

Listing 3.16. Construct a sap.tnt.ToolPage

```
const toolPage = new sap.tnt.ToolPage({
    header: toolHeader,                    See Listing 3.13, "Construct a sap.tnt.ToolHeader"
    sideContent: sideNavigation,           See Listing 3.15, "Construct a sap.tnt.SideNavigation"
    mainContents: [
        new sap.m.Title({
            text: "Main contents area",
            level: "H3", titleStyle: "H3"
        })
    ]
});
```

3.2. A page just to present a Message

We have already used the `sap.m.MessagePage` for our `noRoute` page (see Listing 2.19, "No such route Page"). To allow the user to navigate away from the MessagePage, the property `showNavButton` has to be set to 'true' and a handler function attached to the event `navButtonPress`.

3.3. Summary

In this chapter we learned how to define views and went through various page layouts offered by UI5. The main features of each layout were briefly explained and complemented with code examples. Woven into the chapter are the construction and configuration of responsive toolbars, which are a closely related cross-cutting issue.

Hopefully, the information provided here enables the reader to select the most fitting page layout for the task at hand and start coding.

Chapter 4. Navigation and Routing

After opening the start page of a client web application, the content of the page is modified mostly depending upon user interaction. Technically, this is done by manipulating the HTML DOM (Document Object Model) and the related Cascading Style Sheets (CSS).

As developers, we have to handle user input, request related data and assets, remove and modify current page content and add new content. Meanwhile, the URL in the browser remains the same, because all HTTP requests happen in the background. Such an application doesn't have any routes and navigation doesn't happen either, because we only have one document. Nevertheless, if needed, we can restore some previous state of the application using HTTP request parameters.

With growing size of applications, and particularly with more complex relationships between domain objects, this kind of code becomes difficult to organize and all but trivial changes increasingly expensive. Implementing the concept of different views can help reducing this headache by separating concerns. This does not change the fact that there is still only one HTML document. Basically, a view is something the user sees, which can be developed independently from other views. While this can be very useful, it is important to note that handling and navigating multiple views become itself complex issues, at least if the number of views increases. In this chapter we will look at the UI5 capabilities to help us with these issues.

With UI5, views must be added to aggregations of so-called root elements to be displayed. For the sap.m.App, it is the aggregation pages, while the sap.m.SplitApp has two aggregations named masterPages and detailPages.

4.1. Navigating without routes

The sap.m.App extends the sap.m.NavContainer, which provides full navigational capabilities. It has functions which allow us to manage the pages aggregation.

This kind of navigation works with view IDs. Before we can show a view, we check if it is already available in the associated aggregation or otherwise load the view and add it. Then we can navigate to it. Navigation doesn't change the URL and deep views cannot be reached directly, because the application always reloads to the same point.

Listing 4.1. Load and add view to the App pages aggregation

```
const viewId = "entryView";
if (app instanceof sap.m.App) {
   let view = app.getPage(viewId);              Get view from aggregation 'pages'
   if (view === null) {
      const viewName = "oum.view.entry";
      view = sap.ui.jsview({
         id: viewId,
         viewName: viewName
      });
      app.addPage(view);                        Add view to aggregation 'pages'
   }
   app.to(viewId);                              Navigate to view
}
```

The NavContainer can navigate to any view in the pages aggregation by the view ID. It keeps its own history, so that it can navigate back using the back function. It may also have an associated initialPage or otherwise the top view of the pages aggregation, which are treated like a home page. It navigates to its target using the backToTop function.

The sap.m.SplitApp extends the sap.m.SplitContainer, which basically works like the NavContainer, but with two aggregations for the master and the detail views.

 The SplitApp root element has the unfortunate behavior to only use one SplitContainer when running on a phone. This requires extra work, putting any advantages over the App into question when phones need to be supported.

Listing 4.2. Load and add view to the SplitApp detailPages aggregation

```
const viewId = "helpIntro";
if (splitApp instanceof sap.m.SplitApp) {
   let view = splitApp.getDetailPage(viewId);        Get view from aggregation 'detailPages'
   if (view === null) {
      const viewName = "oum.help.intro";
      view = sap.ui.jsview({
         id: viewId,
         viewName: viewName
      });
      splitApp.addDetailPage(view);                   Add view to aggregation 'detailPages'
   }
   splitApp.toDetail(viewId);                         Navigate to view
}
```

Once added to a page aggregation, the views remain in memory until explicitly destroyed. This means, when the application navigates to another view, the current view is left in its state. When we navigate to that view again later, it is in its previous state. If the view is well designed, restoring the original state should mainly be a matter of resetting the related models.

The NavContainer and SplitContainer provide navigation events, which are triggered before the navigation happens (navigate, masterNavigate, detailNavigate) or after it happened (afterNavigate, afterMasterNavigate, afterDetailNavigate). These events can be used to restore the views to a desired state before navigating to it, or after leaving it. The navigation event object passed to the attached handler function provides parameters concerning the navigation, among them the from and to parameters holding the related view objects.

 And while we are at it, especially for beginners, it won't hurt to attach handlers for navigation events, which add some generally useful logging messages. Here is the revised app.view.js:

Listing 4.3. XML view with sap.m.App using navigate event

```
<View xmlns="sap.m"
      controllerName="oum.controller.app"          Connect controller
      displayBlock="true">

   <App id="oumApp"
        navigate="onNavigate"                       Event 'navigate'
        defaultTransitionName="slide"
   />
</View>
```

The connected `app.controller.js` implements the `onNavigate` function attached to the `navigate` event.

Listing 4.4. App controller with navigate event handler function

```
sap.ui.define([
    "sap/ui/core/mvc/Controller"
], function (oController) {
    "use strict";

    const appController = oController.extend("oum.controller.app", {
        onNavigate: function(oEvent) {
            const from = oEvent.getParameter("from");                    Returns view object
            const to = oEvent.getParameter("to");
            oui5lib.logger.debug("navigate from " + from.getViewName() +
                                  " to " + to.getViewName());

            const firstTime = oEvent.getParameter("firstTime");
            if (firstTime) {
                oui5lib.logger.debug("to be navigated to for the first time");
            }
        }
    });

    return appController;
});
```

While the `logLevel` is set to `DEBUG`, these few lines of code will bring us closer to a 'speaking' console.

For small applications with some sequential views, navigating without routes may be a feasible approach. But for extended applications, we are well advised to primarily use the UI5 routing facilities for navigation.

4.2. Navigating with routes and targets

> OpenUI5 offers hash-based navigation, which allows you to build single-page apps where the navigation is done by changing the hash. In this way the browser does not have to reload the page; instead there is a callback to which the app and especially the affected view can react. A hash string is parsed and matched against patterns which will then inform the handlers.
>
> —openUI5 Developer Guide

In the `sap.ui.core.routing` namespace, we find all the objects related to routing. Instead of navigating by view IDs, we navigate by route or target names.

The `Router` initializes the `sap.ui.core.routing.HashChanger`, which both reacts to URL hash changes and also changes the hash. The related views are provided by the `sap.ui.core.routing.Views` repository. The views are placed and displayed using the `sap.ui.core.routing.Targets`.

The UI5 basic router class is the `sap.ui.core.routing.Router`. There are two extended router implementations. The `sap.m.routing.Router` adds some properties for every route or target: `viewLevel`, `transition` and `transitionParameters`. The `sap.f.routing.Router` additionally adds a property `layout` for every route to be used to navigate a three column layout implemented with a `sap.f.FlexibleColumnLayout`.

For each of the extended `Router` implementations, there are corresponding classes: `Targets`, which handle the additional properties and a `TargetHandler` to show the transitions.

In Chapter 2, *Building a basic responsive Web Application*, we have already explained how to add
and initialize a custom Router with routes and targets defined in the manifest.json. To move forward,
it is assumed here that we have a working oum.Router.

The following examples are building upon Listing 2.5, "Routing section of the manifest", especially
the config section, which sets default values applicable for all routes and targets.

When we configure a route, its name always needs to be unique, or otherwise the following route with
the same name will overwrite the previous. But the target may be shared by multiple routes. We use
the same target for all the following example routes, which we have to add to the targets array of
the manifest.json.

```
"orderEdit": {
   "viewName": "order",
   "title": "View/Edit order"
}
```

We assume to have an order view connected with a controller named oum.controller.order. The controller is in the controller folder and has the name order.controller.js. We prepare it to handle all
the following route examples.

Listing 4.5. Controller implementing pattern-matched handler

```
 1 sap.ui.define([
 2    "oui5lib/controller/BaseController"
 3 ], function(Controller) {
 4    "use strict";
 5
 6    const orderController = Controller.extend("oum.controller.order", {
 7       onInit: function () {
 8          this.getRouter().getRoute("order") ❶
 9             .attachPatternMatched(this._onRouteMatched, this);
10          this.getRouter().getRoute("orderProducts")
11             .attachPatternMatched(this._onRouteMatched, this);
12          this.getRouter().getRoute("orderAddress")
13             .attachPatternMatched(this._onRouteMatched, this);
14          this.getRouter().getRoute("orderAddressParams")
15             .attachPatternMatched(this._onRouteMatched, this);
16       },
17
18       _onRouteMatched: function(oEvent) {
19          const routeName = oEvent.getParameter("name");
20          const routeConfig = oEvent.getParameter("config");
21          const routeParameters = oEvent.getParameter("arguments");
22
23          const routeData = {};
24       }
25    });
26    return orderController;
27 });
```

❶   From the Router we get a Route by its name and then attach a function to its attachPatternMatched
     event.

The routing event object provides the parameters we need to process the event. We can get the route
name (line 19) and configuration (line 20), as well as any parameters (line 21). We will collect useful
information in the routeData object (line 23).

The following route examples have three parts each. The first part is the route configuration, the second part shows how to navigate to it with the router, and the third part is the `_onRouteMatched` code to process the related event.

Each route requires a `pattern`. The URL hash value is sent through the routes to find a match. The order of routes matters because the first matching pattern wins. Let us add some routes to the `routes` array of the manifest.json.

4.2.1. Pattern with optional parameter

```
{
    "pattern": "order/:id:",
    "name": "order",
    "target" : "orderEdit"
}
```

The pattern encloses the parameter id with colons, which make it optional. The pattern will therefore match both "#/order" and "#/order/2". This is quite useful because the same view allows creating a new order, as well as editing an existing order.

To navigate with the Router, we use the following code:

```
router.navTo("order");
router.navTo("order", { id: 2 });
```

In the controller `_onRouteMatched` function, we process the route parameters:

```
if (typeof routeParameters.id === "undefined") {
    routeData.type = "new order";
} else {
    routeData.type = "edit order";
    routeData.orderId = routeParameters.id;
}
```

4.2.2. Pattern with mandatory parameter

In the following route example, we specify a pattern requiring the id parameter, indicated by curly brackets. In this case, we need an order ID for an existing order to get to the related products.

```
{
    "pattern": "order/{id}/products",
    "name": "orderProducts",
    "target": "orderEdit"
}
```

Navigate by Router:

```
router.navTo("orderProducts", {
    id: "000417"
});
```

Process `patternMatched` event:

```
if (routeName === "orderProducts") {
    routeData.orderId = routeParameters.id;
    routeData.type = "products";
}
```

4.2.3. Pattern with multiple parameters

The next route example has two required parameters, the order `id` and the address `type` ("billing" or "shipping"). The pattern will match "#/order/2/address/billing" or "#/order/109428/address/shipping".

```
{
   "pattern": "order/{id}/address/{type}",
   "name": "orderAddress",
   "target" : "orderEdit"
}
```

Navigate by Router:

```
router.navTo("orderAddress", {
   id: 109428,
   type: "shipping"
});
```

Process routeMatched event:

```
if (routeName === "orderAddress") {
   routeData.orderId = routeParameters.id;
   routeData.type = routeParameters.type + "Address";
```

4.2.4. Pattern with additional parameters

Route patterns can also include additional parameters, which will be available from the related routing event object. This allows us to add parameters without the need to change the route pattern. Here, we make them optional by enclosing `?params` in colons. The pattern will match "#/order/109428/addresses" or "#/order/2/addresses?type=billing&mode=edit".

```
{
   "pattern": "order/{id}/addresses/:?params:",
   "name": "orderAddressParams",
   "target" : "orderEdit"
}
```

Navigate by Router:

```
router.navTo("orderAddressParams", {
   id: 2,
   params: "?type=billing&mode=edit"
});
```

Process `patternMatched` event:

```
if (routeName === "orderAddressParams") {
   routeData.orderId = routeParameters.id;
   routeData.type = "addresses";

   const params = routeParameters["?params"];
   const paramsList = [];
   for (let key in params) {
      paramsList.push({ name: key, value: params[key] });
   }
   routeData.params = paramsList;
});
```

4.2.5. Understanding target control parameters

So far, in this chapter all the route examples used the same target ("orderEdit") to be loaded into the default controlId ("oumApp") and controlAggregation ("pages"), which are the default values from Listing 2.5, "Routing section of the manifest".

The controlId may refer to any control with an aggregation for content (controlAggregation). Especially important are the root elements and their aggregations. For flexibility, it is generally useful to have both an App (see Listing 4.3, "XML view with sap.m.App using navigate event") and a SplitApp (see Listing 2.20, "XML view with SplitApp") configured as targets.

```
"targets": {
    "app": {
        "viewName": "app",          View ID is "oumApp"
        "viewType": "XML"
    },
    "splitApp": {
        "viewName": "splitApp",     View ID is "oumSplitApp"
        "viewType": "XML"
    }
}
```

Let us reload our component home page and look at it from the perspective of the UI5 Inspector.

```
▼<sap-ui-area id="oumContent">
  ▼<sap.ui.core.ComponentContainer id="__container0">
    ▼<sap.ui.core.mvc.XMLView id="__xmlview0">
      ▼<sap.m.App id="__xmlview0--oumApp">
        ▶<sap.ui.core.mvc.JSView id="__jsview0">
```

We have the ComponentContainer with a first view, whose content is the sap.m.App. There is only one view loaded into the aggregation pages, which is our entry view. When we navigate to the help, we see some changes.

```
▼<sap-ui-area id="oumContent">
  ▼<sap.ui.core.ComponentContainer id="__container0">
    ▼<sap.ui.core.mvc.XMLView id="__xmlview0">
      ▼<sap.m.App id="__xmlview0--oumApp">
        ▶<sap.ui.core.mvc.JSView id="__jsview0">
        ▼<sap.ui.core.mvc.XMLView id="__xmlview1">
          ▼<sap.m.SplitApp id="__xmlview1--oumSplitApp">
            ▼<sap.m.NavContainer id="__xmlview1--oumSplitApp-Master">
              ▶<sap.ui.core.mvc.JSView id="__jsview1">
            ▼<sap.m.NavContainer id="__xmlview1--oumSplitApp-Detail">
              ▶<sap.ui.core.mvc.JSView id="__jsview2">
```

There is now another view in the pages aggregation (id="__xmlview1"). Its content is the sap.m.SplitApp and it comes along with two sap.m.NavContainer objects, each with one view.

How did this happen? We have never loaded the SplitApp explicitly. Instead, we simply told the Router to navigate to the route "help". The route has two targets.

```
{
   "pattern": "help",
   "name": "help",
   "target": ["helpIndex", "helpIntro"]
}
```

Listing 2.21, "SplitApp target entries" shows the configuration of the related targets. The `parent` property of the `helpIndex` and `helpIntro` targets is the `splitApp` target. This causes the related view to be added to the default `oumApp` pages aggregation. Its content is the `SplitApp`. The targets overwrite the default `controlId`, using the ID of the SplitApp instead, whose `controlAggregation` may either be `masterPages` or `detailPages`.

This is a flexible concept, which works with other controls and aggregations as well, not just with root elements. For this, it is important to understand that a view is not necessarily some kind of a page, but may return any content control tree. A route may have several targets to be added to various aggregations and displayed. The target parent could be any control with an aggregation for content.

4.2.5.1. Using a common layout view

To explore this feature, let us add another route.

```
{
   "pattern": "address/:id:",
   "name": "address",
   "target": "addressForm"
}
```

Instead of a full page layout control, our address view may just construct and return a form.

```
sap.ui.jsview("oum.view.address", {
    createContent : function(oController) {
        const addressForm = new sap.ui.layout.form.SimpleForm(this.createId("addressForm"),{
            title: "SimpleForm 'title'",
            editable: true,
            layout: "ResponsiveGridLayout"
        });

        return addressForm;
    },
    getControllerName : function() {
        return "oum.controller.address";
    }
});
```

We also construct another view as a page template into which we then place the form above.

```
 1 sap.ui.jsview("oum.view.layout", {
 2    createContent : function(oController) {
 3        const headerTitle = new sap.m.Title({
 4            text: "{layout>/titleText}",
 5            level: "H2",
 6            titleStyle: "H4"
 7        });
 8
 9        const headerBar = new sap.m.Bar({
10         design: "Header",
11            contentMiddle: [ headerTitle ],
12            contentRight: [
```

```
13              sap.ui.jsfragment("oum.fragment.BackButton", oController)
14          ]
15      });
16
17      const layoutPage = new sap.m.Page("oumLayout", {        The target 'controlId'
18          customHeader: headerBar,
19          content: [ ],                                        The target 'controlAggregation'
20          footer: sap.ui.xmlfragment("oum.fragment.AppInfoToolbar")
21      });
22      return layoutPage;
23  },
24  getControllerName : function() {
25      return "oum.controller.layout";
26  }
27 });
```

To place the address form into the content aggregation of the Page returned by the layout view, we have to add the related targets to our manifest.json. The parent is our layout target, which provides a sap.m.Page object, whose ID (line 17) is the controlId value of the addressForm target. The controlAggregation provided by the Page is its content aggregation (line 19).

```
"targets": {
    "layout": {
        "viewName": "layout"
    },
    "addressForm": {
        "parent": "layout",
        "viewName": "address",
        "title": "{i18n>target.addressForm.title}",
        "controlId": "oumLayout",
        "controlAggregation": "content"
    }
    ...
}
```

With the address Form placed into the content aggregation of the Page we have two controllers. For the layout view to effectively work as a template, the address controller must be able to set the layout model providing the "titleText" (line 4).

```
sap.ui.define([
    "sap/ui/core/mvc/Controller"
], function (oController) {
    "use strict";

    const addressController = oController.extend("oum.controller.address", {
        onInit: function() {
            const layoutModel = new sap.ui.model.json.JSONModel();
            layoutModel.setData({
                titleText: "Address Form"
            });

            const layoutPage = sap.ui.getCore().byId("oumLayout");
            layoutPage.setModel(layoutModel, "layout");
        }
    });

    return addressController;
});
```

Screenshot of address view as layout Page content

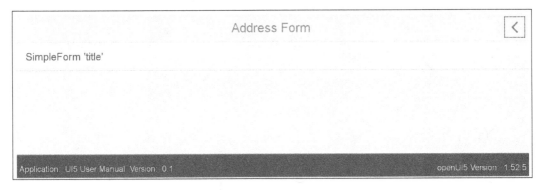

4.2.6. General annotations to targets

It is good practice to declare a target `title` property, simply because it is the only descriptive target property and can be used with the Router.

Here, we don't look into further target properties concerning transitions. Whenever elaborate transitions are needed, play with the `viewLevel`, `transition` and `transitionParameters` properties.

4.3. Ways to navigate

There are different ways to navigate to a target. In the above section you will find several examples, showing how to use the `navTo` function of the `Router`. All of them will add an entry to the browser history.

The `Router` `navTo` function takes three parameters, a route name, an optional parameters object and a boolean indicating if a browser history entry is added. The default is 'false'. If we want a history entry, we use

```
router.navTo(routeName);
```

Otherwise we use

```
router.navTo(routeName, {}, true);
```

We can also pass parameters:

```
router.navTo(routeName,
    {
        key: value,
    }, true);
```

The Router will call the `HashChanger` to change the hash value, which will trigger the actual routing event. Depending upon our choice concerning the history entry, it will use either the `setHash` or the `replaceHash` function. We can also navigate by calling the HashChanger directly:

```
const hashChanger = sap.ui.core.routing.HashChanger.getInstance();
hashChanger.setHash(hashValue);            Add browser history entry
hashChanger.replaceHash(hashValue);        No browser history entry
```

And if we want to navigate without changing the URL hash value, we can use the `Targets` directly.

```
const targets = router.getTargets();
targets.display(targetViewName);
```

 Displaying targets causes no routing event and the related attached handlers will not be called.

4.4. Routing History

After entering the application, the `sap.ui.core.routing.History` keeps the same data as the browser `window.history`. That means, it tells us if the user just entered the application. We can use this information for the 'back' button to not let the user exit the application (see Listing 2.24, "Router function to navigate back").

An application navigation history without duplicates is accessible through the Router. On top of the hash value, it will also keep the title if the target title property is set.

```
function logHistory() {
    const history = router.getTitleHistory();
    history.reverse().forEach(function(historyEntry) {
        oui5lib.logger.info("title: " + historyEntry.title);
        oui5lib.logger.info("hash: " + historyEntry.hash);
    });
};
```

4.5. Summary

In this chapter we looked into the means provided by UI5 to navigate between views, with or without a router. We learned how to configure routes with or without parameters, how to navigate to them and how to handle the routing events. Finally, we looked at a way to access the application routing history.

Based upon the introduction of a custom router in Chapter 2, *Building a basic responsive Web Application*, the details presented here enable the reader to happily navigate between various target views and prepare them according to the route parameters. Using a `Router`, each target may be designed to be self-contained and also control additional dependent views, like for example the master view of a `SplitApp`.

Chapter 5. User Permissions

User (or entity) authentication, session management and access authorization can never be provided on the client-side. It is beyond the scope of this book to deal with these issues. For general information about authentication you may want to read the Authentication Cheat Sheet from the Open Web Application Security Project (OWASP) [https://www.owasp.org/index.php/Authentication_Cheat_Sheet].

In this chapter, we will show how to implement access control to help protect our client application from unauthorized use. Although we use the user's role to grant or deny access, this shall not be understood as a statement for role-based vs. attribute-based access control. [1]

Here, we simply assume that the user already has a verified session and that we can get the user profile from the authorizing server. We further assume, that the response is JSON with some basic information about the user.

```
{
    "firstname": "Carsten",
    "lastname": "Heinrigs",
    "userId": "cahein",
    "token": "562f667540ce09f2a6461920011b341e",
    "roles": [
        "user"
    ]
}
```

5.1. Requesting the current user profile data

To request the user profile, we first add a property userProfileUrl to our config.json and add the related function to the oui5lib.configuration namespace.

```
function getUserProfileUrl() {
    const userProfileUrl = getConfigData("userProfileUrl");
    if (userProfileUrl === undefined) {
        return null;
    }
    return userProfileUrl;
}
configuration.getUserProfileUrl = getUserProfileUrl;
```

Our user object gets the namespace oui5lib.currentuser. Upon initialization, we have to request the user profile and set the related variables.

---

[1]For more information about Role Based Access Control and Attribute Based Access Control you may want to read the following texts provided by the National Institute of Standards and Technology of the U.S. Department of Commerce:

- Role Based Access Control [https://csrc.nist.gov/Projects/Role-Based-Access-Control]

- Economic Analysis of Role-Based Access Control: Final Report [https://csrc.nist.gov/CSRC/media/Publications/white-paper/2010/12/01/economic-analysis-of-rbac-final-report/final/documents/20101219_RBAC2_Final_Report.pdf]

- Guide to Attribute Based Access Control (ABAC) Definition and Considerations [https://nvlpubs.nist.gov/nistpubs/specialpublications/nist.sp.800-162.pdf]

Listing 5.1. Namespace oui5lib.currentuser

```
 1 (function(configuration, request) {
 2    "use strict";
 3
 4    const user = oui5lib.namespace("currentuser"),        Setup namespace and declare variables
 5        _name = null,
 6        _userId = null,
 7        _token = null,
 8        _userRoles = [],
 9        _permissionsMap = null;
10
11    function init() {
12        const userProfileUrl = oui5lib.configuration.getUserProfileUrl();
13        if (userProfileUrl !== null) {
14            requestUserProfile(userProfileUrl);
15        }
16    }
17    user.init = init;                                     Add function to namespace
18
19    function requestUserProfile(userProfileUrl) {
20        oui5lib.request.loadJson(userProfileUrl, ❶
21                                 userProfileRequestSucceeded,   Callback function
22                                 {}, false);                     Set request synchronous
23    }
24
25    function userProfileRequestSucceeded(userProfile) {
26        if (userProfile !== null) {
27            _name = userProfile.firstname + " " + userProfile.lastname;
28            _userId = userProfile.userId;
29            _token = userProfile.token;
30
31            if (userProfile.roles instanceof Array) {
32                _userRoles = userProfile.roles;
33            }
34        }
35    }
36 }(oui5lib.configuration, oui5lib.request));               Pass dependencies as function parameters
```

❶   The oui5lib.request namespace and the loadJson function used here are presented in Listing 11.1, "Namespace oui5lib.request".

So far, the only function added to the oui5lib.currentuser namespace is the init function. In this case we definitely want further processing of our application to be blocked until the issue of authorization is settled. We therefore request the user profile synchronously (lines 20 to 22) since any further steps depend on the response.

If the user doesn't have the required authorization, he or she clearly shouldn't be able to access the application and instead be redirected to a noPermissions page. We add the related route and target to the manifest:

```
"routes": [
   ...
   {
      "pattern": "notAuthorized",
      "name": "notAuthorized",
      "target": "notAuthorized"
   }
],
targets: {
   ...
   "notAuthorized": {
      "viewName": "noPermissions",
      "viewType": "XML"
   }
}
```

As target view, we create a simple MessagePage. For productive environments, the texts below should be multilingual i18n properties.

```
<mvc:View xmlns="sap.m"
          xmlns:mvc="sap.ui.core.mvc">
   <MessagePage
      title="Not Authorized"
      text="This page is not available."
      description="You do not have permission to access the requested page."/>
</mvc:View>
```

Because there are many ways to navigate to views, the only reliable way to check permissions is on the view level. Following widespread practice we configure permissions based upon roles. Let us create a permissions.json and add view entries.

```
{
   "views": {
      "oum.view.entry": {
         "roles": [ "user" ]
      },
      "oum.view.help.index": {
         "roles": [ "noone", "can", "go", "here" ]
      }
   }
}
```

To load the permissions, we request it in the oui5lib.currentuser.init function. Again the request is synchronous for the same reason as stated above.

```
function init() {
   ...
   oui5lib.request.loadJson("permissions.json",
                            permissionsMapRequestSucceeded,      Callback function
                            {}, false);                          Set request synchronous
}

function permissionsMapRequestSucceeded(permissionsMap) {
   _permissionsMap = permissionsMap;
}
```

To check if a user belongs to the required group(s), we add the following function to the oui5lib.currentuser namespace.

Listing 5.2. Check view permission

```
 1 function hasPermissionForView(viewName) {
 2    if (_permissionsMap === null) {
 3       return false;
 4    }
 5
 6    if (typeof _permissionsMap.views[viewName] !== "undefined") {
 7       const roles = _permissionsMap.views[viewName].roles;
 8       return hasPermissions(roles);
 9    }
10    return true;
11 }
12
13 function hasPermissions(authorizedRoles) {
14    if (typeof authorizedRoles === "undefined" ||
15       !(authorizedRoles instanceof Array)) {
16       return false;
17    }
18
19    let authorized = false, i, s;
20    for (i = 0, s = authorizedRoles.length; i < s; i++) {
21       if (hasRole(authorizedRoles[i])) {
22          authorized = true;
23          break;
24       }
25    }
26    return authorized;
27 }
28
29 function hasRole(role) {
30    return _userRoles.indexOf(role) > -1;
31 }
32
33 user.hasRole = hasRole;                              Add functions to namespace
34 user.hasPermissionForView = hasPermissionForView;
```

If the requested permissions.json couldn't be loaded and processed, no authorization is given (line 3). If, however, there is no entry in the permissions map, it is assumed that access is authorized (line 10). In case there is an entry with an empty roles array, no user will be authorized.

To check permission to a particular view, we have to add a few lines to the connected controller onInit function.

```
onInit: function () {
   const view = this.getView();
   if (!oui5lib.currentuser.hasPermissionForView(view.getViewName())) {
      this.getRouter().navTo("notAuthorized");
      return;
   }
   ...                               Without permission, this code will never execute
}
```

Because this needs to be repeated for every view with a target, we should further simplify matters by adding a function to our oui5lib.controller.BaseController (see Listing 2.29, "A custom BaseController").

```
verifyPermission: function() {
   const view = this.getView();
   const viewName = view.sViewName;
   if (!oui5lib.currentuser.hasPermissionForView(viewName)) {
      this.getRouter().navTo("notAuthorized");
      return false;
   }
   return true;
}
```

This significantly reduces the verification code in the onInit function.

```
onInit: function () {
   if (!this.verifyPermission()) {
      return;
   }
   ...
}
```

All our efforts would be in vain, however, if a malicious user could easily circumvent our safety precautions. So far, it would be enough to overwrite the hasPermissionForView function.

```
oui5lib.currentuser.hasPermissionForView = function() {
   return true;
};
```

To make it more difficult we have to freeze the involved objects, so that they cannot be modified afterwards. We add such a function to the oui5lib.util namespace (see Listing 2.25, "Setup custom utility namespace ").

Listing 5.3. Protect objects: deepFreeze function

```
function deepFreeze(o) {
   let prop, propKey;
   Object.freeze(o);
   for (propKey in o) {
      prop = o[propKey];
      if (!(o.hasOwnProperty(propKey) && (typeof prop === "object")) ||
         Object.isFrozen(prop)) {
         continue;
      }
      this.deepFreeze(prop);
   }
}
util.deepFreeze = deepFreeze;
```

Now, we should have everything in place to effectively use oui5lib.currentuser object. The best place to initialize it is the Component init function before initializing the Router.

```
if (typeof oui5lib.currentuser === "object") {
   oui5lib.currentuser.init();
   oui5lib.util.deepFreeze(oui5lib.configuration);
   oui5lib.util.deepFreeze(oui5lib.currentuser);
   oui5lib.util.deepFreeze(oui5lib.request);
}
```

Nothing happens unless the oui5lib.currentuser object is available. We add it to the oui5lib.init dependencies.

```
sap.ui.require([
    "oui5lib/configuration",
    "oui5lib/logger",
    "oui5lib/util",
    "oui5lib/request",
    "oui5lib/currentuser"
], function() {
    oui5lib.logger.info("oui5lib successfully loaded");
});
```

If we add the permissions check to the `oum.controller.entry onInit` function, no user will reach the entry page without the required role.

5.2. Properties to implement user permissions

All the controls introduced here inherit the `visible` property. If set to `false`, both the control and the associated label are excluded from the view. The behavior of the controls can be further specified using the properties `enabled` and `editable`. If not enabled, the control cannot be focused and is excluded from the tab-chain. If enabled, but not editable, just the control value cannot be edited.

These properties can be effectively used to implement user permissions through a permissions model.

```
const permissionsModel = new sap.ui.model.json.JSONModel();
permissionsModel.setData({
    "name": {
        "visible": true,
        "enable": true,
        "edit": false
    }
});
form.setModel(permissionsModel, "permissions");
```

After setting the model so that the control is within its scope (in the above example the 'form' containing the control), the properties can now be set. Changing the permissions model data will now update the view accordingly.

```
new sap.m.Input({
    visible: "{permissions>/name/visible}",      Can the user see the label and control?
    enabled: "{permissions>/name/enable}",       Can the user only see the control?
    editable: "{permissions>/name/edit}"         Can the user edit the value?
});
```

5.3. Summary

In this chapter we have shown how entry to particular views can be effectively denied. We have also introduced a way to implement permissions for controls within a view. While these efforts may not finally prevent access violations by malicious users, we made it harder for them to do so.

Chapter 6. Events and Messages

Software development is a communicative process, which doesn't produce any product in the conventional sense, because, once written, the 'product' can be reproduced without any costs. While the value and benefits of an application are often difficult to evaluate and estimate, the changeability of software can make it the most adaptable aspect of workflow and production processes. This potential is often underutilized and we end up adapting to software instead.

Public websites, and especially online shops, seem to have the greatest incentive to measure the effects of software changes. But they are in a difficult position, because most of their users are anonymous. Regardless of all the tracking, there is very little direct feedback.

In the sphere of business or administrative software where employees have to use the applications their employer provides, software development could be driven by the users. But that rarely happens. Usually, the larger the company, the less influence the users have upon the software they work with. Instead, managers of the various departments come together in meetings to make the general decisions, and IT managers direct the actual implementation and development projects. The primary measure of success for IT managers is not the feedback of the users, but the regard of their superiors. A senior collegue explained to me once, that "no manager was ever fired for hiring IBM".

The big software companies selling applications like regular products are most concerned about their profits, meaning sales. Their salespeople don't advertize their products to the users, but to the IT managers and they speak the language of accountants. Because the applications are designed to fit the greatest possible range of customers, they are generally packed with features.

As software developers, we are usually not directly connected to the users of our work. If we efficiently build an inefficient application the customer asks for, we will be applauded. If we finish a feature in time without noticeable errors, our supervisor is happy. The user often appears as an annoying factor, who makes all kinds of stupid errors. Communication with the user is just a side aspect of our work.

At this point, you may ask: What does all this have to do with the topic of this chapter? Well, depending upon their relationship to the application, different people with different roles look at events and messages from different perspectives. Arguably, the most important perspective is that of the user.

For the user, software applications are just interfaces they have to use. Principally, the user expects that his actions cause a reasonable and predictable behavior of the application. That may mean something different for each user, but some common rules do exist.

The most fundamental rule of software development may sound obvious, but is too often forgotten or ignored: You can never blame the user for any application errors or deficiencies. Next comes the recognition, that the users know best how an application should work for them to help accomplish the tasks at hand. Therefore, whenever possible, we have to ask the users, what they need and want, and learn from them by watching them use the application. Letting the users guide application and feature development is possibly the only way to overcome the negative attitudes of users towards changes, which are often associated with stress.

Now, let's finally get to events and messages. The user generally doesn't like to read messages and, even less, help files. This is partly the result of frustrating experiences with often ridiculously unhelpful messages and partly due to laziness. We can't do much about (other people's) laziness, but there is much left to do to improve the way we communicate with the user.

More concretely, there are some common features, which will likely help the users and should be implemented.

- On every page, the initial focus will give the user a starting point, hinting at what he or she is supposed to do.
- Whenever there is focus on an active element, or a pointer over it, we show a short descriptive text explaining what it does.
- Make sure that the tab navigation works reasonably well, because it is usually the fastest way to work with forms, where the user has to enter text or numbers.
- Whatever input by the user should be validated as soon as possible to give timely feedback. It is not acceptable to let the user run into a bunch of error messages after submitting a form.
- Provide consistent feedback throughout the application.
- Expect the user to make all kinds of 'mistakes' and therefore minimize the options.

6.1. Events

From a developer's perspective, there are two general groups of events. In the first group are events triggered by user actions. These events are both expected as well as essentially unpredictable. In the second group are events which belong to the internal workings of the application and concern its relations to whatever connections and resources it uses. Some of these events require communication with or notification of the user. This means that events and messages are closely related.

6.1.1. User Interface Events

User actions become events if the application has a listener enabled and handlers are called to process the triggered events. Some of these events generate a feedback to the user in the form of messages.

Many controls have properties to attach events, which will call whatever function we attach to it. These calls come with a `sap.ui.base.Event` object, which always has an ID and a source we can get through `oEvent.getSource()`. Other parameters may be available. To find out, which parameters an event provides, we have to look into the UI5 API Reference where we find the available events listed. If we go to an event entry, we find the event object described.

We have already looked at examples how to handle events in Chapter 2, *Building a basic responsive Web Application*. Nevertheless, it may help to look at another example here. The `sap.m.ComboBox` control has several events to attach to. The most important ones are `change` and `selectionChange` events.

UI5 API: ComboBox events

Event Detail

○ **change** (oControlEvent)

This event is fired when the value in the text input field is changed in combination with one of the following actions:

- The focus leaves the text input field
- The *Enter* key is pressed

In addition, this event is also fired when an item in the list is selected.

Parameters:

sap.ui.base.Event	**oControlEvent**	
sap.ui.base.EventProvider	**oControlEvent.getSource**	
object	**oControlEvent.getParameters**	
string	**oControlEvent.getParameters.value**	The new value of the control
boolean	**oControlEvent.getParameters.itemPressed**	Indicates whether the change event was caused by selecting an item in the list

○ **selectionChange** (oControlEvent)

This event is fired when the user types something that matches with an item in the list; it is also fired when the user presses on a list item, or when navigating via keyboard.

Parameters:

sap.ui.base.Event	**oControlEvent**	
sap.ui.base.EventProvider	**oControlEvent.getSource**	
object	**oControlEvent.getParameters**	
sap.ui.core.Item	**oControlEvent.getParameters.selectedItem**	The selected item.

Listing 6.1. Construct a sap.m.ComboBox

```
new sap.m.ComboBox({
   change: function(oEvent) {
      oController.handleChangeEvent(oEvent);          Attach function to 'change' event
   },
   selectionChange: function(oEvent) {
      oController.handleSelectionChangeEvent(oEvent);  Attach function to 'selectionChange' event
   }
});
```

In the controller, we declare the related functions and use the event object.

Listing 6.2. ComboBox event handler functions

```
handleChangeEvent: function(oEvent) {
   const comboBox = oEvent.getSource();
   const value = oEvent.getParameter("value");
   const wasItemPressed = oEvent.getParameter("itemPressed");
},

handleSelectionChangeEvent: function(oEvent) {
   const comboBox = oEvent.getSource();
   const selectedItem = oEvent.getParameter("selectedItem");
}
```

6.1.2. Publish/Subscribe Events

Another category of events is based upon the observer (publish/subscribe) pattern. The pattern helps us to reduce dependencies between objects. This is called loose coupling. These kind of events are usually published because some event occurred which may be of concern for other objects, which have therefore subscribed to the event. The triggering events can come from various sources, which are unknown to the subscribing object.

For example, if a crucial server connection fails, the application needs to inform the user and tell him what to do. If it is merely a matter of a less important request failing, the object expecting the response needs to adjust.

Another example are websocket connections, which allow pushing messages from the server to the client. Using the observer pattern, we can publish the websocket events and thereby allow all potentially affected parts of the application to subscribe to the event for processing.

UI5 implements the observer pattern with the `sap.ui.core.EventBus`. All its functions have a required `eventId` and an optional `channelId`, both strings. Subscribing to an event means to register a function to the list of functions to be notified when a certain event occurs.

There is a one EventBus at the level of the Core and another at the level of the Component. They work the same way, but are independent from each other. We therefore always have to decide if an event is relevant for the whole application, or only related to the Component.

The events are defined by the `channelId` and `eventId`. Subscribing to an event means to add a given function to the event handlers. A synonymous `unsubscribe` call will remove the function from the event handler list.

There is also a `subscribeOnce` function, which is valid only for the first occurrence of a published event.

Let us look at an example controller.

Listing 6.3. Subscribe to an event

```
sap.ui.define([
   "sap/ui/core/mvc/Controller"
], function (oController) {
   "use strict";

   const eventsController = oController.extend("oum.controller.events", {
      onInit: function () {
         // Core EventBus
         const coreEventBus = sap.ui.getCore().getEventBus();
         coreEventBus.subscribeOnce("serviceAvailable", "ldap",          SubscribeOnce
                           this.serviceAvailableHandler);

         // Component EventBus
         const componentEventBus = this.getOwnerComponent().getEventBus();
         componentEventBus.subscribe("dataLoaded", "addresses",          Subscribe
                           this.dataLoadedEvent);
      },

      serviceAvailableHandler: function(channelId, eventId, data) {        Callback for Core event
         if (eventId === "ldap") {
            const host = data.url;
            const port = data.port;
         }
      },

      dataLoadedEvent: function(channelId, eventId, data) {               Callback for Component event
         if (eventId === "addresses") {
```

```
          const ids = data.ids;

          const componentEventBus = this.getOwnerComponent().getEventBus();
          componentEventBus.unsubscribe("dataLoaded", "addresses",      Unsubcribe
                              this.dataLoadedEvent);
      }
    }
  });
  return eventsController
});
```

To publish the event, we have to use the corresponding `sap.ui.core.EventBus`. We can access the Event-Bus anywhere in the code and it can pass any object along with a `channelId` and a mandatory `eventId`.

Although SAP in its "Best Practices for developing SAP Fiori apps" recommends to always use the event bus of the component, there can be situations where we want to use the global event bus.

Listing 6.4. Publish through the Core EventBus

```
const eventBus = sap.ui.getCore().getEventBus();
eventBus.publish("serviceAvailable", "ldap",                    channelId, eventId
            { host: "ldap.example.com", port: "389" }
);
```

Usually we want to use the event bus from the component to publish an event.

Listing 6.5. Publish through the Component EventBus

```
const componentId = "oumComponent";
const component = sap.ui.getCore().getComponent(componentId);
const eventBus = component.getEventBus();
eventBus.publish("dataLoaded", "addresses",                    channelId, eventId
            { ids: [ 1, 2 ] }
);
```

6.1.3. Routing events

We have already touched the issue of routing events in the previous chapter (Listing 4.5, "Controller implementing pattern-matched handler"). Nearly all controllers have to do something when the related route patterns are requested.

The `Router` provides several events which are triggered if any configured route pattern matches. The most important is the `routePatternMatched` event. We can attach a function to the event using the related `attachRoutePatternMatched` function. If we want to be notified before the related targets are loaded and placed, the `beforeRouteMatched` event can be used.

To make use of the `title` property of the targets, we can attach a function to the `titleChanged` event.

In most cases, we don't want to attach a function to all events where a route pattern matches, but only to a particular route pattern. This is achieved using the `Route` object, which we get through the `getRoute` function of the `Router`. It provides similar events and functions, but only for a particular route (`attachPatternMatched`, `attachBeforeMatched`).

6.2. Messages to the user

Some types of messages are needed throughout the application. We could use fragments to make the code reusable. Yet, there is an even simpler way using a custom messages library.

```
(function(logger) {
   const messages = oui5lib.namespace("messages");          Create namespace oui5lib.messages
}(oui5lib.logger));
```

6.2.1. Quick Notitification: MessageToast

The MessageToast shows a message and disappears without user action. It is ideal for success messages, or to give a quick notification of non-essential incoming server messages. A word to the wise: Don't expect the user to have seen and even less to have read it.

Listing 6.6. Function to show a MessageToast

```
function showMessageToast(msg, duration) {
   if (typeof duration !== "number") {
      duration = 3000;                                       Will disappears in 3 seconds
   }
   sap.m.MessageToast.show(msg, { duration: duration });
}
messages.showNotification = showMessageToast;
```

Successfully updated the address

6.2.2. Ask the user: MessageBox

> As MessageBox is a static class, a jQuery.sap.require("sap.m.MessageBox"); statement must be explicitly executed before the class can be used.
>
> —openUI5 API

The MessageBox is the best choice if the user needs to either take notice of something or make some decision. The message popup will block the application until the user chooses one of the actions offered.

The control offers a mix of action buttons and icons, which can be freely combined if we use the sap.m.MessageBox.show function:

Listing 6.7. Use MessageBox

```
jQuery.sap.require("sap.m.MessageBox");
sap.m.MessageBox.show("Some message to show.", {
   title: "Whatever title",
   icon: "INFORMATION"                                       Enumeration sap.m.MessageBox.Icon
   actions: ["OK", "CANCEL"],                                Enumeration sap.m.MessageBox.Action
   initialFocus: "OK",
   onClose: function(sResult) { },
   details: "Some additional information."
});
```

• Enumeration sap.m.MessageBox.Action choices: ABORT, CANCEL, CLOSE, DELETE, IGNORE, NO, OK, RETRY, YES

- Enumeration `sap.m.MessageBox.Icon` choice: ERROR, INFORMATION, NONE, QUESTION, SUCCESS, WARNING

The MessageBox also offers some functions with predefined combinations of icons and actions:

Table 6.1. Predefined MessageBox layouts

Function name	Action Choices	Icon
alert	OK	
confirm	OK, CANCEL	QUESTION
error	CLOSE	ERROR
information	OK	INFO
success	OK	SUCCESS
warning	OK	WARNING

The only event of the MessageBox is `onClose`. It receives a string, which represents one of the action choices from enumeration `sap.m.MessaqeBox.Action`.

6.2.2.1. Show an error message

All applications have errors and UI applications need the ability to show error messages. Instead of repeating the same code, we will add a convenience function to the messages namespace. But let us first look at an example error message:

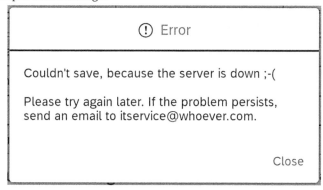

For error messages we use the MessageBox `error` function, which shows an `ERROR` icon and has only a `CLOSE` action. Because we just want to inform the user and don't give her/him any action choice, no handler function is required to process the user action.

Before we will get to the `showErrorMessageBox` function, we have to think about internationalized message texts. If the i18n properties are set to the `Component`, they will not be accessible for the `MessageBox`. The i18n properties could instead be set to the `Core`, but that is a problematic approach, because we may want to use multiple Components together, each having its own set of property keys. Instead, we can simply use a utility function to get the i18n text from the Component. We will add such a function to the `oui5lib.util` namespace (see Listing 2.25, "Setup custom utility namespace "). It gets the component from `getComponent` function of the `oui5lib.configuration` namespace (see Listing 2.13, "Custom namespace for configuration issues").

On top of just returning the property value, the `jQuery.sap.util.ResourceBundle` has the ability to re-place property placeholders of the form '{n}' with the corresponding strings in the provided array (parameter 'args').

Listing 6.8. Utitily function to get I18n resource property

```
function getI18nText(key, args) {
    const component = oui5lib.configuration.getComponent();
    const i18nModel = component.getModel("i18n");              Model name is 'i18n'
    const resourceBundle = i18nModel.getResourceBundle();      Query.sap.util.ResourceBundle
    return resourceBundle.getText(key, args);
}
util.getI18nText = getI18nText;
```

With the utility function to get the text from the resource bundle in place, we can now add a function to show an error message to the `oui5lib.messages` namespace.

Listing 6.9. Function to show an error message

```
function handleErrorMessageBoxClosed(sResult) {
    logger.info("ErrorMessage closed");
}

function showErrorMessageBox(errorMsg, handleClose) {
    if (typeof handleClose !== "function") {
        handleClose = handleMessageBoxClosed;
    }

    const titleText = oui5lib.util.getI18nText("messagebox.error.title");

    jQuery.sap.require("sap.m.MessageBox");
    sap.m.MessageBox.error(errorMsg, {
        title: titleText,
        onClose: handleClose
    });
}
messages.showErrorMessage = showErrorMessageBox;
```

6.2.2.2. Confirm unsaved changes

If the application is going to leave a form with unsaved changes, we may want the user to confirm, that this is really what she/he wants.

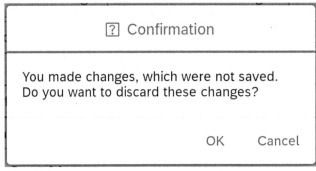

Listing 6.10. Function to ask the user to confirm discarding unsaved changes

```
1 function confirmUnsavedChanges(handleClose, navto) { ❶
2    if (typeof handleClose !== "function") {
3       throw new TypeError("need a function to handle the onClose event");
4    }
5
6    const messageText = oui5lib.util.getI18nText("unsavedChanges.text");
7
8    jQuery.sap.require("sap.m.MessageBox");
9    sap.m.MessageBox.confirm(messageText, {
10      initialFocus: "CANCEL",
11      onClose: function(action) {
12         handleClose(action, navto);
13      }
14   });
15 }
16 messages.confirmUnsavedChanges = confirmUnsavedChanges;
```

❶ Because the application may have to ask the user to confirm discarding pending changes after clicking the 'Back' or 'Home' button (see Listing 16.15, "HomeButton fragment checking for unsaved changes"), we add a navto parameter to be able to continue the requested action after confirmation.

The MessageBox confirm function shows a QUESTION icon and allows an action choice between OK and CANCEL. Because there is a choice, we need a handler function. Therefore, we throw a TypeError if no function is given to handle the user choice (lines 2 to 4).

A simple usage example may look like this:

```
function handleUnsavedChangesConfirmed(action, navto) {
    oui5lib.logger.info("confirm unsaved changes? " + choice);      'OK' or 'CANCEL'
    if (choice === "OK") {
        // discard pending changes

        if (typeof navto === "string) {
            switch(navto) {
            case "home":
                this.getRouter().vNavTo("home");
                break;
            case "back":
                this.getRouter().navBack();
                break;
            }
        }
    }
}

oui5lib.messages.confirmUnsavedChanges(handleUnsavedChangesConfirmed);
```

6.2.2.3. Confirm delete

If the application is going to delete a record, we should ask the user to confirm.

Because the predefined MessageBox layouts (see Table 6.1, "Predefined MessageBox layouts") are not fitting, we have to configure the MessageBox ourselves.

While the above confim unsaved changes message text can be the same throughout the application, we want to show custom messages to warn the user if the application is going to delete a record.

Listing 6.11. Function to ask the user to confirm deleting a record

```
function confirmDelete(msgText, handleClose) {
    if (typeof handleClose !== "function") {
        throw new TypeError("need a function to handle the onClose event");
    }

    const titleText = oui5lib.util.getI18nText("confirmDelete.title");

    jQuery.sap.require("sap.m.MessageBox");
    sap.m.MessageBox.show(msgText, {
        icon: "WARNING",
        title: titleText,
        actions: [ "DELETE", "CANCEL" ],
        initialFocus: "CANCEL",
        onClose: handleClose
    });
}
messages.confirmDelete = confirmDelete;
```

Again, we need to handle the user choice and therefore the confirmDelete function will throw a Type-Error if no such handler function is given.

```
function handleDeleteConfirmed(choice) {
    if (choice === "DELETE") {
        oui5lib.logger.info("user confirmed delete");
        // add code to delete
    }
}

oui5lib.messages.confirmDelete(
    "Are you sure you want to delete this record?",
    handleDeleteConfirmed
);
```

6.2.3. Present a list of messages to the user: MessageStrip

The MessageStrip doesn't require any action by the user. Use it, if there is a list of messages the user should be notified of. There are several types of messages enumerated as `sap.ui.core.MessageType`. The type of the message determines the message icon and color.

As an example, we will assume to have some messages to show after the user submitted a new order. We want the messages to be vertically listed. To hold the messages we therefore create a `sap.m.VBox` with ID "messagesContainer".

```
const msgContainer = new sap.m.VBox(this.createId("messagesContainer"));
```

Let us assume we have just validated the user input and have the following messages to show:

```
const msgs = [
    {text: "Customer email invalid", type: "Error" },
    {text: "No products chosen", type: "Warning" },
    {text: "Shipping Address is different from Billing Address", type: "Information" },
    {text: "Saved despite error and warning ;-)", type: "Success" },
];
```

In the controller, we add a function to add these messages to the message container.

Listing 6.12. Function to show a list of messages: MessageStrip

```
showMessages: function(msgs) {
    const messagesContainer = this.getView().byId("messagesContainer");
    messagesContainer.removeAllItems();

    for (let i = 0, s = msgs.length; i < s; i++) {
        const msg = msgs[i];
        const messageStrip = new sap.m.MessageStrip({
            showCloseButton: true,
            showIcon: true,
            text: msg.text,
            type: msg.type
        });
        messagesContainer.addItem(messageStrip);
    }
}
```

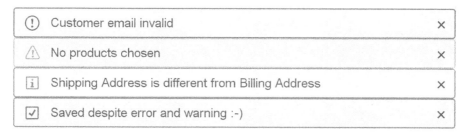

6.2.4. Navigate messages with details: MessagePopover

Another way to show a list of messages is the `sap.m.MessagePopover`. Other than with the MessageStrip, the messages are hidden until the user clicks on a button to open a popover with the messages. The button can be visually modified to indicate that there are messages. The advantage of the Message-Popover is that it presents messages nicely grouped by their type and can show longer descriptions.

Listing 6.13. Construct a sap.m.MessagePopover

```
const messageTemplate = new sap.m.MessageItem({
   type: "{type}",
   title: "{title}",
   subtitle: "{subtitle}",
   description: "{description}",
   groupName: "{group}",
});

const messagePopover = new sap.m.MessagePopover(this.createId("messagePopover"));
messagePopover.bindAggregation("items", {
   path: "/",
   template: messageTemplate
});
```

Put the above code somewhere in the view, but don't add it to the page content. Instead, we add a button, which shows the number of messages and changes its appearance if there are new messages (from type Transparent to Emphasized).

```
new sap.m.Button({
   icon: "sap-icon://message-popup",
   text: "{msgs>/messages_count}",
   type: "{msgs>/messages_buttonType}",          See enumeration sap.m.ButtonType
   press: function(oEvent) {
      oController.showMessagePopover(oEvent);
   }
});
```

In the controller onInit function we set the initial state of the messages button.

```
const msgButtonModel = new sap.ui.model.json.JSONModel({
   "messages_count": 0,
   "messages_buttonType": "Transparent"
});
this.getView().setModel(msgButtonModel, "msgs");
```

Let's assume we have the following messages to present:

```
const msgs = [
   { type: "Error",
     group: "Error Messages",
     title: "Customer email invalid",
     subtitle: "Some subtitle",
     description: "Need a valid email address" },
   { type: "Error",
     group: "Error Messages",
     title: "Customer phone missing",
     description: "Need a phone number" },
   { type: "Warning",
     title: "No products chosen",
     description: "Please select a product" },
   { type: "Information",
     title: "Shipping address is different from billing address" },
   { type: "Success",
     title: "Saved, despite error and warning :-)" }
];
```

To add these messages to the MessagePopover, we set a model to the popover. Additionally, we update the messages button model to visually indicate that there are new messages.

```
const msgsCount = msgs.length;
if (msgsCount > 0) {
    const msgsModel = new sap.ui.model.json.JSONModel(msgs);

    const messagePopover = this.getView().byId("messagePopover");
    messagePopover.setModel(msgsModel);

    const msgButtonModel = this.getView().getModel("msgs");
    msgButtonModel.setProperty("/messages_count", msgsCount);
    msgButtonModel.setProperty("/messages_buttonType", "Emphasized");
}
```

If the user clicks the button, we open the popover from Listing 6.13, "Construct a sap.m.Message-Popover".

```
showMessagePopover: function(oEvent) {
    const popover = this.getView().byId("messagePopover");
    popover.openBy(oEvent.getSource());
}
```

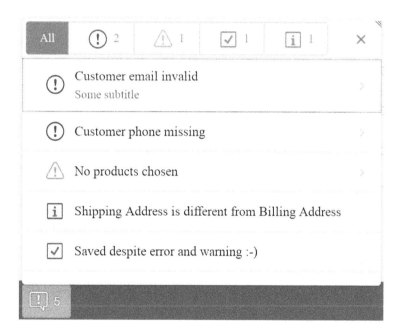

6.2.4.1. MessageView

The sap.m.MessageView works very similar. But while the MessagePopover displays the messages in a Popover container, the MessageView just provides the content for a container, like the sap.m.Popover, sap.m.ResponsivePopover or sap.m.Dialog.

Using the MessageItem from Listing 6.13, "Construct a sap.m.MessagePopover", we construct the MessageView alike.

```
const messageView = new sap.m.MessageView(this.createId("messageView"), {
    showDetailsPageHeader: false,
    groupItems: true
});
messageView.bindAggregation("items", {
    path: "/",
    template: messageTemplate
});
```

As an example, using the same messages as for the MessagePopover, we display the messages in a Dialog. The buttons to close the dialog and navigate back from the message detail to the message list need to be manually added to the dialog.

Listing 6.14. Construct Dialog for the MessageView

```
const msgsModel = new sap.ui.model.json.JSONModel(msgs);

const messageView = this.getView().byId("messageView");
messageView.setModel(msgsModel);

const messageDetailBackButton = new sap.m.Button({          Construct button to navigate to message overview
    icon: "sap-icon://nav-back",
    visible: false,                                         Set invisible
    press: function () {
        messageView.navigateBack();
        this.setVisible(false);
    }
});

messageView.attachItemSelect(function () {
    messageDetailBackButton.setVisible(true);               Show button to navigate to message overview
});

const dialog = new sap.m.Dialog({                           Construct Dialog
    content: [ messageView ],                               Add MessageView as content
    contentHeight: "440px",
    contentWidth: "640px",
    endButton: new sap.m.Button({                           Button to close the Dialog
        text: "{i18n>dialog.button.close}",
        tooltip: "{i18n>dialog.button.close.tooltip}",
        press: function() {
            this.getParent().close();
        }
    }),
    customHeader: new sap.m.Bar({
        contentLeft: [
            messageDetailBackButton                         Place message overview button
        ],
        contentMiddle: [
            new sap.m.Text({ text: "Messages upon saving a new order"})
        ]
    }),
    verticalScrolling: false
});
dialog.open();
```

6.3. Value state messages

UI5 can validate input and show related messages automatically. We will get to an example later (see Section 9.5, "Validation UI5 Style"). Anyway, at this point we want to show the use of the `valueState` and `valueStateText` properties. These properties are available for all controls extending `sap.m.InputBase` (DatePicker, Input, MaskInput/TimePicker, TextArea, ComboBox, MultiComboBox), and also the Select control. The CheckBox only has a `valueState`.

```
control.setValueState("Warning");                          See enumeration sap.ui.core.ValueState
control.setValueStateText("Some warning");
control.openValueStateMessage();
```

Allowed `valueState` values are specified in the enumeration `sap.ui.core.ValueState` ("None", "Success", "Warning", "Error").

6.4. Summary

This chapter began with general thoughts about events and messages, emphasizing the user's perspective. After these introductory words, we looked into user interface events and explained how to attach handler functions to these events. Next we learned how the UI5 implementation of the observer code design pattern works and then revisited the issue of routing events, which we already touched in Chapter 4, *Navigation and Routing*.

After the events, we looked at the various tools provided by UI5 to present messages to the user. We began with quick notifications, moved to dialog boxes, and ways to present a list of messages to the user. We concluded showing how to give visual and textual feedback through input controls.

Chapter 7. Models

UI5 implements the Model View Controller (MVC) pattern, which requires you to separate different concerns of application development: the view part handles the user interface layout, the controller part takes care of handling user interaction and communication and the model part deals with application data and domain logic.

The separation of concerns is crucial to extending the lifetime of applications by avoiding substantial cost increases for future adaptations and modifications. UI5 makes it relatively easy to keep controller and view concerns separated. In this chapter, we will explore only the model part.

The client devices cannot permanently store data used by web applications. Even user preferences stored in client memory are usually erased with the related cookies. With HTML 5 came databases for browsers, which can be used to store and query data, but domain data will have to be continuously synchronized with their server-side source.

In a classical server-client web application, when the server receives a HTTP request, the request URL and parameters determine the queries of data sources. The server generates the HTML response to be presented by the client. The data sources remain hidden from the user interface and only required data are being included in the HTTP response.

When instead various client web applications request data directly from a wealth of services, all these services are being exposed to malicious efforts. To keep the efforts of protecting those services minimal, it is often advisable to send all requests to one server address hiding the services called in the background and returning only required data.

7.1. Where do we use models?

Most importantly, models bind data to the controls. If model data change, the model can automatically update the bound controls. We have already seen this behavior when using the `ResourceModel`. The language specific texts are being automatically refreshed after loading different i18n properties.

Classical example uses are models, which bind a collection of entities to a list or table. Or a model, that binds entity data to a form. These use cases mostly concern the domain entities to be presented and changed through the user interface.

But with models we can also control many aspects of the user interface, like a title text or the visibility and accessibility of controls. As web developers this is not what we are normally used to. In this context, think of controls as document nodes and their children. To change the title, for example, we would get its document node and set its content or style. With UI5 we could do that too, but it is more convenient to change the title property of a model and let the model do the update through the binding. Instead of manipulating the HTML DOM, the controller changes property values of models.

7.2. Which model implementation to use?

We use the `sap.ui.model.resource.ResourceModel` for resource bundles like the i18n property files. If the incoming data are in XML, we use the `sap.ui.model.xml.XMLModel` model, and for data in the JSON format the `sap.ui.model.json.JSONModel`. These are pure client-side model implementations, meaning that, apart from loading data from a given URL, the models don't communicate with a server. The `ODataModel` v2 und v4 are used to connect to OData services.

JSON is a lightweight data interchange format with support in all relevant programming languages. It is most convenient to use in client web applications, because we are programming in JavaScript anyway. If the incoming data are formatted as XML, the XMLModel may be suitable. But be aware that the XMLModel holds an XML document and therefore comes with a performance penalty for large documents. OData services are rarely provided outside the Microsoft/SAP/IBM realm. We will therefore focus on the JSONModel.

7.3. Binding modes

All models have a binding mode. A `ResourceModel` only has binding mode `OneTime`. All other model implementations accept all three binding modes defined as enumeration `sap.ui.model.BindingMode` (OneTime, OneWay or TwoWay). The default binding mode can be overwritten directly after the model instantiation. In the following example, we will use a JSONModel, but the XMLModel works just the same way.

Listing 7.1. Change default binding mode of Model

```
const model = new sap.ui.model.json.JSONModel();
model.getDefaultBindingMode();                        Default: TwoWay
model.setDefaultBindingMode("OneWay");                Change to: OneWay
```

`OneTime` binding is like a snapshot of data from the model to the view. `OneWay` binding means that changes of model data update the views. With `TwoWay` binding, data can be changed both ways between model and view. If the user changes a value of an input, checks a checkbox, or selects an item, the model is updated, as well. Likewise, if the controller changes the data, the user interface is updated, too. Often this is what we want, but it does have side effects, which we need to address. Let us think about this a little deeper.

7.3.1. OneWay or TwoWay?

Using `TwoWay` binding may cause data integrity problems. For example, if we have an edit form with a submit button and the user changes the values, but then wants to cancel or revert, what to do? If we do nothing, the client data are out of sync, because they have been modified without being saved to the source. So, we need to be able to revert to a previous state. It can be done by reloading the data from the source, or by keeping a copy of the original data when entering an edit view to use for reverting. But what happens if the user simply leaves the form without properly canceling or submitting? Is it then better, maybe, to use OneWay binding?

With OneWay binding, changes of model data change the controls, but not the other way. Changes by the user will not effect the model. While that solves our problem of client data integrity, it leads to another problem. With TwoWay binding we get the edited data simply from the model. With OneWay binding the model holds the original data, but we need to get the modifications from the controls, which requires extra coding and makes things more complex.

If we assume that the user interface only allows the user to change data when he is supposed to, the binding mode to use largely depends on preference. Whichever way, the issues remain to be solved.

I recommend keeping the default TwoWay binding of a model, but use cloned data for the model. This way we conveniently get the edited data from the model, validate and send them to a server for permanent storage. Only when the server responds success may we replace the client application data with the modified ones.

On the other hand, if data changes should be real-time without submitting, we need to monitor any user events carefully and immediately handle all kinds of input. OneWay binding helps in this case, because we can validate any input and update the model accordingly. OData services help with many of these problems, but this alone doesn't justify setting them up.

7.4. Loading data

The models can load data and will handle asynchronous loading nicely. We bind a model to a List or Table and don't need to care about the state of the request. Once the data come in, the model will update the view. This is convenient, at least when we don't need to handle multiple asynchronous requests of dependent data.

Listing 7.2. Use the JSONModel to load data

```
const model = new sap.ui.model.json.JSONModel();
model.attachRequestCompleted(function() {
    const data = model.getData();
});
model.attachRequestFailed(function() {
    // handle failure
});
model.attachParseError(function() {
    // the JSON is invalid
});

model.loadData("mockdata/exampleData.json");
```

 The default size limit for models is 100 array entries, but the default can be overwritten using the model setSizeLimit function

The loadData function allows a number of parameters to control the request, with only a URL required. Internally, the function is using jQuery.ajax for the actual request.

loadData (*sURL*, *oParameters*, *bAsync*, *sType*, *bMerge*, *bCache*, *mHeaders*);

sURL string A URL is required;
oParameters object The JavaScript object is converted to a string, url-encoded and appended to the URL;
bAsync boolean Default is async (true);
sType string HTTP request method (usually GET or POST). Default is GET;
bMerge boolean Default is replace (false);
bCache boolean Default is no caching (false);
mHeaders object Additional key/value pairs to be added to the request header;

Asynchronous loading complicates issues of dependent data. Referenced data need to be requested. Yet, while we cannot ensure the sequence of asynchronous responses, we often need data from particular requests to continue. If we only have an ID reference to some entity, we may have to wait for the related data to be available before we can show anything to the user. Only if the related data is not critical can we enrich the model once the data comes in and refresh the bindings.

7.5. Setting and getting model data

Instead of letting the model request and load the data, we can also set any data to the model using `model.setData(data)`, or `model.setData(data, true)` to merge data in. This way we can set whatever JavaScript data we have to a JSONModel.

Listing 7.3. Set data to a model

```
const authors = {
   "Dostoyevsky": {
      books: [
         { title: "Crime and Punishment", published: "1866" },
         { title: "The Idiot", published: "1869" },
         { title: "Demons", published: "1872" }
      ]
   },
   "Camus": {
      books: [
         { title: "The Myth of Sisyphus", published: "1942" },
         { title: "The Plague", published: "1947" },
         { title: "The Rebel", published: "1951" }
      ]
   }
};
const model = new sap.ui.model.json.JSONModel();
model.setData(authors);
```

After setting the data to the model, we can get the current data from a model using the `getData` function. Because the function returns a reference to the model data, all changes to the data are also changing the model data.

If we just need a particular value from the model data, we can use the `getProperty` function. It requires a property `path` and we can optionally specify a `context` for the path.

getProperty (*sPath, oContext*);
sPath string;
oContext object;

The following example code gives you an idea of binding path and context. Surely, it will be most instructive to use the browser console and experiment for yourself with data, contexts and paths.

Listing 7.4. Get model data values by path and context

```
model.getProperty("/Camus/books");              Use absolute path
model.getProperty("/Camus/books/2/title");

let context = model.getContext("/Camus/books/2");   Get Context object
model.getProperty("published", context);            Use relative path with Context

context = model.getContext("/Dostoyevsky");         Get Context object
model.getProperty("books/0/title", context);        Use relative path with Context
```

 If a binding path notation is syntactically valid, but the path does not exist, the model returns `undefined`. If the path notation is invalid, the model will return `null` instead.

To set or update model properties, the `setProperty` function can be used. It requires a property `path` and a `value`. We can optionally set the `context` for the path. The boolean `asyncUpdate` specifies if the update of dependent bindings should happen asynchronously. The function returns `true` if the property was successfully updated and `false` if an error occurred.

setProperty (*sPath*, *oValue*, *oContext*, *bAsyncUpdate*);
sPath string;
oValue object;
oContext object;
bAsyncUpdate boolean;

Listing 7.5. Set model data values by path and context

```
model.setProperty("/Dostoyevsky/born", "1821");                          Add property
const context = model.getContext("/Dostoyevsky");                        Get Context object
model.setProperty("died", "1881", context);

const books = model.getProperty("books", context);
model.setProperty("books/" + books.length,
                  { title: "The Brothers Karamazov", published: "1880" },
                  model.getContext("/Dostoyevsky"));

model.setProperty("editions",
                  [ { year: "1996", publisher: "Bantam Classics" } ],
                  model.getContext("/Dostoyevsky/books/0"));
```

 The above example data (see Listing 7.3, "Set data to a model") are well structured to access a particular author because the author's name is the key. But if we want to show all the books as a list, this data structure is troublesome, because for the list items binding we need an array.

```
const books = [
    { author: "Dostoyevsky", title: "Crime and Punishment", published: "1866" },
    { author: "Dostoyevsky", title: "The Idiot", published: "1869" },
    { author: "Dostoyevsky", title: "Demons", published: "1872" },
    { author: "Camus", title: "The Myth of Sisyphus", published: "1942" },
    { author: "Camus", title: "The Plague", published: "1947" },
    { author: "Camus", title: "The Rebel", published: "1951" }
];
```

On the other hand, at least if there are many records to deal with, it is not efficient to always filter through all the entries of an array in order to identify those belonging to one author. Instead of working with model data not fitting for the task at hand, it is often better to transform the data for a tailored model.

7.6. Setting and getting models

The `setModel` and `getModel` functions are defined in the `sap.ui.base.ManagedObject`, which is subclassed by numerous UI5 classes and all controls.

The scope of a model depends on the object it is being set to. The broadest scope is the `Core`. Then comes the `Component`, where we have set the i18n ResourceModel. More limited in scope models may be set to a `View`, a `SimpleForm` or `FormContainer`, or even particular controls like a `Select`.

Use this function to set or unset a model with an optional model name. Valid model names are any non-empty strings except "null" and "undefined". The model to be set may be null or undefined.

setModel (*oModel*, *sName*);
oModel sap.ui.model.Model;
sName string;

Use this function to get a model previously being set. The model is taken either from the `ManagedObject` itself or the first found in its parent hierarchy. If no model exists, `undefined` is returned.

`getModel (sName);`
`sName string;`

7.7. Binding context and path

In the JavaScript views and fragments we mostly use references to model paths. These references are strings of paths enclosed in curly braces.

`"{}"`

The ResourceModel holds simple key value data. To reference the values, use

`"{modelName>key}"`

Binding paths of other models depend on the structure of the data they hold, but generally they follow the following pattern:

`"{modelName>path}"`

If the path begins with a forward slash, it denotes an absolute path.

`"{modelName>/}"`

The model name part of the path is only required for named models. Otherwise, the absolute path to the model data is simply

`"{/}"`

This is synonymous with

`model.getData();`

To get the second item of an array, use

`"{modelName>/1}"`

Forward slashes also separate further portions of the path. To get a property from the fifth array item

`"{modelName>/4/propertyName}"`

7.7.1. Complex binding syntax

In Listing 2.1, "sap-ui-bootstrap", we set the `data-sap-ui-bindingSyntax` to `complex`. This allows us to not just use binding paths, but so called expression binding. To begin with a simple example of embedded binding, the following expression combines the values of two relative model property paths into a concatenated string:

`"{lastname}, {firstname}"`

Apart from such still very basic expressions, we can also use a subset of JavaScript for the expressions. Note, that the rules of character data escaping in XML apply:

> The ampersand character (&) and the left angle bracket (<) MUST NOT appear in their literal form, except when used as markup delimiters, or within a comment, a processing instruction, or a CDATA

section. If they are needed elsewhere, they MUST be escaped using either numeric character references or the strings " & " and " < " respectively. ...
—W3C Recommendation: Extensible Markup Language (XML) 1.0 (Fifth Edition)

There are two general variants of expression binding:

1. `"{:= expression}"`

   The expression is evaluated and processed only once. This variant should be preferred because is takes less resources.

2. `"{= expression}"`

   The expression is re-processed upon any change of the model values.

Let us look at some example expressions. Sometimes, we need to use conditional statements. Be aware, that the following expression will return a boolean, which makes it only suitable for properties requiring a boolean value.

`"{:= typeof ${valueState} === 'undefined'}"`

We can also express more complex conditions:

`"{:= ${valueState} === 'None' &amp;&amp; ${orderTotal} < 1000}"`

If we need an if..else conditional evaluation, we would write something like this:

`"{:= (${status} !== 'Pending') ? 'Error':'None'}"`

Basic value manipulations are also possible. The following expression will uppercase the whole string:

`"{:= ${billingName}.toLocaleUpperCase()}"`

Let's assume we want to show the order total formatted as a money value. Aware that the order total may change, we would write:

`"{= parseFloat(${orderTotal}).toFixed(2)}"`

To compute the order line total, we could use the following expression:

`"{= String(${quantity} * ${price})}"`

These expressions quickly become difficult to read, like this one printing the order date as a string:

`"{:= ${orderDate}.getDate()}.{:= ${orderDate}.getMonth() + 1}.{:= ${orderDate}.getFullYear()}"`

 Use the complex binding syntax with care. After all, why care about MVC and the separation of concerns when we litter our views with complex code expressions difficult to read and test?

7.7.2. Formatting values for display

We have just seen, how complex binding expressions can be used to format and convert values. In this section, we look at other means offered by UI5 for these cases.

If we just need to format a certain value, the UI5 types under namespace `sap.ui.model.type` provide simple formatting options. Three static classes under namespace `sap.ui.core.format` provide the format constraints for the model types: `DateFormat`, `NumberFormat` and `FileSizeFormat`.

- Type sap.ui.model.type.Float: NumberFormat.getFloatInstance()
- Type sap.ui.model.type.Integer: NumberFormat.getIntegerInstance()
- Type sap.ui.model.type.Currency: NumberFormat.getCurrencyInstance()
- Type sap.ui.model.type.Date: DateFormat.getDateInstance()
- Type sap.ui.model.type.Time: DateFormat.getTimeInstance()
- Type sap.ui.model.type.DateTime: DateFormat.getDateTimeInstance()
- Type sap.ui.model.type.FileSize: FileSizeFormat.getInstance()

For example, if we have a float value 2.54721 and want to show only two fraction digits, we can use the `Float` type to display the properly rounded value 2.55 (`maxFractionDigits`). And if the user inserts "2", the value will be automatically converted to 2.00 (`minFractionDigits`).

Listing 7.6. Using type Float to format displayed value

```
const floatType = new sap.ui.model.type.Float(
   {                                        Format options
      minFractionDigits: 2,                 See new sap.ui.core.format.NumberFormat
      maxFractionDigits: 2
   },
   {}                                       Value constraints
);
const floatInput = new sap.m.Input({
   value: {
      path: "/float_example",
      type: floatType
   }
});
```

If the complex binding syntax and the model types are not sufficient, we can use JavaScript functions to return whatever value programmatically.

Let us look at a simple input control with a model property path binding:

```
new sap.m.Input({
   value: "{modelName>/somePropertyPath}"
});
```

If we need prior processing based on the value of the property, we can use the path/formatter notation:

Listing 7.7. Use path/formatter notation

```
new sap.m.Input({
   value: {
      path: "modelName>/somePropertyPath",
      formatter: function(propertyValue) {
         return oController.formatFunction(propertyValue);
      }
   }
});
```

Or, if we need to bind more than one property, the parts/formatter notation:

Listing 7.8. Use parts/formatter notation

```
new sap.m.Input({
    value: {
        parts: [
            { path: "modelName>/somePropertyPath" },
            { path: "modelName>/anotherPropertyPath" }
        ],
        formatter: ".formatFunction" ❶
    }
});
```

❶   The dot in front of formatFunction indicates that the function is expected to be found in the connected controller. Otherwise, the function is looked for in the global namespace.

 Use formatter functions carefully and only to format values for display. Surely, they can also be used to handle all kinds of issues with the model data, but don't go that way. In both cases, when we have a model value which always needs to be converted for display, and when the model data need processing logic to generate a display value, it will usually be better to enhance the model data to fit the user interface requirements.

For example, the order total could be computed from the ordered items using a formatter function. Every time the related control is rendered or the model bindings have to be refreshed, the formatter function would be called. Instead, we can add an orderTotal property to the model once when the order data become available and only recompute the value when the ordered items changed. This separates the issue from the UI control and also avoids unnecessary function calls. Maybe the most important aspect is an improved readability of the view code constructing the control.

7.7.3. Using a factory function

To bind an array to a control aggregation, UI5 has the bindAggregation of sap.ui.base.ManagedObject. Usually, the function uses a template control for displaying the entries. Each entry of the array is applied to the template and added to the content. The template is always the same. In most cases, this is what we want.

Listing 7.9. Construct a sap.m.StandardListItem

```
const itemTemplate = new sap.m.StandardListItem({
    icon: "sap-icon://machine",
    title: "{equipmentNumber}",
    description: "{equipmentDescription}"
});
```

We use the bindAggregation function to connect the model path and item template with the List items aggregation.

```
const list = new sap.m.List();
list.bindAggregation("items", {
    path: "/",
    template: itemTemplate
});
```

But sometimes, we need to use a different control, depending on the context. In these cases, we can use a factory function. With a factory function we can first inspect the context and then construct the UI control to be returned.

```
list.bindAggregation("items", {
   path: "/",
   factory: function(sId, oContext) {
      const propValue = oContext.getProperty("somePropertyPath")
      // Construct and return whatever suitable control with ID "sId"
   }
});
```

7.8. Simple model example

The following example shows a use case of model binding and how to provide the data in the controller. The specifics of the controls used are explained in later chapters. Often, a good place to set a model not dependent upon route parameters is the controller onInit function. Here, we assume to add user interface controls to sort a list of books.

```
onInit: function() {                                     Controller onInit
   const sortModel = new sap.ui.model.json.JSONModel();
   sortModel.setData({
      sortOptions: [                                     Select control: aggregation 'items'
         { key: "", text: "Please select a sort option" },  Placeholder option
         { key: "author", text: "Author" },
         { key: "title", text: "Book Title" },
         { key: "published", text: "First Published" }
      ],
      sortBy: "author",                                  Select control: property 'selectedKey'
      sortDescending: false                              CheckBox control: property 'selected'
   });
   this.getView().setModel(sortModel, "sort");           Model is named "sort"
}
```

For the sort options, we use a Select control. It uses an item template to display the array of sortOptions.

Listing 7.10. Select control for the sort options

```
const sortSelect = new sap.m.Select({
   tooltip: "sort list by",
   selectedKey: "{sort>/sortBy}",                 Model path of the currently selected sort option
   change: function () {
      oController.sortBy();                        Handler function triggered if another sort option is selected
   }
});

const itemTemplate = new sap.ui.core.Item({ ❶
   key : "{sort>key}",
   text : "{sort>text}"
});

sortSelect.bindAggregation("items", { ❷
   path: "sort>/sortOptions",
   template: itemTemplate
});
```

❶ The paths we use for the item template depend on the path we use to bind the aggregation, which sets the context for the items. The name of the model is "sort", which is the "sort>" part of all the paths in this example. The path of `bindAggregation` "/sortOptions" refers to the array of objects. The `Item` template paths `key` and `text` are relative paths to properties of the sort option objects.

❷ The `bindAggregation` function binds the model property path to the `items` aggregation of the `Select` control, using the item template for presentation.

For the sort order, we use a `Checkbox` control. Its `selected` property is of type boolean. Our default is to sort ascending (`sortDescending` is set to `false`), its path notation is "/sortDescending" and the model name part is "sort>".

Listing 7.11. Checkbox control for the sort order

```
const sortOrderCheckbox= new sap.m.CheckBox({
   tooltip: "sort list descending"
   selected: "{sort>/sortDescending}",
   select: function () {
      oController.sortBy();              Handler function triggered if the checkbox status is changed
   }
});
```

Both controls attach the `sortBy` function of the controller as event handler, triggered when the user selects another item or changes the state of the checkbox. In the controller, we conveniently get the model and access the data to work with.

Listing 7.12. Example controller function getting model properties

```
sortBy: function() {
   const sortModel = this.getView().getModel("sort");
   const sortBy = sortModel.getProperty("/sortBy");
   const sortDesc = sortModel.getProperty("/sortDescending");
   if (sortDesc) {
      this.debug("sort is descending");
   }
   // do the sorting ❶
}
```

❶ Model data sorting is explained in Section 8.5, "Sorting".

7.9. Scope and design of models

Throughout an application, many models will be used with various names or remain nameless. Binding models to their smallest possible scope helps to avoid interference and simplifies debugging. In our example above, we should have wrapped the various sort controls (Label, Select, Checkbox) in an `OverflowToolbar` control and set the model to it, instead of setting it to the whole View.

The scope obviously depends on the context. The language properties were set to the `Component`. And if a model is used globally, we can set and get the model from the `Core`.

```
let model = sap.ui.getCore().getModel("modelName");
if (model === undefined) {
   model = new sap.ui.model.json.JSONModel();
   model.loadData(url);
   sap.ui.getCore().setModel(model, "modelName");
}
```

It is also good practice to provide each model only with the data needed, and separate issues with different models. Better use more models and keep their scope limited. This will help to avoid errors and to keep the controller code readable.

7.10. In client memory vs. constant reloading

Client JavaScript applications can have major benefits towards requesting whole pages generated by whichever web application server. First, they are more responsive to user interaction, because no server roundtrip is required. This benefit largely depends upon using async requests of resources, because otherwise the user interface might freeze. Secondly, the use of client resources (memory, processor) reduces load on the server(s). This benefit may be largely canceled by requesting all data with each page view.

Generally speaking, it is not desirable to always reload the same data. On the other hand, users expect the data they see to be up-to-date. This is understandable, but more importantly, we need to ensure, that all relevant information is presented to the user to make a qualified decision. For this, it may be irrelevant if the user sees the latest updates during the current session.

There are different types of data in any application. Some change frequently, others very rarely. Some have many records, others just a few. Some collections need to be sorted and filtered frequently. Some records just take a few bytes, while others may contain long texts. Some large dataset could be stored in a client *IndexedDB*, especially when they don't change too frequently.

It is clear that we don't want to load many thousands of records into client memory. But what about a few hundred? And how often do we need to update loaded records? Surely, when editing a record, we had better not use an old copy to begin with.

 All model data are accessible from the browser console. It needs some inspection, but we get to the binding contexts and models. UI5 provides all necessary functions to explore the whole control tree like we see done by the UI5 Inspector extension. Confidential data should obviously never be available in client memory in an unencrypted form without requiring prior authorization to decrypt them. This applies generally, but it can't be repeated often enough!

We should handle different data differently. A proper evaluation of data requirements and security policies is necessary to make qualified decisions about which data to load into client memory, which to keep, and when to refresh them.

7.11. Limits to Models

The controllers set the models for the views and handle user events. They may modify models to meet the view requirements. But programming domain logic of the data in the controller will lead to overblown controllers doing too much and mixing issues.

The models are well integrated with views, controls and events. Models make requests and handle the response, bind paths and update them, process messages and events. We could write custom models extending whatever UI5 model and add domain logic there, but why not simply write separate objects?

Instead of becoming masters of handling contexts and binding paths to relate our data, and of extensively using formatters to convert model values into whatever we want to show in the user interface, we may better use custom domain objects to enhance, transform and relate the incoming data according to our needs. The custom objects provide the data for the models. We can keep issues separated and will have simple binding paths and leaner controller code. We will show how this can be done in Chapter 12, *Custom data objects*.

7.12. Summary

This chapter covers the use of models to bind data to user interface controls.

We began by briefly explaining the various model implementations and binding modes. Then we looked at ways to load, set and modify model data and explained the use of context and path to access model data. Building upon this information, we saw how model data are bound to user interface controls and how we can process and format model values for display.

After the more theoretical part, an example was presented to show the use of models and controls in practice. The chapter closed with general considerations about model design and data loading strategies.

Chapter 8. Lists and Tables

8.1. Common features and behavior

List and Table both extend the sap.m.ListBase and therefore share its properties. And table rows are list items of type ColumnListItem, which extends the sap.m.ListItemBase. Both bind an array of data to the aggregation items and use a template to present the data object. Both are sorted and grouped with the same code.

8.1.1. ListBase

The sap.m.ListBase provides numerous properties, aggregations and events to specify how a List or Table looks and behaves.

Either a headerText or a headerToolbar can be added to the top of the list or table. An additional info-Toolbar can be placed below the header. And at the bottom a footerText string may be added.

Be aware, that the header elements will disappear out of view when the user scrolls down the list. Since UI5 version 1.54, the Table has a property sticky, which can be set to HeaderToolbar, InfoToolbar or ColumnHeaders. The feature has limited browser support.

For the List, we have to use a workaround. To make header elements always stay on top, we first construct a List just with top elements but without data and the property showNoData set to false. Then we construct another List without those top elements and take it as content for a sap.m.ScrollContainer with the height property set to some percentage value. If we add both the List without data and the ScrollContainer to the main content, we get something like a sticky header.

For styling, we can use the width and inset properties. By default, the width is "100%", but it can be set to any valid CSS expression. Property inset is a boolean. If true, a CSS class with a padding directive will be added to create space around the list or table.

For touch screens, there are properties swipeDirection, swipe and swipeContent. If the user swipes in the specified direction, the swipe event is triggered to show the swipeContent. With an attached swipe function, we can therefore modify the swipeContent according to the swiped item.

Sometimes, it is useful to provide an additional explanatory text spoken by a screen reader. For this purpose we use the ariaLabelledBy association. If the text should be invisible, we use the sap.ui.core.InvisibleText control and don't forget to add it to the page content. For an example, see Listing 9.6, "Construct a sap.m.MaskInput".

8.1.1.1. ListMode

The mode property refers to the sap.m.ListMode enumeration. The default is None, which means that no event is triggered selecting an item. Delete adds a delete icon to each list item, which, if pressed, will trigger the delete event and call the attached function. SingleSelectMaster causes the whole item to be selectable. Similar modes are SingleSelect, SingleSelectLeft and MultiSelect, all of which result in a selection control (checkbox) to be added to each item. Selecting an item will trigger the selectionChange event.

8.1.1.2. Growing

If there are many items, the behavior of the list or table may show unacceptable delays. At least in these cases, we have to implement paging, which means that we only show some items and require navigation to see others. Unfortunately, UI5 doesn't offer paging functionality, but a growing feature instead.

To activate this feature, we set property `growing` to true. The initial number of items shown is set with property `growingThreshold`, which defaults to 20. Depending upon the `growingDirection`, the navigation element appears below (`Downwards` - default) or above (`Upwards`) the list items. Setting `growingScroll-ToLoad` true will trigger loading more items when the user scrolls to the end of the currently shown items.

As re-rendering may be automatically triggered by data changes, sorting, filtering or searching, we need to be careful with a large number of items. The `updateStarted` event is triggered before such an update happens and `updateFinished` afterwards. The event object gives us a `reason`, which can be "Binding", "Filter", "Sort", "Growing", "Change", "Refresh", or "Context". It also gives us the `actual` and `total` number of items.

8.1.2. ListItemBase

The `sap.m.ListItemBase` provides base functionality for an item of a list, or a table row. UI5 has numerous variations to present list items. For an overview of available list item implementations, look into the Samples/Explored section of the UI5 documentation and filter the examples by 'ListItem'.

8.1.2.1. ListType

The `type` property refers to an enumeration `sap.m.ListType`. The default is `Inactive`. Setting the type to `Active` causes the list item, if pressed, to trigger the `press` event. Type `Detail` will add a button to the list item which triggers the event `detailPress`. Both features can be combined with type `DetailAndActive`. Type `Navigation` does the same as `Active`, but also adds an icon to the list item.

8.2. A List example

The following list example shows the use of features from the `ListBase` and `ListItemBase`. First, we construct the list item template.

Listing 8.1. Construct an ObjectListItem

```
 1 const listitemTemplate = new sap.m.ObjectListItem({        Item template
 2    title: "{customerName}",
 3    number: "{orderTotal}",
 4    numberUnit: "{currency}",
 5    type: "Detail",                                          Enumeration sap.m.ListType
 6    detailPress: function (oEvent) {
 7       oController.handleShowDetail(oEvent);
 8    }
 9 });
10
11 const orderStatus = new sap.m.ObjectStatus({
12    title: "{i18n>order.status}",
13    text: "{status}",
14    state: "{valueState}"                                    Set ValueState for coloring
15 });
```

```
16 listitemTemplate.setFirstStatus(orderStatus);
17
18 const orderDateAttr = new sap.m.ObjectAttribute({
19    title: "{i18n>order.date}",
20    text: "{orderDate}"
21 });
22 listitemTemplate.addAttribute(orderDateAttr);
```

The above item template is a `sap.m.ObjectListItem`, which is one of the many subclasses of `sap.m.ListItemBase`.

Listing 8.2. Construct a sap.m.List

```
 1 const list = new sap.m.List(this.createId("exampleList"), {      Let the View create the id
 2    mode: "SingleSelectMaster",                                    Enumeration sap.m.ListMode
 3    selectionChange: function(oEvent) {
 4       oController.handleItemSelected(oEvent);
 5    }
 6 });
 7
 8 list.bindAggregation("items", {
 9    path: "/",
10    template: listitemTemplate
11 });
```

The code above will show an empty list until we set a model to it to provide the data. We can do that in the controller `onInit` function. We load data into the model and set it to the list. In this example, we won't give the model a name. Without a model name the binding path of aggregation `items` is "/".

```
const list = this.getView().byId("exampleList");
list.setModel(model);
```

 We use the View `byId` function to get the `List` control, which corresponds to the View `createId` we used in Listing 8.2, "Construct a sap.m.List" line 1.

After reloading the view, we see the list items.

Elke Lüke	19.60 US-$ ✎
Order Date: Thu Nov 30 2017	Status: Shipped
Ines Gedat	13.09 € ✎
Order Date: Thu Nov 30 2017	Status: Pending
Michael Fatima	97.67 US-$ ✎
Order Date: Wed Nov 29 2017	Status: Invoiced
Robert Müller	20.67 € ✎
Order Date: Wed Nov 29 2017	Status: Payment Overdue

8.3. Controller functions handling events

Referring to Listing 8.2, "Construct a sap.m.List" we set the `ListMode` to "SingleSelectMaster" (line 2) and attached the `handleItemSelected` function to the `selectionChange` event provided by the `ListBase` (lines 3 to 5). In the controller, we want to get the related data.

The event source is the object itself. In the case of the `selectionChange` event, it is the `List`. The event parameter `listItem` gives us the selected list item. Using the `getBindingContext` function, we get to the selected record data.

Listing 8.3. How to get the item data from a ListBase event

```
handleItemSelected: function(oEvent) {
    const list = oEvent.getSource();

    const selectedItem = oEvent.getParameter("listItem");
    const bindingContext = selectedItem.getBindingContext();
    const model = bindingContext.getModel(); ❶
    const data = model.getProperty(bindingContext.getPath());
}
```

❶   If the model is named, the `getModel` function requires the name of the model.

Refering to Listing 8.1, "Construct an ObjectListItem", we set the `ListType` to "Detail" (line 5) and attached the `handleShowDetail` function to the `detailPress` event provided by the `ListItemBase` (lines 6 to 8).

In this case, the event source is the `ObjectListItem`. Apart from the binding context and path, which is a general way to get data from an event, the ObjectListItem provides its own accessor functions to get the `title` and `number` properties we set in lines 2 and 3.

Listing 8.4. Controller function to get ObjectListItem properties

```
handleShowDetail: function(oEvent) {
    const selectedItem = oEvent.getSource();
    const customerName = selectedItem.getTitle();
    const orderTotal = selectedItem.getNumber();
}
```

8.4. A Table example

Whatever we said about the `sap.m.List` applies to the `sap.m.Table` also. The events and handlers described above work the same, except for those functions specific to the `sap.m.ObjectListItem`.

The `sap.m.Table` has a `columns` aggregation, which is an array of `sap.m.Column` elements.

To prepare a table to adjust to different visible widths, we have to use a combination of properties. If we just set the `minScreenWidth` property, the column will be hidden once the screen width reaches the minimum set. If we use the `minScreenWidth` and set the `demandPopin` to `true`, the column label and value will appear below the column (pop-in). With the `popinDisplay` property we can specify how the popped-in column is to be displayed (`Block` - default, `Inline`, `WithoutHeader`).

Listing 8.5. Construct a sap.m.Table

```
const table = new sap.m.Table(this.createId("exampleTable"), {
    columns: [
        ...
        new sap.m.Column({
            width: "120px",                       Set column width
            header: new sap.m.Label({
                text: "{i18n>order.customer.name}"
            })
        }),
        new sap.m.Column({
            hAlign: "End", ❶
            header: new sap.m.Label({
                text: "{i18n>order.total}"
            }),
            footer: new sap.m.Text({ ❷
                text: "{summary>/totalSum}"
            })
        }),
        new sap.m.Column({
            minScreenWidth: "Tablet",             Enumeration sap.m.ScreenSize
            demandPopin: true,                    Column will pop-in
            popinDisplay: "Inline",               Enumeration sap.m.PopinDisplay
            header: new sap.m.Label({
                text: "{i18n>order.date}"
            })
        })
        new sap.m.Column({                        Column will be hidden on a phone
            minScreenWidth: "Small",
            header: new sap.m.Label({
                text: "{i18n>order.shipped.date}"
            })
        })
        new sap.m.Column({
            header: new sap.m.Label({
                text: "{i18n>order.status}"
            })
        })
        ...
    ]
});
```

❶ To align the text, we can set the hAlign property. Allowed values are enumerated under sap.ui.core.TextAlign. The vAlign property values are enumerated under sap.ui.core.VerticalAlign.

❷ We can set any Control to the footer aggregation of the Column. This is especially helpful to show column sums.

 Since UI5 version 1.52, we can activate alternate row coloring by setting the alternateRowColors property of the sap.m.Table to true.

The ListItemBase implementation for the sap.m.Table is the sap.m.ColumnListItem, which provides the cells aggregation, which is an array of Control objects. The order of the cells aggregation should match the order of the columns aggregation of the Table.

Listing 8.6. Construct a sap.m.ColumnListItem

```
 1 const rowTemplate = new sap.m.ColumnListItem({
 2    type: "Navigation",
 3    press: function(oEvent) {
 4       oController.handleRowPressed(oEvent);
 5    },
 6    cells : [
 7       ...
 8       new sap.m.Text({ text: "{customerName}" }),
 9       new sap.m.Text({
10          text: {
11             path: "orderTotal",
12             formatter: function(value) {          Use path/formatter notation
13                return value.toFixed(2);
14             }
15          }
16       }),
17       new sap.m.Text({ text: "{orderDateString}" }),
18       new sap.m.Text({ text: "{shippedDateString}" }),
19       new sap.m.ObjectStatus({                    Construct ObjectStatus
20          text: "{status}",
21          state: "{valueState}"
22       })
23       ...
24    ]
25 });
```

Binding for the table works the same as for the list.

```
table.bindAggregation("items", {
   path: "/",
   template: rowTemplate
});
```

ID	Customer Name	Total	Currency	Order Date	Payment ...	Ship Date	Status	
210	Julian Levett	50.40	US-$	Thu Nov 30 2017	Sat Dec 02 2017	Sun Dec 03 2017	Shipped	>

ID	Customer Name	Total	Status	
210	Julian Levett	50.40	Shipped	>
Currency: US-$				
Order Date: Thu Nov 30 2017				

The code of the handleRowPressed function we attached to the ColumnListItem press event in Listing 8.6, "Construct a sap.m.ColumnListItem" lines 3 to 5 may be the same as we already saw in Listing 8.3, "How to get the item data from a ListBase event".

8.5. Sorting

The bindAggregation function to bind an array of objects to an aggregation allows an additional optional property sorter. Let us begin by adding an initial sorter in the view.

The constructor for a sap.ui.model.Sorter takes up to four parameters:

- sPath The path string is required.
- bDescending The sort order. Default is 'false' (sort ascending).
- vGroup Either 'true' or a grouper function.
- fnComparator A comparator function to sort the items.

Listing 8.7. Binding items with a Sorter

```
const initialSorter = new sap.ui.model.Sorter("orderDate", true);
list.bindAggregation("items", {
   path: "/",
   template: listitemTemplate,
   sorter: initialSorter
});
```

Building upon the Listing 7.12, "Example controller function getting model properties" we can add the code to sort the list items. For this example, we have expanded the sorting to use an array of Sorter objects.

Listing 8.8. How to sort items

```
const aSorter= [];
if (sortData.firstSortBy !== "") {
   aSorter.push(
      new sap.ui.model.Sorter(sortData.firstSortBy,
                              sortData.firstSortAsc)
   );
}
if (sortData.secondSortBy !== "") {
   oSorter.push(
      new sap.ui.model.Sorter(sortData.secondSortBy,
                              sortData.secondSortAsc)
   );
}
const control = this.getView().byId("exampleList");
const binding = control.getBinding("items");
binding.sort(oSorter);
```

To allow the user to re-sort the list items, we add a sorter toolbar to the headerToolbar or infoToolbar of the List or Table. For the code to construct the sort Select and Checkbox, look up Section 7.8, "Simple model example".

```
const sortToolbar = new sap.m.OverflowToolbar({
    content: [
        new sap.m.Input({ width: "120px", enabled: false, value: "First sort by" }),
        firstSortSelect,
        firstSortOrderCheckbox,
        new sap.m.ToolbarSeparator(),
        new sap.m.Input({ width: "120px", enabled: false, value: "Then sort by" }),
        secondSortSelect,
        secondSortOrderCheckbox
    ]
});
list.setHeaderToolbar(sortToolbar);
```

| First sort by | Order Date ⌄ | ✓ Descending | Then sort by | Please select a sort option ⌄ | ☐ Descending |

8.5.1. Grouping

Besides sorting, the Sorter can also group the items. First, the items are sorted and then the group determined. It won't make much sense to group by a property which has no recurrent content, because every item would have its own group. But if we search by a recurrent property value, for example an order status, we can add grouping easily.

```
new sap.ui.model.Sorter("status", true, true);
```

Instead of just grouping items by the path, we can write a custom grouper. For example, we might want to group the orders by month.

```
const group = function(v) {
    if (v instanceof Date) {
        var month = v.getMonth();
        switch(month) {
        case 0:
            return "January";
            break;
        ...
        case 11:
            return "December";
            break;
        }
    } else {
        return "Error";
    }
};
const grouper = function(oContext) {
    const v = oContext.getProperty("orderDate");
    const month = group(v);
    return month;
};
new sap.ui.model.Sorter("orderDate", true, grouper);
```

8.6. Filtering and Searching

With UI5, searching is filtering. The bindAggregation function has a property named filters, which can be used to filter the items. Another way to filter is to use the filter function of sap.ui.model.List-

`Binding`. The difference is mainly a timing issue. Binding happens mostly in the view, at a time when we can do some initial filtering. Filtering by user input happens after the binding has already happened. Let us first look at a basic filter searching for items with the status "Processing".

Listing 8.9. Binding model with a filter

```
const filterArray = [];
filterArray.push(new sap.ui.model.Filter("status", "EQ", "Processing"));

list.bindAggregation("items", {
   path: "/",
   template: listitemTemplate,
   filters: filterArray
});
```

In the user interface, we add a search input field to allow the user to specify the search string.

Listing 8.10. Construct a sap.m.SearchField

```
var searchField = new sap.m.SearchField({
   width: "300px",
   placeholder: "{i18n>searchfield.placeholder}",
   tooltip: "{i18n>searchfield.tooltip}",
   search: function(oEvent) {
      oController.filterItems(oEvent);
   }
});
```

The related controller function first gets the query string from the event object. Next, two filters are added to the filters array to test if the value returned with the model property path contains the given query string. These filters are then conjunct as a logical OR.

Listing 8.11. Controller function to filter list items

```
filterItems: function(oEvent) {
   let filters = [];

   const searchString = oEvent.getParameter("query");      The search event provides parameter 'query
   if (searchString !== "") {
      const orFilters = [];
      orFilters.push(new sap.ui.model.Filter({             Add a filter for "status"
         path: "status",
         operator: "Contains",                             Enumeration sap.ui.model.FilterOperator
         value1: searchString
      }));
      orFilters.push(new sap.ui.model.Filter({             Add a filter for "customerName"
         path: "customerName",
         operator: "Contains",
         value1: searchString
      }));

      filters = new sap.ui.model.Filter({
         filters: orFilters,
         and: false                                        Each filter can match
      });
   }
```

```
    const list = this.getView().byId("exampleList");
    const binding = list.getBinding("items");
    binding.filter(filters);                        Filter the items
}
```

We find the list of available filter operators under enumeration `sap.ui.model.FilterOperator`. Note that some of the filter operators require two values.

8.6.1. Facet Filter

Faceted navigation is a search pattern where the user is offered a variety of criteria (called facets) to navigate potentially large result sets. The available criteria inform about critical distinctive attributes and available values. Selecting values progressively narrows the search by filtering. Most e-commerce shops use faceted navigation for their category pages to assist the user to find what he or she is looking for.

UI5 has the `sap.m.FacetFilter`, which can be used to provide interface elements for filtering. A `FacetFilter` has an aggregation `lists`, which is an array of `FacetFilterList` objects, which extends `sap.m.List` and therefore inherits all its features. The `FacetFilterList` has an aggregation `items` and uses a `FacetFilterItem` as a template.

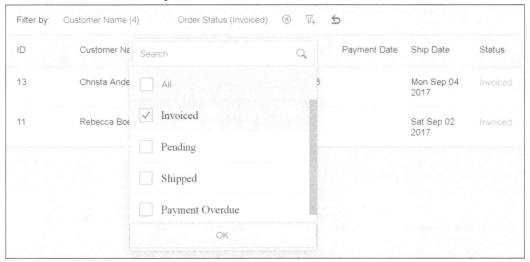

Listing 8.12. Construct a sap.m.FactetFilter

```
 1 const facetFilter = new sap.m.FacetFilter(this.createId("exampleFacetFilter"), {
 2    type: "Simple",
 3    showPersonalization: true,
 4    showPopoverOKButton: true,
 5    confirm: function(oEvent) {
 6       oController.filterByFacet(oEvent);
 7    },
 8    reset: function(oEvent) {
 9       oController.resetFacetFilter(oEvent);
10    }
11 });
12
13 const filterList = new sap.m.FacetFilterList({
14    title: "{listTitle}",
15    key: "{listKey}"
16 });
17
18 facetFilter.bindAggregation("lists", {        Bind path to FacetFilter aggregation 'list'
19    path: "/",
20    template: filterList
21 );
22
23 const filterItem = new sap.m.FacetFilterItem({
24    key: "{key}",
25    text: "{text}"
26 });
27
28 filterList.bindAggregation("items", {         Bind path to FacetFilterList aggregation 'items'
29    path: "values/",
30    template: filterItem,
31    templateShareable: true ❶
32 });
```

❶ By default, "the template will be shared which means that it won't be destroyed or cloned automatically". Anyway, in this case, without explicitly setting the `templateShareable` property, we get the following error message in the console: "During a clone operation, a template was found that neither was marked with 'templateShareable:true' nor 'templateShareable:false'. The framework won't destroy the template. This could cause errors (e.g. duplicate IDs) or memory leaks (The template is used in aggregation 'items' of object '__list0'). For more information, see documentation under 'Aggregation Binding'.

With asynchronous loading the `FilterList items` aggregation can only be populated after the related data request has been successfully completed. But, nevertheless, we want the `FacetFilter` to appear on the initial page. To achieve that, we can use the controller `onInit` function to set the model to the `FacetFilter` without item data.

```
onInit: function () {
   const facetFilterData = [
      {
         title: "Customer Name",
         key: "customerAddressId",
         values: []                                 The array remains empty
      },
      {
         title: "Order Status",
         key: "status",
         values: []
      }
   ];
   const facetModel = new sap.ui.model.json.JSONModel(facetFilterData);
   const facetFilter = this.getView().byId("exampleFacetFilter");
   facetFilter.setModel(facetModel);
}
```

After the data has become available we update the model.

```
const customers = [
   { key: 1, text: "Some Name" },
   { key: 2, text: "Another Name" },
   ...
];
const statuses = [
   { key: "processing", text: "Processing" },
   { key: "pending", text: "Pending" },
   ...
];

const facetFilter = this.getView().byId("exampleFacetFilter");
const facetModel = facetFilter.getModel();
facetModel.setProperty("/0/values", customers);
facetModel.setProperty("/1/values", statuses);
```

In Listing 8.12, "Construct a sap.m.FactetFilter", we attached handler functions to the FacetFilter confirm and reset events (lines 5 to 10). The filterByFacet function first collects the active filters, which are those where the user selected any items. Then the Filter is constructed from the array of active FacetFilterList objects.

We construct a Filter containing an array of Filter arrays. The active list filters are conjunct with a logical AND and the item filters conjunct with a logical OR. The effect is that all records are shown which match one of the selected items of each of the filter lists.

Listing 8.13. Controller functions for the FacetFilter

```
 1 filterByFacet: function(oEvent) {
 2    const facetFilter = oEvent.getSource();
 3    const filterLists = facetFilter.getLists();
 4
 5    const activeLists = [];                        Collect active filters
 6    filterLists.forEach(function(filterList) {
 7       if (filterList.getSelectedItems().length > 0) {
 8          activeLists.push(filterList);
 9       }
10    });
11
```

```
12    const filters = new sap.ui.model.Filter({
13       filters: activeLists.map(                              Array of Filter objects
14         function(filterList) {
15            return new sap.ui.model.Filter({
16               filters: filterList.getSelectedItems().map(    Array of Filter objects
17                 function(selectedItem) {
18                    return new sap.ui.model.Filter({
19                       path: filterList.getKey(),
20                       operator: "EQ",
21                       value1: selectedItem.getKey()
22                    });
23                 }),
24                 and: false                                    Combined: OR
25            });
26         }),
27       and: true                                               Combined: AND
28    });
29
30    this.filterList(filters);
31 },
32
33 resetFacetFilter: function(oEvent) {
34    const facetFilter = oEvent.getSource();
35    const filterLists = facetFilter.getLists();
36    filterLists.forEach(function(filterList) {
37       filterList.setSelectedKeys();                           Reset selected keys
38    });
39    this.filterList([]);
40 },
41
42 filterList: function(filters) {
43    const list = this.getView().byId("exampleList");
44    list.getBinding("items").filter(filters);
45 }
```

 The code in Listing 8.13, "Controller functions for the FacetFilter" is lacking functionality to handle the available items of non-active filter lists. After filtering the data, only a subset of the original items remains, because some of the items may no longer be available. With the AND conjunction (line 27) selecting such an item will result in an empty list. Therefore, the FacetFilter model has to be changed accordingly.

8.7. Summary

In this chapter we learned that in UI5 lists and tables are basically the same thing and the common base was explained. After that we went through examples of a list and a table. Building on these examples we learned how to sort, filter and search the model data bound to the list or table. The chapter closed with an example showing how faceted navigation can be realized with UI5.

Chapter 9. Forms and Input Validation

A HTML form is a container for interactive controls and associated labels, which allows the user to edit and submit data from a web page to a web server. In this chapter, we will learn how to construct forms with UI5 and introduce the main form controls.

9.1. Form

You might expect to find a 'sap.m.Form' control included in UI5, but there is none. Instead there is a namespace sap.ui.layout.form, where we find the classes involved, which construct a form.

A Form has an aggregation formContainers where we add at least one FormContainer. Each FormContainer has an aggregation formElements where we add rows represented as FormElement objects. These objects have a label and an aggregation fields to which the form controls are added.

Listing 9.1. Construct a sap.ui.layout.form.Form

```
const formContainer = new sap.ui.layout.form.FormContainer({
    formElements: [
        new sap.ui.layout.form.FormElement({
            label: "{i18n>some.formelement.label}",
            fields: [ ]                                    Array of form controls
        })
    ]
});
const form = new sap.ui.layout.form.Form({
    title: "{i18n>some.form.title}",
    formContainers: [ formContainer ],                    Add formContainer to aggregation
    layout: [
        new sap.ui.layout.form.ResponsiveGridLayout()
    ],
    editable: true
});
```

Regarding the Form layout property we can read in the API documentation that the ResponsiveGridLayout is generally suggested, "as its responsiveness allows the available space to be used in the best way possible."

The documentation also states that the editable property "has no influence on the editable functionality of the form's content". But, because it sets the aria-readonly attribute of the HTML output, it is important to set anyway.

To add a row to the FormContainer, we need to construct a FormElement with a label and a fields array of controls.

Listing 9.2. Add FormElement to FormContainer

```
const formElement = new sap.ui.layout.form.FormElement();
formElement.setLabel(label);                    Can be a string or a Label object
formElement.addField(formControl);
formElement.addField(anotherFormControl);

formContainer.addFormElement(formElement);
```

9.2. SimpleForm

Luckily, we don't need to always repeat the form code above. As a kind of standard form, we can use
the SimpleForm. It requires fewer lines of code at the price of requiring to respect certain conventions.
For example, adding a title will add a new FormContainer. And if we add a Label to the SimpleForm
content aggregation, it will add a new FormElement.

Listing 9.3. Construct a sap.ui.layout.form.SimpleForm

```
const simpleForm = new sap.ui.layout.form.SimpleForm({
    layout: "ResponsiveGridLayout",        Enumeration sap.ui.layout.form.SimpleFormLayout
    title: "{i18n>simpleForm.title}",
    editable: true,
    content: []
});
```

Form layout is a tricky part, given the many interacting properties involved. If the form is not supposed to take up the whole space, the singleContainerFullSize needs to be set to 'false'. For the ResponsiveGridLayout there are "labelSpan" and "emptySpan" properties, each with the sizes "S", "M",
"L" and "XL". The sizes are defined by a "breakpoint" for "M", "L" and "XL". And the "column"
properties also have no "S" size. The properties are named as a concatenation of name and size, for
example "emptySpanS" or "columnM". Begin with the default values and play with the properties
to get to the expected layout behavior.

Figure 9.1. Screenshot of UI5 Inspector ResponsiveGridLayout properties

```
Properties   Bindings (0)

#__jsview0--exampleForm--Layout (sap.ui.layout.form.ResponsiveGridLayout)
    labelSpanXL: -1
    labelSpanL: 4
    labelSpanM: 2
    labelSpanS: 12
    adjustLabelSpan: true
    emptySpanXL: -1
    emptySpanL: 1
    emptySpanM: 0
    emptySpanS: 0
    columnsXL: -1
    columnsL: 1
    columnsM: 1
    singleContainerFullSize: false
    breakpointXL: 1440
    breakpointL: 1024
    breakpointM: 600
```

To add controls to the `SimpleForm`, we add them to the aggregation `content`. Remember, that adding a `Label` to the `SimpleForm` content will add a new `FormElement` and thereby start a new row.

```
simpleForm.addContent(label).addContent(formControl);
```

9.3. InputBase

One of the subclasses of the `Control` is the `sap.m.InputBase`, which handles the `change` event. It is triggered when

- the text in the input field has changed and the focus leaves the input field,
- the Enter key is pressed,
- the item is clicked on.

The `InputBase` contributes further important properties

- to control the interactive behavior of the control (`editable`, `enabled`),
- to give feedback to the user (`valueState`, `valueStateText`, `showValueStateMessage`),
- to hold the input value (`value`) or show a hint if there is no value yet (`placeholder`),
- to set the HTML input element attribute name (`name`),
- to style the HTML input element (`width`) and the input value (`textAlign` and `textDirection`).

For all the properties, there are getter and setter functions.

If a `tooltip` is not sufficient, to improve usability for users with a screen reader, the `InputBase` provides the association `ariaLabelledBy`, which maintains an array of controls, usually some invisible text, to be read to the user when the focus moves to the HTML input element.

Form controls using the InputBase are the `Input`, `MaskInput`, `TextArea`, `ComboBox`, `MultiComboBox`, and the `DatePicker`.

9.4. Selected Form Controls

The following selection of form controls does not include all form controls, but, hopefully, the most prominent and useful ones.

9.4.1. Label

A `sap.m.Label` is used to provide text for other controls. It can be associated with a particular control using the `labelFor` property. Setting the `required` property to `true` will add a visual marker next to the label indicating that the associated form control requires user input.

Listing 9.4. Construct a sap.m.Label

```
const label = new sap.m.Label({
    text: "{i18n>name.label}",
    design: "Standard",           LabelDesign: "Standard" or "Bold"
    required: true,               Indicates visually, if input/selection is required
    labelFor: formControl         The associated control
});
```

9.4.2. Input

The most important form control is the Input, which generates an HTML input element.

Listing 9.5. Construct an sap.m.Input

```
const nameInput = new sap.m.Input({
    placeholder: "{i18n>name.input.placeholder},
    tooltip: "{i18n>name.input.tooltip}",
    value: {
        path: "/name"                    Model absolute path
    },
    maxLength: 30,                       Sets the HTML input maxlength attribute
    width: "200px",                      Sets the HTML width attribute for the control
    change: function(oEvent) { },
    liveChange: function(oEvent) { }
});
```

To get the input value from the Input control, we use its getValue function. From the Event object we get it as a parameter (oEvent.getParameter("value");).

9.4.2.1. Specifying the InputType

The sap.m.InputType sets the HTML type attribute of the input element. Apart from the password type, which causes the user input to be obscured replacing each character by a placeholder symbol, setting the type is mostly a convenience feature for the user, since it specifies the keyboard being displayed on devices with a touchscreen software keyboard.

Available types are implemented as an enumeration sap.m.InputType: 'Email', 'Number', 'Password', 'Tel', 'Text' (default), 'Url'. HTML5 compliant browsers can actually validate the input according to the type, but UI5 doesn't use these abilities yet.

9.4.2.2. Value help and autocomplete features

The input can be further enhanced with a help button and an autocomplete feature.

To add a help button to the input and attach the controller handleHelpRequest function when requested, we add the following code:

```
nameInput.setShowValueHelp(true);                    Add help button
nameInput.attachValueHelpRequest(function(oEvent) {  Attach handler function
    oController.handleHelpRequest(oEvent);
});
```

The autocomplete feature is activated by setting the showSuggestion property to true. The suggestions are stored in either the suggestionItems or the suggestionRows aggregation. The following example code expects an array of objects with a property name under the model path "/suggestedNames".

```
nameInput.setShowSuggestion(true);
const itemTemplate = new sap.ui.core.Item({
    key: "{name}",
    text: "{name}"
});
nameInput.bindAggregation("suggestionItems",
                          "/suggestedNames",
                          itemTemplate);
```

For more elaborate examples showing how to use these features, be sure to have a look at the InputAssisted, InputAssistedTabularSuggestions, InputAssistedTwoValues examples to be found in the `test-resources/sap/m/demokit/sample` folder of the UI5 SDK.

9.4.3. MaskInput

A variation of an input control is the `sap.m.MaskInput`. It allows setting a mask for the input value and related rules to allow only matching input. This control is quite efficient to enforce a certain input format.

Listing 9.6. Construct a sap.m.MaskInput

```
const maskInputExplain = new sap.ui.core.InvisibleText({
    text: "First we expect two digits followed by two lower case letters"
});
new sap.m.MaskInput({
    value: "{/maskValue}",
    mask: "dd ll",
    rules: [
        new sap.m.MaskInputRule({              Rule to allow only digits for the d in the mask
            maskFormatSymbol: "d",
            regex: "[0-9]"
        }),
        new sap.m.MaskInputRule({              Rule to allow only letters for the l in the mask
            maskFormatSymbol: "l",
            regex: "[a-z]"
        }),
        ariaLabelledBy: [ maskInputExplain ]   The control needs to be added to the page content
    ],
    change: function(oEvent) { }
});
```

MaskInput: `2_ __`

9.4.4. TextArea

The `sap.m.TextArea` control works like a regular HTML `textarea`. Use it if the input allows linebreaks or is too long for a normal input field.

Listing 9.7. Construct a sap.m.TextArea

```
const textarea = new sap.m.TextArea({
    placeholder: "{i18n>description.input.placeholder}",
    value: "{/description}",
    maxLength: 200,                    Sets the HTML textarea maxlength attribute
    rows: 2,                           Sets the HTML textarea rows attribute
    cols: 20,                          Sets the HTML textarea cols attribute
    growing: true,                     Allow the textarea to grow with the user input
    growingMaxLines: 10,
    change: function(oEvent) { }
});
```

Instead of the `rows` and `cols` properties, we can also use the `width` and `height` properties, which both require a valid CSS size value. Be aware, that the `height` property is ignored, when the `growing` property is set to `true`.

9.4.5. ComboBox and MultiComboBox

The `sap.m.ComboBox` is a useful control. It is a combination of a dropdown list and an input field with autocomplete functionality.

Listing 9.8. Construct a sap.m.ComboBox

```
const combobox = new sap.m.ComboBox({
    placeholder: "{i18n>location.combobox.placeholder}",
    selectedKey: "{/location}",
    selectionChange: function(oEvent) { },        Triggered if an item matches
    change: function(oEvent) { }                   Triggered upon any input value change
});
```

Let us quickly revisit the issue of how to bind an array of data objects from a model to an aggregation of any object extending the `ManagedObject`[1]. For this, we can use the `bindAggregation` function. The array entries are presented using an item template. Here, we can choose to have the objects in the array sorted or filtered.

Listing 9.9. Binding data to an aggregation

```
const itemTemplate = new sap.ui.core.Item({
    key: "{keyValue}",
    text: "{textValue}"
});

const textValueSorter= new sap.ui.model.Sorter("textValue", false);

const control = new sap.m.SelectList();          Has aggregation named 'items'
control.bindAggregation("items", {
    path: "modelName>/pathToArray",              Model property path
    template: itemTemplate,
    sorter: textValueSorter
});
```

The above example shows how to bind an array of objects to the aggregation 'items'. The `bindAggregation` function of the `sap.ui.core.ManagedObject` allows a number of additional parameters, which are listed in the API Reference. To bind a value to a property, use the `bindProperty` function.

To use the `ComboBox` as a replacement of an HTML `select`, we need to change the default behavior of the control which allows the user to input a value which is not among the options. To warn the user in case of an input value without a selected item, we attach a handler function to the `change` event.

```
combobox.attachChange(function() {
    oController.checkComboBox(comboBox);
}
```

The controller function may look like this:

```
checkComboBox: function(comboBox) {
        const vlue = comboBox.getValue();              Get the input value
        const selectedItem = comboBox.getSelectedItem();   Get the selected item
    if (selectedItem === null) {
        if (!vlue === "") {
```

---

[1]See Listing 8.2, "Construct a sap.m.List", Listing 8.7, "Binding items with a Sorter", Listing 8.9, "Binding model with a filter".

```
            comboBox.setValueState("Warning");
            comboBox.setValueStateText("No item selected");
            return;
        }
    }
    comboBox.setValueState("None");
}
```

The sap.m.MultiComboBox is similar to the ComboBox, but the user can select multiple items. Accordingly, instead of a selectedKey property, the MultiComboBox has a selectedKeys property expecting an array of keys.

```
sap.m.MultiComboBox({
    placeholder: "{i18n>location.multicombobox.placeholder}",
    selectedKeys: "{/locations}"
});
```

The binding is the same as in the ComboBox example above.

A problem occurs with the MultiComboBox if the user selects multiple entries with a box representation wider than the space available.

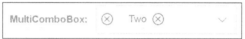

9.4.6. Date/TimePicker

For date or time input or display, UI5 has special controls. The sap.m.DateTimePicker and sap.m.DateRangeSelection extend the sap.m.DatePicker, while the sap.m.TimePicker extends sap.m.MaskInput.

Using the DatePicker and subclasses, the user can select a date from a calendar, or insert the date directly in the input field. The property displayFormat specifies the expected input pattern. If not configured, the calender type and formats are dependent upon the current locale.

Listing 9.10. Construct a sap.m.DatePicker

```
new sap.m.DatePicker({
    valueFormat: "yyyyMMdd",            How the value is formatted
    displayFormat: "short",             How the date is displayed
    dateValue : "{/someDate}",          Model property path to JavaScript Date instance
    change: function() {}
});
```

Properties valueFormat and displayFormat expect a string. The API Reference tells us, how the string has to be formatted: "Supported format options are pattern-based on Unicode LDML Date Format notation." UI5 understands shortcuts 'short, 'medium', 'long' or 'full'. By default, the `displayFormat` is used as a `placeholder`.

The date can be set either with `dateValue` as a JavaScript Date, or with `value` as a string. Both values are synchronized internally.

Further useful properties are `minDate` and `maxDate`, both requiring a JavaScript Date instance. To limit valid dates to the past, we set the `maxDate` to `new Date()`. But remember, that the views are usually kept in memory in their last state. Therefore, we need to ensure that the date is updated, when the view is visited again. Otherwise the `maxDate` could remain to be set to the time when the view was initialized.

The `DateTimePicker` is constructed likewise. Just the format patterns need to include the time as well. A special variant of the DatePicker is the `DateRangeSelection`. It allows the user to select a date range with the calendar.

Listing 9.11. Construct a sap.m.DateRangeSelection

```
new sap.m.DateRangeSelection({
    from: "{/fromDate}",
    to: "{/toDate}",
    change: function() {}
});
```

To get the dates from the control, use the functions `getDateValue` and `getSecondDateValue`.

9.4.7. CheckBox and Switch

We often need the user to make a yes/no decision. For this, HTML has an `input type checkbox`. The UI5 implementation is the `sap.m.CheckBox`.

Listing 9.12. Construct a sap.m.CheckBox

```
new sap.m.CheckBox({
    selected: "{/checkboxState}",
    name: "someName",                          Sets the HTML input name attribute
    text: "{i18n>checkbox.text}",              Adds text next to the square box
    textAlign: "Begin",
    tooltip: "{i18n>checkbox.tooltip}",
    select: function() {}
});
```

The `select` event is triggered when the user changes the state of the checkbox. To get the value from the checkbox, use the `getSelected` function.

Another control to set a boolean value is the `sap.m.Switch`. The main difference is visual.

Listing 9.13. Construct a sap.m.Switch

```
new sap.m.Switch({
    state: "{/switchState}",
    tooltip: "{i18n>switch.tooltip}",
    type: "AcceptReject",                      Enumeration sap.m.SwitchType
    change : function() {}
});
```

The type can either be 'AcceptReject' or 'Default'. The texts for type 'Default' can be changed with the properties customTextOn and customTextOff.

9.4.8. Select

The Select control emulates the HTML select behavior.

Listing 9.14. Construct a sap.m.Select

```
new sap.m.Select({
    textAlign: "Begin",                     Enumeration sap.ui.core.TextAlign
    autoAdjustWidth: true,                  Sets width, so that all item texts are visible
    selectedKey: "{/selected}",
    change: function(oEvent) {}
});
```

Bind an array of objects to the aggregation items to provide a list of entries. Note that the Select has no placeholder property. Instead, we have to add a placeholder item to the aggregation. This can be done by adding a placeholder item to the model data (see Section 7.8, "Simple model example").

Regarding property forceSelection, the UI5 API recommends, "that you always set this property to false and bind the selectedKey property to the desired value for better interoperability with data binding." Oddly, the default is true. But following the recommendation results in enabling the autoAdjustWidth property, which requires a selected item. If the key value is null or an empty string, it will not match any Item and the width will not be calculated properly.

9.4.9. RadioButton

Another way to have the user choose among a number of given choices is a group of HTML input elements of type radio.

Listing 9.15. Construct a sap.m.RadioButtonGroup

```
new sap.m.RadioButtonGroup({
    columns: 4,
    selectedIndex: 0,
    select: function(oEvent) {
        oController.radioButtonSelected(oEvent);
    },
    buttons: [
        new sap.m.RadioButton({ text: "Air" }),
        new sap.m.RadioButton({ text: "Water"}),
        new sap.m.RadioButton({ text: "Earth", editable: false }),
        new sap.m.RadioButton({ text: "Fire", enabled: false })
    ]
});
```

We can also bind an array of objects to the aggregation buttons.

```
const radioTemplate = new sap.m.RadioButton({
    text: "{textValue}"
});
```

```
radioGroup.bindAggregation("buttons", {
   path: "/pathToArray",
   template: radioTemplate
});
```

9.5. Validation UI5 Style

OpenUI5 offers automated input validation and will show a related message if the input value doesn't validate. The predefined types are under the namespaces sap.ui.model.type and sap.ui.model.oda-ta.type for EDM types.

To see how it works, let us look at an example. Types have formatting options and constraints. Type String doesn't have any formatting options, but has various constraint properties.

```
const nameType = new sap.ui.model.type.String(
    {},                                        No formatting options
    { minLength: 3, maxLength: 20 }            Constraint properties
);
```

Now, we only have to set the type for the value to get the input validated.

```
new sap.m.Input({
   value: {
      path: "/name",
      type: nameType
   }
});
```

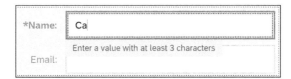

There are several model types included in UI5. And custom types are not too complicated to create. The following listing provides a simple model type Email, assigned to the custom namespace oum.lib.type.

Listing 9.16. Basic custom type: Email

```
sap.ui.model.SimpleType.extend("oum.lib.type.Email", {
   formatValue: function(oValue) {
      return oValue;
   },
   parseValue: function(oValue) {
      return oValue;
   },
   validateValue: function(oValue) {
      const regex = /[A-Z0-9._%+-]+@[A-Z0-9.-]+\.[A-Z]{2,4}/;    Regular expression for basic email validation
      if (!regex.test(oValue)) {
         throw new sap.ui.model.ValidateException(
            oui5lib.util.getI18nText("invalid.email")
         );
      }
   }
});
```

The Email type neither has formatting options nor constraint properties. This is how it is constructed:

```
const emailType = new oum.lib.type.Email({}, {});
```

9.6. Summary

This chapter introduced two ways to construct forms with UI5, one more flexible and another simplifying construction through conventions. Then we went through examples of common form controls. We round the chapter out with an example how to implement validation of user input with UI5 means.

We will revisit the issues of form control construction and user input validation in later chapters. Chapter 14, *Form Control Generation* presents a unified way to automate the generation of form controls. Chapter 13, *Validation* introduces a way to meet all validation needs.

Part II. Providing and using metadata for domain entities

It may appear odd to have whole chapters without dependency to UI5 in a UI5 User Guide. But to use UI5 efficiently it is critical to understand where the toolkit helps us and where it becomes a burden. UI5 shines generating a responsive user interface and allowing us to conveniently handle user events. But we are well advised to not see it as the one-stop solution to building the whole application.

As a developer with an open source attitude and practice, I am used to cherry-picking features and functionality from a wide range of tools and applications. OpenUI5 is open source and it allows us to rapidly develop responsive data-centric applications without having to write HTML and CSS. It is convenient to build a user interface with lists, tables and forms. Let us use the toolkit for its strengths and choose a different path where it limits our flexibility and leads to problematic code, mixing domain-specific concerns with UI5 object code.

After initializing the oui5lib namespace Listing 2.12, "Initialize custom namespace", we have created several sub-namespaces and added functions to these namespaces. So far, these functions were just supportive without seriously altering the way we work with UI5.

This part of the book goes further by introducing metadata for domain entities. This mostly concerns situations where we don't have OData services available, or at least, have mixed data sources and services leaving us with missing metadata about the data handled by the application. Collecting metadata into configuration files allows us to avoid spreading information about domain entities and their relations throughout the application.

Very often, terms are not precise. The same term can be used for different things and multiple terms can fit for one thing. Many terms are loaded with meaning coming from a particular context. As context changes meaning, mixing contexts makes terms ambiguous.

For example, we use the term "domain entity" without implicating that we follow the "Domain-Driven Design" approach. The term should therefore be taken lightly here. It is just an abstract term to speak about the data which are being presented and edited by the application.

It proved tricky to find terms speaking about metadata for domain entities. In particular, because the code uses the metadata to deal with the entity data and is written in the JavaScript language. These are different contexts using the same terms. Keeping the code itself readable forces us to find distinguished terms to avoid having to think much about the relative context.

Metadata for domain entities are not really a configuration, because they don't configure the entities in any way. They also don't define the entity. They partly just describe the entity and also specify particular aspects like how to validate values or construct user interface elements.

Writing readable code is more important than using the academically 'correct' terms. And writing about code only adds an additional layer of misunderstanding. When we write code, especially code fragments spread around files, using the same terms for the same things is crucial. Therefore, we need to set a particular language and terms and use them consistently.

After these general words about language and terms, I will now introduce the terms being used for the rest of the book.

We speak about domain entities with attributes. The attributes have a name and a value. The related entity metadata are collected into mappings with a entity and a request section. The entity section contains entity attribute specifications. Each entity attribute has an attribute specification.

Each entity belongs to a collection of entity items of the same type identified by a primary key.

Requests have a name and are configured. They don't have attributes, but parameters. Each parameter is specified. Therefore, we speak about a request configuration with parameter specifications.

The entity attribute and request parameter specifications have various properties. The value of the property name is used as reference to a property of an entity data object. The combined entity name and attribute name are expected to be unique and identify both specifications and values.

In the first chapter of this part, we will introduce the metadata JSON. Next we will show how the request configurations can be used to run requests. This is followed by chapters using entity attribute specifications to validate user input and construct form controls.

Separating HTTP request handling from UI5 and using the standard JavaScript XMLHttpRequest instead - at least, for requests not using OData services and the OData protocol, enables us to test the connection issues without any dependencies.

We will also present a way to separate domain entities and the related collections from UI5. Developing domain logic and conventions apart from UI5 has major advantages. The most important advantage concerns the readability and stability of the related code base. By exclusively focusing on expressing the core information and expertise of the customer about his field we stand the best chance of developing a stable base upon which we can build whatever user interface.

Separating the domain data logic and related request handling from the data binding to the user interface elements allows us to develop and test these concerns independently from each other. This works on the basis of specifications of data required by the user interface. Whatever data are received and held by the client have to be transformed to meet the user interface requirements. If the incoming data structure changes, the transformation may also have to be changed, but the user interface can function without interruption.

Table of Contents

Chapter 10. Entity specifications: Mapping

Providing metadata for domain entities

The so called 'client-side' models lack all metadata. This lack of metadata doesn't mean we don't need them. We need to know the domain data, which attributes they have and their types, how the entities relate to each other and how we can request the entity data with which query parameters. We need to validate user input and post change requests. Not having the required metadata in one place only means that we will spread the information throughout the application wherever we deal with these aspects.

To provide metadata for the domain entities we use JSON-formatted files called mappings. By convention, we name these files after their entity, for example order.json, address.json or product.json.

The mappings are not based upon a well defined specification like OData. Instead, they are made up from scratch to collect whatever metadata we discover in the process of learning about the domain entities and their attributes. The mappings express a current understanding of the domain entities, which can be communicated between all participants in the development process. The more we let our application be driven by the collected domain metadata, the easier we can modify it by improving our metadata.

Let us begin with the general outline of a mapping. A mapping must specify the primary key of the entity to be able to access it from the related collection. It has an entity and a request section.

Listing 10.1. General outline of a mapping

```
{
  "description": "Always describe the entity with a few words",
  "primaryKey": "keyName",
  "entity": [
    {
      "name": "keyName"
    }
  ],
  "request": {
    "defaults": { }
  }
}
```

10.1. Describe an entity

As a general rule, we expect all incoming data to be formatted as JSON. Let us look at a simplified order entry as an example entity:

Listing 10.2. Example order

```
{
    "id": 1,
    "status": "shipped",
    "billingAddressId": 1,
    "shippingAddressId": 1,
    "currency": "US-$",
    "orderDate": "2017-05-16 10:01:23",
    "items": [
        {
            "productId": "0394718747",
            "quantity": 2,
            "unitPrice": 4.80
        },
        {
            "productId": "0889610356",
            "quantity": 1,
            "unitPrice": 19.90
        }
    ]
}
```

We use the `entity` section of the mapping to describe the entity as an array of objects with various properties, of which only the `name` is required. The default `type` is "string" and the default value for `required` is `false`.

An initial and incomplete order entity mapping may look like this:

```
 1 {
 2     "description": "Metadata for an Order",
 3     "primaryKey": "id",                                                What is the primary key?
 4     "entity" : [
 5         {
 6             "name": "id"                                               The primary key
 7         },{
 8             "name": "status",
 9             "default": "new",                                          Set a default value
10             "referenceTo": "status.status",
11             "allowedValues": ["new", "pending", "processing", "shipped"]   Allowed values
12         },{
13             "name": "billingAddressId",
14             "referenceTo": "address.id",
15             "required": true
16         },{
17             "name": "shippingAddressId",
18             "referenceTo": "address.id",
19             "description": "If no shipping address is given, the billing address is used"
20         },{
21             "name": "currency"
22         }
23     ]
24 }
```

The property `description` is reserved for holding descriptive notes and can be added anywhere in the mapping without any repercussions. It is good practice to annotate important parts of the mapping with short descriptions to help the reader understand it more easily.

The property `referenceTo` (lines 10, 14, 18) is used to point to another entity object, for example the order addresses to an address entity or the ordered products to a product entity. We mainly use this to provide important information.

So far, all the above entity attributes have had the default `type` "string". The IDs (lines 6, 13, 17) may actually be numbers but string representations fulfil the same purpose and can't cause problems with the user interface, where control value properties mostly require strings.

The `orderDate` is a different type. It comes in as a string but for the application we need to convert it to a JavaScript Date object. For this conversion we may need a `dataFormat` property.

```
{
   "name": "orderDate",
   "type": "Date",                                   Type is a Date instance
   "dateFormat": "yyyy-MM-dd HH:mm:ss",              Incoming date format pattern
   "required": true                                  An orderDate is required
}
```

Apart from the primitive values (string, number) and literal name tokens (true, false, null), JSON has two basic data structures: array and object. Let us first consider the array.

The ordered `items` (see Listing 10.2, "Example order") are an array of objects with a `productId`, `quantity` and `unitPrice`. The mapping uses the `type` "array" for this kind of structure and an additional property `arrayItem` which holds an array of objects describing each individual item attribute.

```
{
   "name": "items",
   "description": "The list of ordered items",
   "type": "array",                                  Type is an instanceof Array
   "arrayItem": [                                     Define the item object
     {
        "name": "productId",
        "required": true,
        "referenceTo": "product.isbn"
     },{
        "name": "quantity",
        "type": "int",                               The quantity is a JavaScript Number
        "default": 1,
        "required": true
     },{
        "name": "unitPrice",
        "type": "float",                             The unitPrice is a float
        "required": true
     }
   ]
}
```

There is another kind of array. Instead of an array of objects, we may just have an array of strings. Here is an example mapping entry:

```
{
   "name": "roles",
   "required": true,
   "type": "array",
   "allowedValues": ["developer", "user", "editor", "administrator"]
}
```

This leaves only the JSON object data structure uncovered. Let us look at an example of a product entry:

```
{
   "isbn": "0521560241",
   "title": {
      "a": "A forest of time :",
      "b": "American Indian ways of history /",
      "c": "Peter Nabokov."
   },
   ...
}
```

Here the `title` is not a primitive value or an array, but an object. The related part of the mapping uses a `type` "object", which expects an `objectItem` as an array of objects specifying the title attributes of the product entity.

```
{
   "description": "Metadata for a Product",
   "primaryKey" : "isbn",
   "entity" : [
      {
         "name": "isbn"
      },{
         "name": "title",
         "type": "object",
         "objectItem": [
            {
               "name": "a",
               "required": true
            },{
               "name": "b"
            },{
               "name": "c",
               "required": true
            }
         ]
      },
      ...
   ]
}
```

10.2. Describe Requests

We can also use the mapping to describe related requests. The available requests are put under the `request` section (see Listing 10.1, "General outline of a mapping").

The JavaScript `document.location` has several parts: `protocol`, `host` and `pathname` We use these names for the request configuration properties. In order to avoid repeating the same protocol and host for every request, we may set `defaults`.

Each request has a unique name to access the request configuration object, which requires at least a `pathname`. The request property `method` refers to the HTTP verbs. The only ones used here are GET and POST. The default is GET. Additionally, we may specify an array of `parameters`. The properties to describe the parameters are a subset of the entity attribute specification properties. Other than the entity attribute the parameter specifications are flat name/ value pairs without multi-level data structures (types 'array/ object).

Listing 10.3. Example mapping: specify order requests

```
{
    "primaryKey": "id",
    "request": {
        "defaults": {                           Set default protocol and host
            "protocol": "http",
            "host": "localhost:3000"
        },
        "queryOrders": {                        Request name
            "pathname": "getOrders",
            "method": "GET",
            "parameters": [
                {
                    "name": "startDate",        Required parameter
                    "type": "Date",
                    "dateFormat": "yyyy-MM-dd",  Needed to convert Date object into string
                    "required": true
                },{
                    "name": "endDate",
                    "type": "Date",
                    "dateFormat": "yyyy-MM-dd"
                },{
                    "name": "statuses",
                    "type": "Array"
                }
            ]
        },
        "getOrder": {                           Request name
            "pathname": "getOrder",
            "method": "GET",
            "parameters": [
                {
                    "name": "id"
                }
            ]
        },
        "saveOrder": {                          Request name
            "protocol": "https",                Overwrite defaults
            "host": "localhost:3010"
            "pathname": "saveOrders",
            "method": "POST",
            "parameters": [
                {
                "name": "orderString",
                "type": "json",
                "description": "The value is a stringified JSON order object"
                }
            ]
        }
    }
}
```

10.3. Access the mappings

Up to this point, we have only introduced a way to express entity metadata. This would be of limited use if we didn't provide easy access to these metadata. So, let us take care of that now.

All mappings go into a folder, whose path we set in the `config.json` (see Listing 2.11, "Custom configuration"), where we add a `mappingDirectory` property. To access the value we add a corresponding function to the `oui5lib.configuration` namespace.

```
function getMappingDir() {
    return getConfigData("mappingDirectory");
}
configuration.getMappingDir = getMappingDir;
```

When needed, we have to load the mapping. Loading JSON files is a generally useful function to have available. Request handling is a particular issue, which we cover in the following Chapter 11, *Request Handling*. For now, we just assume to have the functionality available.

For the sake of providing convenient access to the mappings data we put the related code into the namespace `oui5lib.mapping` and therefore create a file `mapping.js` in the `oui5lib` folder.

Listing 10.4. Namespace oui5lib.mapping

```
(function() {
    /** @namespace oui5lib.mapping */
    const mapping = oui5lib.namespace("mapping");
}());
```

We begin with the inner functions. If we plan to actually use the mappings, we need to normalize them by adding default values to all the attribute specifications of the `entity` section, as well as the request `parameters`. This allows us to count on certain properties being available and avoids unnecessary checks for undefined keys down the line.

All entity attribute and request parameter specifications have a `name`, a `type` and a `required` property. The following function sets default values for the `type` and `required` properties for entity attribute and request parameter objects omitting them.

```
function setDefaultProperties(spec) {
    if (typeof spec.type !== "string") {
        spec.type = "string";                    Default type "string"
    }
    if (typeof spec.required !== "boolean") {
        spec.required = false;                    Default is not required
    }
}
```

While the request parameters are only used to send requests, the entity attributes are presented in the user interface and may be modifiable. Therefore, we have additional defaults which concern the validation of values, multilingual support and form generation. We will explain and use these properties in the following chapters.

For the time being, we will just introduce a `validate` property as an array of strings, which we are going to use to validate user input (see Chapter 13, *Validation*). As a first validation string we add "required" if indeed the attribute is set to `required`.

```
function setEntityAttributeDefaults(attributeSpec) {
   let tests = [];
   if (typeof attributeSpec.validate !== "undefined" &&
       attributeSpec.validate instanceof Array) {
      tests = attributeSpec.validate;
   }
   if (attributeSpec.required) {
      tests.push("required");                        Add test 'required'
   }
   if (tests.length > 0) {                           Without tests 'validate' remains undefined
      attributeSpec.validate = tests;
   }

   if (typeof attributeSpec.i18n === "undefined") {  I18n section
      attributeSpec.i18n = {};
   }
   if (typeof attributeSpec.ui5 === "undefined") {   UI5 section
      attributeSpec.ui5 = {};
   }
}
```

The above functions need to be called for all related objects of the mapping. This includes the "arrayItem" and "objectItem" arrays of entity attribute specifications.

Listing 10.5. Process entity attribute and request parameter specifications

```
function procArrayOfSpecifications(specs, isEntityAttr) {
   if (specs === undefined) { return; }
   if (typeof isEntityAttr !== "boolean") { isEntityAttr = false; }

   specs.forEach(function(spec) {                    Loop the specifications
      setDefaultProperties(spec);                    Set general default properties
      if (isEntityAttr) {
         setEntityAttributeDefaults(spec);           Set entity attribute defaults
      }
      switch(spec.type) {
      case "array":
         procArrayOfSpecifications(spec.arrayItem); ❶
         break;
      case "object":
         procArrayOfSpecifications(spec.objectItem); ❷
         break;
      }
   });
}
```

❶❷ We set defaults for all levels of entity attributes by recursively calling the procArrayOfSpecifications function when we encounter a type "array" or "object".

After dealing with the entity attribute and request parameter specifications, we need to take care of normalizing the request configurations. All requests need a protocol and host to build the URL for the request. Some applications use a multitude of services with different URLs from which to request their domain data. Other applications basically use one URL as source for all or most of their data requests. Setting defaults to be overwritten by the individual request configuration provides us with the required flexibility.

Listing 10.6. Set defaults for request configurations

```
function setRequestDefaults(requestConfig, requestDefaults) {
   const defaultKeys = ["protocol", "host"];                Possible request defaults
   defaultKeys.forEach(function(key) {
      if (requestConfig[key] === undefined) {
         if (requestDefaults[key] !== undefined) {
            requestConfig[key] = requestDefaults[key];        Use default
         }
      }
   });
   if (typeof requestConfig.method === "string" &&           GET or POST
       ["GET", "POST"].indexOf(requestConfig.method) > -1) {
      return;
   }
   requestConfig.method = "GET";
}
```

All the above functions would be useless if not called. The best moment to normalize the mappings is directly after loading them.

The source of the mapping data is a file in the mappings directory named after the entity. Each mapping file is loaded only once, processed to add default values and then stored in a mappings object in client memory. The drawback of this is that any changes of the mappings will not become effective until we reload the application and unfortunately may also require a clearing of the browser cache.

The request to load a mapping carries the entity name to the function mappingLoaded, which is called when the response was successful. Note that the request here is set to run synchronously to reduce complexity, but also because without valid mapping much of the following code won't work anyway. As the mappings are small files loaded from the application webspace, hopefully this should not be a big issue.

Listing 10.7. Load and process entity mapping

```
const _mappings = {};

function getMapping(entityName) {
   if (typeof mappings[entityName] === "undefined") {
      loadMapping(entityName);                               The mapping has to be loaded
   }
   if(typeof _mappings[entityName] === "undefined") {
      throw new Error("couldn't load mapping for entity " + entityName);
   }
   return _mappings[entityName];
}

function loadMapping(entityName) {                           Load the mapping file
   const mappingDir = oui5lib.configuration.getMappingDir();
   const url = mappingDir + "/" + entityName + ".json";

   oui5lib.request.loadJson(url, mappingLoaded
                           { entity: entityName },
                           false);                           Synchronous request
}

function mappingLoaded(mappingData, requestProps) {          Handles successful response
```

```
    const entityName = requestProps.entity;

    if (typeof mappingData === "object") {
        if (mappingData.entity !== undefined) {
            procArrayOfSpecifications(mappingData.entity, true); ❶
        }
        if (mappingData.request !== undefined) {
            const requestDefaults = mappingData.request.defaults;

            for (let requestName in mappingData.request) {          Loop the request configurations
                if (requestName === "defaults") {                   Skip "defaults"
                    continue;
                }
                const requestConfig = mappingData.request[requestName];
                if (requestDefaults !== undefined) {
                    setRequestDefaults(requestConfig, requestDefaults);  Set request defaults
                }
                if (requestConfig.parameters !== undefined &&
                    requestConfig.parameters instanceof Array) {
                    procArrayOfSpecifications(requestConfig.parameters); ❷
                }
            }
        }
        _mappings[entityName] = data;                               Store normalized mapping
    }
}
```

❶❷ See Listing 10.5, "Process entity attribute and request parameter specifications". The first call is for an entity attribute specification and the second for a parameter specification.

Now, let's look at the 'public' methods to get the primary key (getPrimaryKey), a request configuration (getRequestConfiguration) and the entity attribute specifications (getEntityAttributeSpecs).

```
function getPrimaryKey(entityName) {
    return getMapping(entityName).primaryKey;
}
mapping.getPrimaryKey = getPrimaryKey;

function getRequestConfig(entityName, requestName) {
    return getMapping(entityName).request[requestName];
}
mapping.getRequestConfiguration = getRequestConfig;

function getEntityAttributeSpecs(entityName) {
    return getMapping(entityName).entity;
}
mapping.getEntityAttributeSpecs = getEntityAttributeSpecs;
```

The function to get a single attribute specification by its path is a little tricky because it has to deal with the array and object types allowing multiple levels of properties.

```
function getEntityAttributeSpec(entityName, propertyPath) {
   let attributeSpecs = getEntityAttributeSpecs(entityName);

   const pathLevels = propertyPath.split("/");
   if (pathLevels.length > 1) {
      let subPath, attributeSpec;
      for (let i = 0, s = pathLevels.length; i < s - 1; i++) {
         subPath = pathLevels[i];
         attributeSpec = listHelper.getItemByKey(attributeSpecs, "name", subPath);
         if (attributeSpec === null) {
            return null;
         }

         switch(attributeSpec.type) {
         case "object":
            attributeSpecs = attributeSpec.objectItem;
            break;
         case "array":
            attributeSpecs = attributeSpec.arrayItem;
            break;
         }
      }
      propertyPath = pathLevels[pathLevels.length - 1];
   }
   return listHelper.getItemByKey(attributeSpecs, "name", propertyPath);
}
mapping.getEntityAttributeSpec = getEntityAttributeSpec;
```

 As an attentive reader, you surely have noticed that the above code uses a `listHelper.getItem-ByKey` function. This is just a helper function to find an item in an array by its key value.

10.4. Summary

The first part of this chapter introduced the reader to a simple way to collect and store metadata about the data handled by the application. We call it mappings. This is critical to understand because it is the basis for Chapter 11, *Request Handling*, Chapter 13, *Validation*, and Chapter 14, *Form Control Generation*.

The second part presented the code to access and normalize these metadata. It is not absolutely necessary to understand this because you can simply download and use the code from https://github.com/cahein/oui5lib. It is merely explanatory and will help the reader to extend the mappings.

Chapter 11. Request Handling

In the previous chapter we needed to load the mapping files. We also mapped requests which we wanted to activate. Because the Fetch API does not allow any synchronous requests and we don't want to duplicate functionality, we will use the standard `XMLHttpRequest` for the requests.

Instead of using Promise objects, which are designed to handle both the fulfilled (success) and rejected (failure) states, our request function handles success and failure in different ways. The function has a parameter `handleSuccess` which requires a `typeof "function"`. In case the request is successful, the given `handleSuccess` function is called (callback). In case the request is successful, but the JSON won't parse, we have our code throw an `Error`. In case of a request failure, a related event is published. This way, our data requests are made optimistically and don't deal with request failure. Instead, the application in general and controllers in particular will take care of failure scenarios by subscribing to the related events.

Figure 11.1. Request Flow

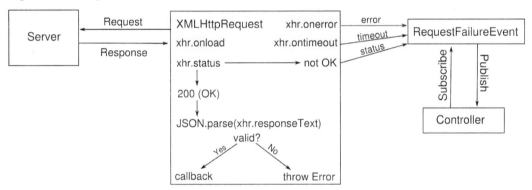

The most fitting namespace for this kind of functionality seems to be `oui5lib.request`. We therefore create a file `request.js` in the `oui5lib` folder and begin coding.

11.1. Request URL returning JSON

The following code listing is quite long, but actually not very complicated to follow. It begins with JSDoc comment tags describing the `fetchJson` function parameters. For the request we use the standard W3C XMLHttpRequest. The relevant events handlers are attached with the `addHandlers` function.

Listing 11.1. Namespace oui5lib.request

```
(function() {
    /**
     * Send XMLHttpRequest expecting JSON.
     * @memberof oui5lib.request
     * @param {string} url              The URL to request.
     * @param {function} handleSuccess  The function to call when the request
     *                                  is completed with response status 'Success'.
     * @param {object} requestProps     Properties to be passed with the request.
     * @param {boolean} isAsync         Load asynchronously? Defaults to 'true'.
```

```
 * @param {string} httpVerb              Either GET or POST. Defaults to GET.
 * @param {string} encodedParams         A URL-encoded parameter string.
 */
function fetchJson(url, handleSuccess, requestProps, isAsync, httpVerb, encodedParams) {
    if (typeof isAsync !== "boolean") { isAsync = true; }            Set default values
    if (typeof httpVerb !== "string") { httpVerb = "GET"; }

    if (typeof encodedParams === "string" && httpVerb === "GET") {
        const protocolRegex = /^https?.*/;
        if (protocolRegex.test(url)) { ❶
            url += "?" + encodedParams;
        }
    }

    const xhr = new XMLHttpRequest();
    xhr.overrideMimeType("application/json");
    try {
        xhr.open(httpVerb, url, isAsync);
    } catch(e) {
        oui5lib.logger.error(e.message);
    }

    addHandlers(xhr, handleSuccess, requestProps, isAsync);

    if (httpVerb === "POST") {
        xhr.setRequestHeader("Content-type", "application/x-www-form-urlencoded");
        xhr.send(encodedParams);
    } else {
        xhr.send();
    }
}

function addHandlers(xhr, handleSuccess, requestProps, isAsync) {
    xhr.onload = function() {
        const status = xhr.status + "";
        if (status.match(/^20\d$/) || status === 0) {              Response status code 'Success'?
            let responseData = null;
            try {
                responseData = JSON.parse(xhr.responseText);
            } catch(e) {
                throw new Error("JSON is invalid");                 Invalid JSON
            }
            if (typeof handleSuccess === "function") {
                handleSuccess(responseData, requestProps);
            }
        } else {
            oui5lib.event.publishRequestFailureEvent("status",
                                            xhr, requestProps); ❷
        }
    };

    xhr.onerror = function() {
        oui5lib.event.publishRequestFailureEvent("error",
                                            xhr, requestProps); ❸
    };

    if (isAsync) {
        xhr.timeout = 500;
```

```
        xhr.ontimeout = function() {
            oui5lib.event.publishRequestFailureEvent("timeout",
                                                xhr, requestProps); ❹
        };
    }
}

/** @namespace oui5lib.request */
const request = oui5lib.namespace("request");          Create namespace
request.fetchJson = fetchJson;                          Add function to namespace
}());
```

❶   The encoded parameters will only be added to a URL using the protocol scheme http or https.
     This will allow us to request mockdata from files.

❷❸❹ In case of failure, the oui5lib.event.publishRequestFailureEvent function is called. It will publish
     a Component-level event on channel "xhr" for the failure events "status", "error" and "timeout".
     Because these events are request-related, the XMLHttpRequest object is sent along with the
     original request properties object for inspection.

The above fetchJson function is sufficient to request some URL and handle the related events. But
the mapping requests need prior additional processing.

11.2. Running requests configured in the mapping

 This section builds upon Chapter 10, *Entity specifications: Mapping*, especially Section 10.2,
"Describe Requests".

In the mappings, we configure requests with parameters. These parameters need to be prepared from
the provided data. This should not be done in the controllers because it only concerns the request.

To process the correct request parameters, we need to first collect all matching values and then URL-
encode the parameter values to generate the request parameter string.

11.2.1. Process request parameters

It is assumed, that all parameters being sent along with requests need to be strings. The mapping
request configuration allows the processing and conversion of the data provided for the request. The
following procParameters function will loop through the request parameters configured in the mapping
and collect values either from the data object or take a default value from the mapping. In case a
required parameter is missing, the function will throw an error.

Listing 11.2. Process request parameters

```
1  function procParameters(data, requestConfig) { ❶
2      const paramsConfig = requestConfig.parameters;
3      if (paramsConfig === undefined || paramsConfig.length === 0) {   A request without parameters?
4          return {};
5      }
6      if (data === undefined || data === null) {                        No data for the parameters?
7          data = {};
8      }
9
10     const requestParams = {};
11     let paramName, paramValue;                                        Declare loop variables
```

```
12    paramsConfig.forEach(function(paramSpec) {
13        paramName = paramSpec.name;                               Get parameter name
14        paramValue = null; ❷
15        if (data[paramName] === undefined) {
16            if (typeof paramSpec.default === "string")
17                paramValue = paramSpec.default;                   Use the default value
18            }
19        } else {
20            paramValue = data[paramName];
21            if (paramSpec.type !== "string") {
22                paramValue = convertToString(paramValue, paramSpec);
23            }
24        }
25
26        if (paramSpec.required && paramValue === null) { ❸
27            throw new Error("required parameter missing: " + paramName);
28        }
29        if (paramValue !== null) {
30            requestParams[paramName] = paramValue;
31        }
32    });
33    return requestParams;
34 }
35
36 function convertToString(value, paramSpec) {
37    switch (paramSpec.type) {
38        ...
39    }
40    return value;
41 }
```

❶   To get the request configuration we use the getRequestConfiguration function of Listing 10.4, "Namespace oui5lib.mapping".

❷   The parameter value for the request is initially set to null (line 14). If there is no property with the given name in the request data object, the default value from the mapping is used (line 17). Else, the parameter value is used and eventually converted if a type other than "string" is specified (lines 20 to 23).

❸   If there is no value for a required parameter, the function throws an error (line 27).

11.2.2. Encode the parameter values

To safely append the parameters to the URL (GET) or send them in the request body (POST), they need to be encoded.

```
function getEncodedParams(params) {
   let encodedString = "";
   for (let prop in params) {
      if (params.hasOwnProperty(prop)) {
         if (encodedString.length > 0) {
            encodedString += "&";
         }
         encodedString += encodeURI(prop + "=" + params[prop]);
      }
   }
   return encodedString;
}
```

11.2.3. Prepare environments

Requesting domain data always depends upon the environment. Let us assume an ideal project with four different environments: testing, development, staging and production. The environment is an application configuration issue. We, therefore, add a property `environment` to the oui5lib configuration file. And to access the value we add another function to the `oui5lib.configuration` namespace:

```
function getEnvironment() {
    const environment = getConfigData("environment");
    if (environment === undefined) {
        return "production";
    }
    return environment;
}
configuration.getEnvironment = getEnvironment;
```

Normally, we get the URL for a mapping request from the `protocol`, `host` and `pathname` of the request configuration. Knowing about the environment allows us to write the mapping for the production environment and, at the same time, configure a different URL for each environment.

Listing 11.3. Get the request URL depending upon the configured environment

```
function procUrl(requestConfig) {
    const pathname = requestConfig.pathname;

    switch (oui5lib.configuration.getEnvironment()) {
    case "development":
        if (typeof oui5lib.request.getDevelopmentUrl === "function") {
            return oui5lib.request.getDevelopmentUrl(pathname);
        }
        break;
    case "testing":
        if (typeof oui5lib.request.getTestingUrl === "function") {
            return oui5lib.request.getTestingUrl(pathname);
        }
        break;
    case "staging":
        if (typeof oui5lib.request.getStagingUrl === "function") {
            return oui5lib.request.getStagingUrl(pathname);
        }
        break;
    }
    const protocol = requestConfig.protocol;
    const host = requestConfig.host;
    const requestUrl = protocol + "://" + host + "/" + pathname;
    return requestUrl;
}
```

With this in place, we can maintain a set of functions configuring requests for each of the environments. That's all. Moving from one environment to another is as simple as changing the configuration file.

11.2.4. Send and process the request

Bringing the pieces together, we now get to the function running the requests defined in the mappings. Getting the request configuration from the mapping requires both the name of the domain entity, as well as the name of the request. If there are any mandatory request parameters, a data object is also needed which contains the properties for the request parameters. Additionally, we can provide a function to be called when the request completed sucessfully. Lastly, just in case, we can tell the request to wait for the response by setting the async parameter to false.

Listing 11.4. Function to send a request defined in the mapping

```
/**
 * Run XMLHttpRequest defined in the mapping.
 * @memberof oui5lib.request
 * @param {string} entityName     The name of the entity.
 * @param {string} requestName    The name of the request.
 * @param {object} data           The data provided for the request.
 * @param {function} handleSuccess  The function to call if the request
 *                                is successfully completed.
 * @param {boolean} isAsync       Load asynchronously? Defaults to 'true'.
 */
function sendMappingRequest(entityName, requestName, data, handleSuccess, isAsync) {
    if (typeof oui5lib.mapping !== "object") {
        throw new Error("oui5lib.mapping namespace not loaded");
    }

    if (typeof isAsync !== "boolean") {
        if (oui5lib.configuration.getEnvironment() === "testing") { ❶
            isAsync = false;
        } else {
            isAsync = true;
        }
    }

    const requestConfig = oui5lib.mapping.getRequestConfiguration(entityName,
                                                                  requestName);

    const requestParams = procParameters(data, requestConfig);        Process request parameters
    const encodedParams = getEncodedParams(requestParams);            Parameters are URL-encoded

    const httpVerb = requestConfig.method;
    const url = procUrl(requestConfig);                               Get the request URL

    fetchJson(url, handleSuccess, { "entity": entityName,
                                    "request": requestName,
                                    "requestParameters": requestParams
                                  }, isAsync, httpVerb, encodedParams);
}
request.sendMappingRequest = sendMappingRequest;
```

❶   In order to conveniently use the function in a testing environment, we prepare it to run requests synchronously by default. This setting can be overwritten by the function parameter if we want to test the asynchronous aspects of the code.

11.3. Testing the new functionality

So far, we have only written a lot of code which does not effectively accomplish anything. Following best practices of testing, we should have developed the code test-first all the way, but that would be too much for the purposes of this book. Nevertheless, we have now reached a point where we want to present at least some tests to ensure that we can load data with the help of our request mapping.

11.3.1. Setup for testing

We will now assume you have the following `test` folder setup:

```
.
├── helper
│   ├── fixtures.js
│   ├── jquery.js
│   ├── oumSetup.js
│   └── requestSetup.js
├── jasmine
│   ├── boot.js
│   ├── console.js
│   ├── jasmine.css
│   ├── jasmine_favicon.png
│   ├── jasmine-html.js
│   └── jasmine.js
├── mockdata
│   ├── addresses.json
│   ├── order.json
│   ├── orders.json
│   ├── products.json
│   └── statuses.json
├── spec
├── config.json
└── SpecRunner.html
```

We have not created any dependency from UI5 for our mapping and request namespaces. But we have used the `sap.ui.require` function in the `oui5lib/init.js`. Because we don't want to load UI5 we have to provide the namespace and function to avoid JavaScript errors. For this, we use the `ui5.js` file in the `helper` folder.

```
sap = {};
sap.ui = {};
sap.ui.require = function(libs, callback) {};
```

Our `Component` name is "oum". The mappings belong to the application domain and so do the related mapping requests. Our test environment doesn't know about the namespace. We need to set it up using the `oumSetup.js` file in the `helper` folder.

```
if (typeof oum === "undefined") {
   var oum = {};
}
if (typeof oum.do === "undefined") {          We are soon going to use this namespace
   oum.do = {};
}
oum.namespace = function(string) {
   const levels = string.split(".");
   let object = this;
   for (let i = 0, l = levels.length; i < l; i++) {
      if (typeof object[levels[i]] === "undefined") {
         object[levels[i]] = {};
      }
      object = object[levels[i]];
   }
   return object;
};
```

To allow the mappings to be found and to set the environment, we also have to provide a basic `config.json`.

```
{
    "logLevel": "INFO",
    "environment": "testing",
    "mappingDirectory": "../domainObjects/mapping"
}
```

We have already prepared the request functions for different environments (see Listing 11.3, "Get the request URL depending upon the configured environment"). Why not use that feature and provide a function to load JSON files as test fixtures? To do that we can use the requestSetup.js file in the helper folder.

```
oui5lib.request.getTestingUrl = function(pathname) {
    switch(pathname) {
    case "getOrders":
        return "mockdata/orders.json";
    case "getOrder":
        return "mockdata/order.json";
    case "getProducts":
        return "mockdata/products.json";
    case "getAddresses":
        return "mockdata/addresses.json";
    case "getStatuses":
        return "mockdata/statuses.json";
    default:
        return null;
    }
};
```

To unit test functions in isolation we don't want to go through the request but instead set data directly. We also need parameters for the orders request, which we don't want to repeat in the test specifications. Therefore, we need to provide further test fixtures through the fixtures.js file.

```
oum.fixture = {};
oum.fixture.startDate = "2017-10-01";
oum.fixture.endDate = "2017-12-01";
oum.fixture.statuses = [ "processing" ];
oum.fixture.orderId = 8;
oum.fixture.ordersData = [ ... ];
oum.fixture.productsData = [ ... ];
oum.fixture.addressesData = [ ... ];
oum.fixture.statusesData = [ ... ];
```

The final step to setting up the test environment is creating the Jasmine SpecRunner.html to run the actual tests.

Listing 11.5. Jasmine Standalone SpecRunner.html

```
 1 <!DOCTYPE html>
 2 <html>
 3   <head>
 4     <meta charset="UTF-8"/>
 5     <title>Jasmine Spec Runner</title>
 6     <link rel="shortcut icon" type="image/png" href="jasmine/jasmine_favicon.png"/>
 7     <link rel="stylesheet" href="jasmine/jasmine.css"/>
 8     <script src="jasmine/jasmine.js"></script>
 9     <script src="jasmine/jasmine-html.js"></script>
10     <script src="jasmine/boot.js"></script>
```

```
11      <script src="helper/ui5.js"></script>
12      <script src="../oui5lib/init.js"></script>
13      <script src="../oui5lib/lib/listHelper.js"></script>
14      <script src="../oui5lib/configuration.js"></script>
15      <script src="../oui5lib/logger.js"></script>
16      <script src="../oui5lib/event.js"></script>
17      <script src="../oui5lib/request.js"></script>
18      <script src="../oui5lib/mapping.js"></script>
19
20      <script src="helper/oumSetup.js"></script>
21      <script src="../domainObjects/Loader.js"></script>
22
23      <!-- test fixtures -->
24      <script src="helper/requestSetup.js"></script>
25      <script src="helper/fixtures.js"></script>
26
27      <!-- include spec files here... -->
28      <script src="spec/request.js"></script>
29      <script src="spec/Loader.js"></script>
30    </head>
31    <body>
32    </body>
33 </html>
```

Without dependency loading, we will need to load the oui5lib namespace files in a particular order (lines 12 to 18). The init sets up the namespace and adds the namespace function. The listHelper is just a collection of useful functions for arrays. The configuration is required for the logger. The event is required for the request. The mapping depends upon the request to load the mappings, which depends upon the mapping to send any mapping requests.

After loading the oui5lib code, we set up our Component oum namespace (line 20) and load the code we are about to develop (line 21). Then we set up the testing environment and load test fixtures (lines 24 and 25). Finally, the actual test specifications are loaded.

11.3.2. Specifying our expectations

Let us begin to clarify our expectations. Our mappings describe requests and their parameters. The actual requests are sent by the sendMappingRequest function of the oui5lib.request namespace (see Listing 11.4, "Function to send a request defined in the mapping"). It is a generic function designed to use any normalized mapping request configuration.

Let us first see if the function will send a request and hand the response data to our handleSuccess function, thereby verifying some expectations. The second function call is expected to throw an error because we fail to provide a value for the required startDate parameter.

The next expectation (spec/request.js) is an integration test. We will test a functionality provided by connecting separately developed units of code. For the test to succeed, the order mapping has to be loaded and the request configuration returned. That means, we are not unit testing the sendMappingRequest function.

Listing 11.6. Describe oui5lib.request expectations

```
describe("Request namespace object", function() {
   it ("should send the getOrders request with startDate parameter",
      function() {
         function handleSuccess(responseData, requestProps) { ❶
            expect(requestProps.entity).toEqual("order");
            expect(requestProps.request).toEqual("getOrders");

            expect(responseData.result).toBe(true);
            expect(responseData.value instanceof Array).toBe(true);
            expect(responseData.value.length).toEqual(2);

            hasEvaluatedExpectations = true;
         }

         var hasEvaluatedExpectations = false;
         oui5lib.request.sendMappingRequest(
            "order", "getOrders",
            { "startDate": oum.fixture.startDate },
            handleSuccess
         );
         expect(hasEvaluatedExpectations).toBe(true);
      }
   );
   it ("should throw an Error if the required parameter startDate is omitted",
      function() {
         let errorThrown = false;
         try {
            oui5lib.request.sendMappingRequest(
               "order", "getOrders",
               { "statuses": oum.fixture.statuses },
               function() {});
         } catch (e) {
            expect(e.name).toEqual("Error");
            expect(e.message).toEqual("required parameter missing: startDate");
            errorThrown = true;
         }
         expect(errorThrown).toBe(true);
      }
   );
});
```

❶   The expectations are based upon setting up our test environment to request JSON files synchro-
     nously. This is not bad for a test designed to give us some confidence that our function works.
     But if our code has external dependencies, we can never solely rely upon tests only simulating
     the real environment.

We can't test the procParameters function (see Listing 11.2, "Process request parameters") directly
without adding it to the namespace. But we can, at least, see it working in the console:

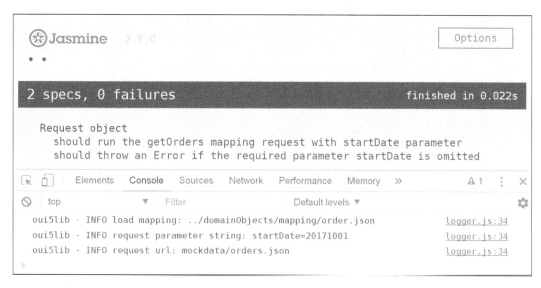

We can call the sendMappingRequest function directly anywhere in our code. Do we want that to happen with the requests to load the domain data? Isn't it better to have a dedicated Loader object call the requests and also provide the function or functions to handle the successful response? This will avoid redundant code and also allow us to use more expressive function names and simplify the function parameters, as well.

The mappings describe domain entities, which belong to the application namespace. Because the Loader is concipated to request and receive domain data, we want to add it to the namespace of our example UIComponent, which is named "oum".

Our resource root settings specify that "oum" resolves to "./". If we choose the namespace oum.Loader, UI5 will request it as "./Loader.js". However, this is not at all what we want, as we would like to avoid adding more files to our web application root folder. It is possible to work around this because the namespace has nothing to do with the resource path. Nevertheless, this would result in inconsistencies and workarounds, for example, requiring a resource as "/what/ever/path/Loader" to get the "oum.Loader".

Luckily, we can combine any namespace but the plain "oum" with another UI5 resource root entry to separate resource path and namespace. The Loader is about loading domain data. A reasonable namespace choice could be "oum.domainObjects.Loader". However, this seems a little too long and cumbersome for my own taste. Instead, we will use the namespace oum.do.Loader here and add a related resource root entry.

```
data-sap-ui-resourceroots='{
    "oum" : ".",
    "oum.do" : "./domainObjects",
    "oui5lib" : "./oui5lib"
}'
```

The mapping example above (see Listing 10.3, "Example mapping: specify order requests") configures a getOrders request with three parameters: "startDate", "endDate" and "status". The Loader is expected to call the sendMappingRequest function of the oui5lib.request namespace with an object containing properties to match the request parameters and also to provide a common function to handle successful requests named `handleSuccessfulResponse`. Let us describe these expectations in detail (`spec/Loader.js`):

Listing 11.7. Jasmine specification of the mapping request Loader

```
describe("Namespace oum.do.Loader", function() {
    const loader = oum.do.Loader;
    beforeAll(function() {
        spyOn(oui5lib.request, "sendMappingRequest"); ❶
    });
    afterEach(function() {
        oui5lib.request.sendMappingRequest.calls.reset(); ❷
    });

    it ("should call function to request orders data by startDate", function() {
        loader.queryOrders({ "startDate": oum.fixture.startDate });

        expect(oui5lib.request.sendMappingRequest.calls.count()).toEqual(1); ❸
        expect(oui5lib.request.sendMappingRequest)
            .toHaveBeenCalledWith("order", "getOrders", ❹
                                { "startDate": oum.fixture.startDate },
                                loader.handleSuccessfulResponse);
    });

    it ("should call function to request orders even without a required parameter", function() {
        loader.queryOrders({ "statuses": oum.fixture.statuses });

        expect(oui5lib.request.sendMappingRequest.calls.count()).toEqual(1);
        expect(oui5lib.request.sendMappingRequest)
            .toHaveBeenCalledWith("order", "getOrders",
                                { "statuses": oum.fixture.statuses },
                                loader.handleSuccessfulResponse);
    });
});
```

❶   The `spyOn` function will record any calls of the specified namespace function. The function itself will not be called, unless we append `.and.callThrough()`.

❷   After each specification, the spy calls count and records are reset for fresh expectations.

❸❹   The spy counts all calls and also keeps record of the parameters with which the function was called.

 The Loader unit tests only verify that the `sendMappingRequest` function of the `oui5lib.request` namespace is being called with the expected parameters. We have already looked at test specifications for the function itself in the previous Listing 11.6, "Describe oui5lib.request expectations".

Like usual, when applying test-driven development, the test will fail unless we provide the namespace under test (`oum.do.Loader`). Because we added a resource root entry replacing "oum.do" with "./domainObjects", the `Loader.js` file is expected to be found in the `domainObjects` subfolder of our web application root folder.

Listing 11.8. Namespace oum.do.Loader: loading domain data

```
 1 (function() {
 2   const loader = oum.namespace("do.Loader");              Namespace oum.do.Loader
 3
 4   function queryOrders(query) {
 5     oui5lib.request.sendMappingRequest(
 6       "order", "getOrders",
 7       query,
 8       handleSuccessfulResponse
 9     );
10   }
11   loader.queryOrders = queryOrders;
12
13   function loadOrder(orderId) {
14     oui5lib.request.sendMappingRequest(
15       "order", "getOrder",
16       { "id": orderId },
17       handleSuccessfulResponse
18     );
19   }
20   loader.loadOrder = loadOrder;
21
22   function handleSuccessfulResponse(responseObject, requestInfo) {
23     const entity = requestInfo.entity;
24     if (responseObject.result) {
25       const data = responseObject.value;
26     } else {
27       oui5lib.logger.error("Data source error: " + entity); ❶
28     }
29   }
30   // add for testing only
31   loader.handleSuccessfulResponse = handleSuccessfulResponse;
32 }());
```

❶   Of course, a professional application can't just log an error message but would need to either publish an event or throw an error.

With the oum.do.Loader code loaded, the test results should now be all green:

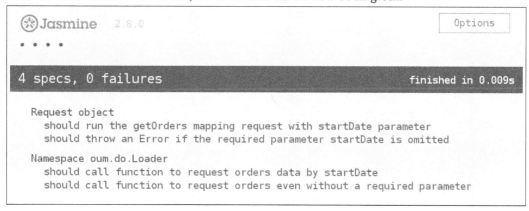

The `handleSuccessfulResponse` function (lines 22 to 29) expects the `responseObject` to follow a certain scheme which loosely resembles the OData notation. The `result` property of the response JSON tells us about an error on the data source level, for example a database SQL error. A `false` value means the request itself was successful, but we didn't get the requested data anyway.

Carrying an array of objects we get:

```
{
    "result": true,
    "value": [ ]
}
```

And for a single object:

```
{
    "result": true,
    "value": { }
}
```

If the `result` is `false`, the JSON may include the error message(s) as well:

```
{
    "result": false,
    "errors": [
        { "errorcode": "08006", "errorname": "connection_failure" }
    ]
}
```

11.4. Summary

This chapter presented code to standardize request handling. It cannot be emphasized enough that a common approach is necessary to handle requests. Otherwise, how can you avoid spreading related code fragments throughout the application?

Step by step, the request is prepared, sent and the response handled. After going through the code to run the requests, we learned by way of an example how to write tests for a request and verify our expectations using the Jasmine testing framework.

Chapter 12. Custom data objects

Separating domain logic from UI5 models

In the previous chapter, namely Chapter 11, *Request Handling*, we looked at loading domain data. We introduced a `oum.do.Loader` namespace providing functions to call the `sendMappingRequest` function of the `oui5lib.request` namespace and to handle incoming data following a successful response. In this context, a 'successful response' means that the server or service could be reached in time and did respond with a HTTP status 200 (OK) (or any other HTTP successful response status code). Now, let us take a look at what to do with this data.

In the context of client web application development, the model-view-controller (MVC) pattern needs to be rethought. While the view and controller parts are running on the client, the model part always has server aspects and components, because the client cannot be the source of the domain data. Data are requested from and saved to a server or services. Communicating the server and client-side aspects of model development is critical for client web application development. To be effective, developers on both 'sides' of the model development need to work closely together.

Domain objects, their rules, logic and relations must be understood and corresponding responsibilities assigned. Some aspects will always be primarily server-side issues, like access authorization and securing data integrity, connecting to data sources and running queries, or the final validation of posted data. But many aspects are negotiable. For example, work can be done with SQL or with client JavaScript. Unclear responsibilities can easily lead to trouble with all sides claiming to have done their part while the integration fails. It cannot be emphasized enough how important it is to continuously deploy and test even small changes to a staging environment, which should resemble the expected production environment as closely as possible.

The UI5 documentation speaks about 'client-side' and 'server-side' models. This is misleading because all model implementations run on the client. The main difference is that the OData 'server-side' models use the metadata and build-in functionality provided by the OData REST services while the JSON and XML 'client-side' models are basically just containers for data binding.

The server-side of the model provides the domain data. The incoming data structure can be more or less custom-tailored to the user interface. Nevertheless, the client-data need to be related according to the domain logic. Additionally, the incoming data often need to be transformed and supplemented according to user interface requirements. And the outgoing data from the client to the server-side, sending the edited model data from the views to the server, often need to be prepared for change requests back to the server.

The close integration of UI5 models with the views and controllers means that server-side response changes often directly affect the user interface. This is troublesome, because developing services on the server-side to provide required data, and requesting and processing them on the client-side frequently leads to user interface errors. For example, if the sales order lines are accessible through a certain path of the order model and the server-side request changes to no longer include the order lines but have them requested separately, at least the line editing parts of the UI will no longer work. If we have an order object in between the server/service requests and the UI, we only have to modify this object layer but leave the UI as it is.

It seems much more promising to largely separate the issues of server-client communication and the domain logic from the UI5 models. This separation will allow us to develop and test the domain objects without UI5 dependency. If incoming data sources change, we modify the domain objects, but the models we use for the UI can continue to work as expected. And instead of spreading domain logic throughout controllers and models, we keep it all in one place. There we collect our knowledge about the domain.

Figure 12.1. Scheme of MVC Pattern

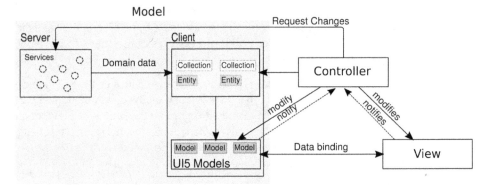

12.1. Provide common functions for domain objects

We begin with entity collection objects acting as the authoritative source of entity data for the user interface. The individual entity objects get their data from the collections. The collections get their data from service requests. We may temporarily clone entity data for editing, but after successfully saving the changes to the server or a service the client collection data are updated. Keeping a snapshot of data in the client-side memory can greatly reduce the number of service requests from the server-side, and also enhance the flow of the application to provide an improved user experience.

Each domain entity gets a collection namespace. The collection data are an array of objects, which are accessed either as an array, or as an entity object through their primary key. To avoid repeating the same code, we use base objects for collections and entities. As a general rule, these objects are separate from the mappings and UI5.

The collections are essentially a snapshot of data currently loaded and can be reset to replace the current snapshot with another one. Depending upon how we manage the collections data, we can reduce the number of requests for data by optimizing the use of collections data.

12.1.1. Collection

For the collection base object, we use the namespace `oui5lib.listBase`. Under this namespace we collect functions generally useful for collection objects. The code is plain JavaScript and too long to list here. But remember that the code examples can be viewed and downloaded from the oui5lib repository [https://github.com/cahein/oui5lib].

Here, it will be enough to list the common functions of the collection objects.

- addData (*data, reset*);
  data object|array;
  reset boolean ;

  Add or update data. The given data may either be a single item object or an array of item objects. If reset is true, the collection is emptied first.

- resetData ();

  Reset the collection. Clears all data.

- registerProcFunction (*procFunction*);
  procFunction function;

  Register a function to process all incoming data. If set, the addData function will call it with the data as only parameter.

- addItemDataChangedListener (*callback, context*);
  callback function;
  context object;

  Add a callback function to be notified when item data were added or updated after being processed. The context is usually the object the function belongs to and is used to set 'this' to the receiving object. The addData functions will call all registered listeners with the primary key as parameter.

- removeItemDataChangedListener (*callback, context*);
  callback function;
  context object;

  Remove a callback function from the array of listeners to the itemDataChanged event.

- addDataChangedFunction (*callback, context*);
  callback function;
  context object;

  Add a callback function to be notified when data were changed. The context is usually the object the function belongs to and is used to set 'this' to the receiving object. The addData function will call all registered listeners at the end.

- removeDataChangedListener (*callback, context*);
  callback function;
  context object;

  Remove a callback function from the array of listeners to the dataChanged event.

- getData ();

  Returns the array of items.

- getItemCount ();

  Returns the number of items currently loaded.

- isItemLoaded (*keyValue*);
  keyValue string|number;

  Check if the item with the given primary key value is loaded.

- `getItem (keyValue)`;
  keyValue string|number;

  Returns an item by its primary key value.

- `addItem (itemData)`;
  itemData object;

  Add an item object to the array. Will not update any already loaded item with the same primary key. Returns a boolean telling if the item was added or not.

- `updateItem (itemData)`;
  itemData object;

  Update an item. The primary key value will be used to identify the item to be updated. Returns a boolean telling if the item was updated or not.

- `removeItem (keyValue)`;
  keyValue string|number;

  Remove an item by its primary key. Returns the removed object or null, if no such item could be found in the collection.

- `filterBy (key, value)`;
  key string;
  value string|number;

  Simple key/value filter. Returns the filtered data.

- `sortBy (key)`;
  key string;

  Sort data by a key. Returns the sorted data.

- `getModel ()`;

  Convenience function to get a JSONModel holding the collections data. It always returns the same model object with updated collection data. The model sizeLimit is adjusted to hold all data. Returns `null` if there are no data.

A basic custom collection object is easily set up by extending the `oui5lib.listBase`. Instead of introducing jQuery as a dependency, we quickly add such an `extend` function to the `oui5lib.util` namespace.

Listing 12.1. Utility function to extend an object

```
function extend(){
    for (let i = 1; i < arguments.length; i++) {
        for (let key in arguments[i]) {
            if (arguments[i].hasOwnProperty(key)) {
                if (typeof arguments[0][key] === "object"
                    && typeof arguments[i][key] === "object") {
                    extend(arguments[0][key], arguments[i][key]);        Recursive function call
                } else {
                    arguments[0][key] = arguments[i][key];
                }
            }
        }
    }
    return arguments[0];
}
util.extend = extend;                                          Add function to oui5lib.util namespace
```

In some cases, for example to get a i18n property or to format a date, we want to use UI5 functionality in the custom objects. At the same time, we don't want UI5 to be a permanent dependency. This can be avoided with conditional statements.

```
function isUI5Env() {
    if (typeof sap === "undefined" || typeof sap.ui === "undefined" ||
        typeof sap.ui.getCore !== "function") {
        return false;
    }
    return true;
}
util.isUI5Env = isUI5Env;
```

For the domain objects, we may also use the namespace oum.do. Putting the pieces together, the initial object for a collection of orders only has a few lines of code.

Listing 12.2. A basic orders collection object

```
(function() {
    const primaryKey = oui5lib.mapping.getPrimaryKey("order");
    const listBase = oui5lib.listBase.getObject(primaryKey);

    let orders = oum.namespace("do.orders");                      Namespace oum.do.orders
    orders = oui5lib.util.extend(orders, listBase);               Merge listBase into orders object
}());
```

 We use the mapping to get the primaryKey, but the primary key string works as well. This means that the custom objects are generally independent from the mappings.

Likewise, mappings and collection objects for addresses, products, statuses and countries are to be created. The order statuses and countries collections are different because the data are essentially static objects which don't change and need to be loaded only once. The status of these collections is either initialized or not. Here, we list the statuses collection object.

Listing 12.3. A statuses collection object

```
(function() {
   const primaryKey = oui5lib.mapping.getPrimaryKey("status");
   const listBase = oui5lib.listBase.getObject(primaryKey);

   let statuses = oum.namespace("do.statuses");
   statuses = oui5lib.util.extend(statuses, listBase);

   let _initialized = false;

   function init(data) {
      if (data instanceof Array) {
         statuses.addData(data, true);                    Add data after resetting the collection

         if (oui5lib.util.isUI5Env()) {
            addStatusTexts();
            sap.ui.getCore().attachLocalizationChanged(addStatusTexts); ❶
         }

         _initialized = true;
         oui5lib.event.publishReadyEvent("statuses");      Publish event that statuses are loaded
      }
   }
   function isInitialized() {
      return _initialized;
   }

   statuses.init = init;                                   Add functions to namespace
   statuses.isInitialized = isInitialized;

   function addStatusTexts() {
      const statusList = statuses.getData();
      statusList.forEach(function(statusItem) {
         statusItem.statusText = oui5lib.util.getI18nText(
            "orderStatus." + statusItem.status);
      });
   }
}());
oum.do.Loader.loadStatuses();                              Call the Loader to request the status list
```

❶ Because the status text is language dependent, we use the `attachLocalizationChanged` function to add a function to be called in the event of any change of localization settings like the language.

Figure 12.2. Browser console: listing available functions of the oum.do.products namespace

```
> oum.do.products.addData
                 addData                    Object
                 addDataChangedListener
                 addItem
                 addItemDataChangedListener
                 filterBy
                 getData
                 getItem
                 getItemCount
                 getModel
                 isItemLoaded
                 registerProcFunction
```

12.1.2. Entity

In addition to the collection object, which is concerned with the array of entity data and related functions, entity objects provide access to a particular entity and its relations to other entities.

For the entity base, we use the namespace `oui5lib.itemBase`.

- `getData ();`

  Get the data object.

- `setData (data);`
  data object;

  Set the data object.

- `getProperty (path);`
  path string;

  Get a property value by its property path.

- `setProperty (key, value);`
  key string;
  value any;

  Set the value for the given property path. Will set the record to modified and update the model data.

- `isNew ();`

  Check if it is a new record.

- `setNew (isNew);`
  isNew boolean;

  Set the record to new. A new record is instantiated with default properties and values.

- `wasModified ();`

  Check if the record was modified.

- `setModified ();`

  Set the record to modified.

- `isLoading ();`

  When data are requested asynchronously, the object is set to loading until the HTTP response provides the data.

- `setLoading (isLoading);`
  isLoading boolean;

  Set the object to loading.

- `isClone ();`

  Returns boolean indicating if the object is using cloned data

- setIsClone (*isClone*);
  isClone boolean;

  Configure the object to use cloned data.

- getModel ();

  Convenience function to get a JSONmodel holding the entity object data.

The oum.do.Order entity prototype is created from the oui5lib.itemBase with additional functions added to it. An Order may either be an existing order, or a new order. If an existing order is not already loaded, and therefore available from the orders collection, it needs to be loaded and added to the collection. While loading, the object's loading status is set to true.

Listing 12.4. A basic order entity object

```
(function () {
    function Order(id, isClone) {
        if (!(this instanceof oum.do.Order)) {
            return new oum.do.Order(id, isClone);
        }

        if (typeof isClone !== "boolean") { isClone = false; }    Default is not to use cloned data
        this.setIsClone(isClone);

        if (id === undefined || id === null) {                    No ID was given
            this.setData(getNewOrder());                          Set new order object
            this.setNew(true);
        } else {                                                  Order ID given
            this.id = id;
            if (oum.do.orders.isItemLoaded(id)) {                 Are the order data already loaded?
                let orderEntry = oum.do.orders.getItem(id);
                if (isClone) {
                    orderEntry = oui5lib.util.cloneData(orderEntry); ❶
                }
                this.setData(orderEntry);                         Set order object
            } else {                                              The order data have to be loaded
                this.setLoading(true);
                oum.do.orders.addItemDataChangedListener(         Add itemDataChanged event listener
                    dataAvailable, this);
                oum.do.Loader.loadOrder(id);                      Use the Loader function
            }
        }
    }

    function dataAvailable(orderId) {                             Callback function
        if (this.id === orderId) {
            oum.do.orders.removeItemDataChangedListener(          Remove itemDataChanged event listener
                dataAvailable, this);
            let orderEntry = oum.do.orders.getItem(orderId);
            if (this.isClone()) {
                orderEntry = oui5lib.util.cloneData(orderEntry);
            }
            this.setData(orderEntry);
            this.setLoading(false);
        }
    }
```

```
    function getNewOrder() {                              Provide new order object
        const newOrder = {
            "id": -1,
            "status": "new",
            "billingAddressId": null,
            "customerAddressId": null,
            "items": []
        };
        if (oui5lib.util.isUI5Env()) {
            newOrder.statusText = oui5lib.util.getI18nText("orderStatus.new");
        }
        return newOrder;
    }

    Order.prototype = Object.create(oui5lib.itemBase);
    oum.do.Order = Order;
}());
```

❶   Since, unfortunately, there is no simple function capable of cloning our data objects without loss, we will use jQuery.extend(true, {}, data);.

Figure 12.3. Browser console: listing available functions of the oum.do.Order object

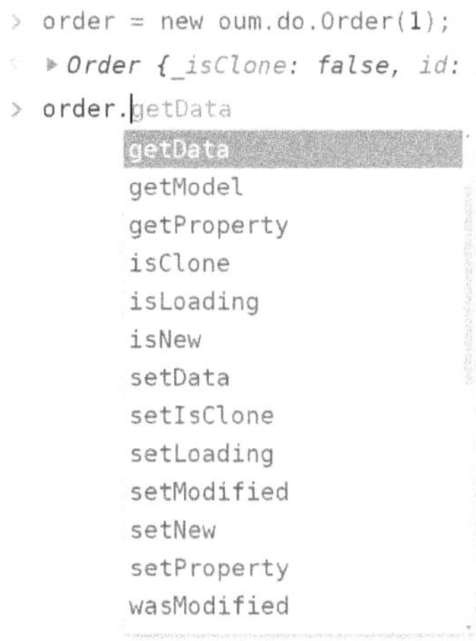

```
> order = new oum.do.Order(1);
  ▶ Order {_isClone: false, id: 1, _data: {…}}
> order.getData
        getData
        getModel
        getProperty
        isClone
        isLoading
        isNew
        setData
        setIsClone
        setLoading
        setModified
        setNew
        setProperty
        wasModified
```

12.2. Adding data to the collections

Remember, that we develop data objects isolated from UI5. Consequently, we have nothing to show here. The best way to ensure that our code actually does what it is supposed to, is simply through testing. The general test setup is explained in Section 11.3.1, "Setup for testing".

At this point, we assume to have collection objects for all our example entities: orders, products, addresses and statuses. We also assume that the oum.do.Loader (see Listing 11.8, "Namespace oum.do.Loader: loading domain data") has functions to load the entities data and that its handleSuccessfulResponse function handles the successful responses.

Let us begin to formulate expectations about our general goal. In short, we expect that the Loader adds data to the orders collection object. While in a testing environment, the mock data come from JSON files synchronously requested. This removes unnecessary complexity from the tests.

The following integration tests can easily fail if we change anything they depend upon. Nevertheless, it is important to have these kind of tests to ensure that we don't get lost writing and unit testing pieces of code which never integrate to provide any useful functionality.

Listing 12.5. Test the loading of orders

```
describe("Loading data into Domain Collection Objects", function() {
    beforeEach(function() {
        oum.do.orders.resetData();                     Reset the collections
        oum.do.products.resetData();
        oum.do.addresses.resetData();
    });

    const loader = oum.do.Loader;
    it ("should load orders into the orders collection object", function() {
        loader.queryOrders({ "startDate": oum.fixture.startDate });

        const data = oum.do.orders.getData();
        expect(data instanceof Array).toBe(true);
        expect(data.length).toEqual(2);
    });
    it ("should load an order into the orders collection object", function() {
        loader.loadOrder(oum.fixture.orderId);

        const data = oum.do.orders.getData();
        expect(data instanceof Array).toBe(true);
        expect(data.length).toEqual(1);
    });
});
```

The above-stated expectations will fail, unless we actually add incoming data to the collection objects. Because, so far, our Loader handles all successful responses, it only requires a small addition to meet said expectations:

Listing 12.6. Loader function to handle the successful response

```
function handleSuccessfulResponse(responseObject, requestInfo) {
    const entity = requestInfo.entity;
    if (responseObject.result) {
        let data = responseObject.value;
        if (!(data instanceof Array) && data instanceof Object) {
            data = [ data ];
        }
        if (data.length === 0) {                        Is the result empty?
            oui5lib.event.publishReadyEvent(entity);    Publish 'loading ready' event
            return;
        }

        switch(entity) {
        case "order":
            oum.do.orders.addData(data);                Add orders
            break;
        case "product":
            oum.do.products.addData(data);              Add products
            break;
        case "address":
            oum.do.addresses.addData(data);             Add addresses
```

```
        break;
      case "status":
        oum.do.statuses.init(data); ❶
        break;
      case "countries":
        oum.do.countries.init(data); ❷
        break;
      default:
        break;
    }
  } else {
    oui5lib.logger.error("Data service reports error");
  }
}
```

❶❷ Statuses are different because there is only a short list of static entries. We, therefore, use the `init` function, which clears the collection before adding the incoming status data, sets the collection object initialized and publishes a 'loading ready' event (see Listing 12.3, "A statuses collection object"). Countries are a longer list but are handled just like the statuses.

12.3. Unit testing the entity collection and item objects

For unit testing, we want the object being tested to function in isolation. Therefore, we will use test fixtures for the following test specifications. That means, we don't request any data but set them directly to the collection objects. We also use spies to record function calls without actually calling them.

We will begin with some example specifications for the order collection and entity objects. Basically, these specifications test the functionality provided by the `oui5lib.listBase` and `oui5lib.itemBase`. The main reason for presenting them here is to give the reader an idea of how the objects work.

Jasmine has several functions to prepare the setup for specifications. Here, we will use the `beforeAll` handle to initially set test data to the orders collection and the `beforeEach` handle to (re)set the state of the orders collection.

Listing 12.7. Specifications for orders collection object

```
describe("Orders collection object", function() {
  const orders = oum.do.orders;

  beforeAll(function() {
    oum.do.addresses.resetData();                    Reset referenced entity collections
    oum.do.products.resetData();
  });
  beforeEach(function() {
    orders.addData(
      JSON.parse(JSON.stringify(oum.fixture.ordersData)), ❶
      true
    );
  });

  it ("should return the orders collection", function() {
    const data = orders.getData();
    expect(data instanceof Array).toBe(true);
    expect(data.length).toBe(2);
```

```
   });

   it ("should return the item count", function() {
      expect(orders.getItemCount()).toBe(2);
   });

   it ("should allow us to check if an order is loaded", function() {
      expect(orders.isItemLoaded(1) instanceof Date).toBe(true);
      expect(orders.isItemLoaded(2) instanceof Date).toBe(true);
      expect(orders.isItemLoaded(3)).toBe(false);
   });

   it ("should return order data by id", function() {
      const data = orders.getItem(1);
      expect(data.id).toBe(1);
   });
});
```

❶   Some of the tests change the orders data. Using cloned data ensures that the test data are always
      the same. Here, we use a very simple way to get cloned data via JSON. The limitation is that
      this is not a lossless procedure, because it only works for the JSON types.

Testing the order entity object works in a similar fashion. Again, we will initially add the test data to
the orders collection. This is necessary to allow constructing an Order with an ID of already loaded
data. The last specification constructs an Order with an ID not yet loaded and uses a spy on the
Loader.loadOrder function

Listing 12.8. Specifications for the order entity object

```
describe("Order entity object", function() {
   beforeAll(function() {
      oum.do.products.resetData();                            Reset referenced entity collections
      oum.do.addresses.resetData();
   });
   beforeEach(function() {
      oum.do.orders.addData(
         JSON.parse(JSON.stringify(oum.fixture.ordersData)),
         true);
   });

   describe("Instantiation", function() {
      it ("should get a new Order", function() {
         const order = new oum.do.Order();
         expect(order instanceof oum.do.Order).toBe(true);
         expect(order.getProperty("id")).toEqual(undefined);
         expect(order.isNew()).toBe(true);
      });

      it ("should get an existing Order already loaded", function() {
         const order = new oum.do.Order(2);
         expect(order instanceof oum.do.Order).toBe(true);
         expect(order.getProperty("id")).toEqual(2);
         expect(order.isNew()).toBe(false);
      });
   });

   describe("Accessing and modifying properties", function() {
```

```
    it ("should get the Order id as property", function() {
       const order = new oum.do.Order(1);
       expect(order.getProperty("id")).toEqual(1);
    });

    it ("should get the Order id directly", function() {
       const order = new oum.do.Order(1);
       expect(order.id).toEqual(1);
    });

    it ("should allow the modification of Order data", function() {
       const order = new oum.do.Order(2);
       expect(order.getProperty("status")).toEqual("processing");
       expect(order.wasModified()).toEqual(false);

       order.setProperty("status", "shipped");
       expect(order.getProperty("status")).toEqual("shipped");
       expect(order.wasModified()).toEqual(true);
    });
  });

  it ("should call the Loader to request an Order not in the collection", function() {
    spyOn(oum.do.Loader, "loadOrder");                          Initiate spy

    expect(oum.do.orders.isItemLoaded(8)).toBe(false);
    const order = new oum.do.Order(8);
    expect(oum.do.Loader.loadOrder).toHaveBeenCalledWith(8);    Evaluate spy result
  });
});
```

When we run the test specifications, we will hopefully get the all green test results:

```
❋ Jasmine  2.8.0                                               Options

 • • • • • • • • • • • •

 12 specs, 0 failures                              finished in 0.024s


   Domain Objects
     should load orders into the orders collection object
     should load an order into the orders collection object

   Orders collection object
     should return the orders collection
     should return the item count
     should allow us to check if an order is loaded
     should return order data by id

   Order entity object
     should get a new Order
     should get an existing Order already loaded
     should get the Order id as property
     should get the Order id directly
     should allow modification of Order data
     should call the Loader to request an Order not in the collection
```

So far, our domain data objects meet the specified expectations, so that we can move on to add further expectations and functionality.

12.4. Handle referenced data

The orders have references to records, which may need to be loaded to show them in the user interface. There are the customer and billing addresses, which may be the same. Likewise, whatever products are ordered need at least a name.

 Because we are going to resolve the order references to addresses and products, some of the following code depends upon minimal product and address mappings specifying at least the primary key and configuring a request to getProducts and getAddresses. We also assume that the related functions loadProducts and loadAddresses are added to the oum.do.Loader namespace. Minimal address and product collection and entity objects also need to be available, as well as mock data not just for orders but also for the related addresses and products.

Having committed ourselves to the test driven development approach, we will begin by writing a test to define the desired behavior. First, we add expectations for the Order entity object to ensure the availability of functions dealing with getting the customer and billing addresses. Also, these functions are expected to return address entity objects.

Listing 12.9. Additional Order Specifications

```
it ("should have functions to get the customer and billing address", function() {
    const order = oum.do.Order();
    expect(typeof order.getCustomerAddress).toEqual("function");
    expect(typeof order.getBillingAddress).toEqual("function");
});

it ("should get referenced address entity objects", function() {
    oum.do.addresses.addData(oum.fixture.addressesData, true);          Provide referenced addresses

    const order = new oum.do.Order(2);
    const billingAddress = order.getBillingAddress();
    expect(billingAddress instanceof oum.do.Address).toBe(true);
    expect(billingAddress.getProperty("id")).toEqual(2);

    const shippingAddress = order.getShippingAddress();
    expect(shippingAddress instanceof oum.do.Address).toBe(true);
    expect(shippingAddress.getProperty("id")).toEqual(3);
});
```

The above tests expect that the oum.do.Order entity object has getBillingAddress and getShippingAddress functions and that they return a oum.do.Address entity object. Let us add the expected functions:

```
function getBillingAddress() {
    const id = this.getProperty("billingAddressId");
    return getAddress.call(this, id);
}

function getShippingAddress() {
    const id = this.getProperty("shippingAddressId");
    return getAddress.call(this, id);
}
```

```
function getAddress(id) {
    if (oum.do.addresses.isItemLoaded(id)) {
        return new oum.do.Address(id, this.isClone());
    }
    return null;
}

Order.prototype.getBillingAddress = getBillingAddress;
Order.prototype.getShippingAddress = getShippingBillingAddress;
```

 The above getBillingAddress and getShippingAddress functions call the getAddress function to get the Address object, which is using this. Normally, the calling context determines this. To avoid errors we have to explicitly set the context using the call function.

The functions are now available and the above tests succeed. Bear in mind, however, that we have achieved this by adding the address data as test fixtures and haven't actually loaded the referenced addresses. Before sorting this out, let us think about the orders data.

In general, the orders collection data are used for lists and the order entity for details and editing. When the user Interface normally requires certain values to be shown which are not included in the incoming data, it is easiest to enrich these data as soon as they come in, to have the issue covered once and for all. For example, the orders collection object holds order data without a customer name. To show a list of orders without the customer name is not really acceptable.

Accordingly, we want to enrich the order data with address names. Where do we get the address name from? This is a job for the Address entity object. The related expectation is quickly formulated:

```
describe("Address entity object", function() {
    beforeAll(function() {
        oum.do.addresses.addData(oum.fixture.addressesData, true);
    });

    it ("should return the name for an Address", function() {
        const addressData = oum.fixture.addressesData[0];
        const addressName = addressData.firstname + " " + addressData.lastname;

        const address = new oum.do.Address(addressData.id);
        expect(typeof address.getName === "function").toBe(true);
        expect(address.getName()).toEqual(addressName);
    });
});
```

To make the specification succeed, we will have to add and assign the expected function to the oum.do.Address object:

```
function getName() {
    const firstName = this.getProperty("firstname");
    const lastName = this.getProperty("lastname");
    return firstName + " " + lastName;
}
Address.prototype.getName = getName;
```

Now, we can move on to add a specification of the orders collection object. At this point, we will assume that the addresses are already loaded.

```
it ("should add address names to the order data", function() {
   oum.do.addresses.addData(oum.fixture.addressesData);
   const orderData = oum.fixture.ordersData[0];

   orders.procAddresses(orderData);
   expect(typeof orderData.billingName === "string").toBe(true);
   expect(typeof orderData.shippingName === "string").toBe(true);
});
```

Our example orders have two types of addresses ("billing" and "shipping"). The procAddresses function is expected to add the address name for each address type to the order data. To actually retrieve the name, we use the getName function of the Address entity object.

Listing 12.10. Function to add address names to orders

```
const _addressTypes = ["billing", "shipping"];
function getAddressTypes() {
   return _addressTypes;
}

function procAddresses(order) {
   let address, addressId;
   getAddressTypes().forEach(function(type) {
      addressId = order[type + "AddressId"];

      if (oum.do.addresses.isItemLoaded(addressId)) {
         address = new oum.do.Address(addressId);
         order[type + "Name"] = address.getName();          Add address name
      }
   });
}

orders.getAddressTypes = getAddressTypes;                   Add functions to namespace
orders.procAddresses = procAddresses;
```

The handling of referenced entity data (addresses and products) has to cover a scenario where we have these data already available and another where we have to first fetch them from whatever service. This issue concerns the relations between the domain objects in general and the handling of references in particular. Hence, we will refer the handling of references to a oum.do.RefsHandler namespace:

```
(function() {
   const refsHandler = oum.namespace("do.RefsHandler");
}());
```

Before we proceed, let us take a look at a figure illustrating the involved objects and the flow being triggered by the incoming orders data.

Figure 12.4. Domain Data Handler Objects

"E" stands for Event and "DO" for Domain (Collection) Object. Both the Loader and RefsHandler are emitting Events for any registered listener.

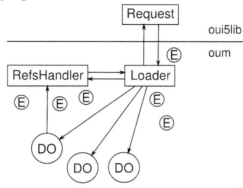

When we add orders data to the orders collection, we expect the RefsHandler to be called. It goes through the orders, collects all references not yet loaded and then calls the Loader to request any missing references. Because of the asynchronous request, the RefsHandler registers these references as missing. When data come in the Loader adds them to the domain entity collections and notifies the RefsHandler which then deletes any loaded reference as no longer missing. When an order is completely loaded (with references) we expect the above procAddresses function to be called and an event to be published that the order is ready.

We begin coding with the 'private' functions, which are not added to the namespace and therefore cannot be tested directly. More specifically, we begin with a function to be called when all referenced data are available:

```
function completeOrder(orderId) {
    const order = oum.do.orders.getItem(orderId);
    if (order !== null) {
        oum.do.orders.procAddresses(order);          Add billingName and shippingName properties

        oui5lib.event.publishReadyEvent({            Publish 'loading ready' event
            entity: "order",
            id: orderId
        });
    }
}
```

The goal is to emit events for each individual entity, as well as a collection. These events have a common channelId (loading) and eventId (ready). Parameters carried by the event are either the entity name with its ID for a single entity or the plural of the entity name for a collection. This allows us to have the controllers subscribe to one channel/event and handle all dependencies in a common handler function. Handling of error scenarios is centralized Component-wide.

Because we request the referenced data asynchronously and don't know if and when they come in, we have to keep track of orders waiting for data to be able to notify their listeners that the loading of referenced data is complete. Therefore, we need to temporarily store the necessary information by registering the references as missing.

```
let _missingData = {};

function addToMissing(orderId, entityName, id) {
   const idString = "order" + orderId;
   if (_missingData[idString] === undefined) {
     _missingData[idString] = {};
   }

   const orderEntry = _missingData[idString];
   if (orderEntry[entityName] === undefined) {
     orderEntry[entityName] = [ id ];
   } else {
     const ids = orderEntry[entityName];
     if (ids.indexOf(id) == "-1") { ❶
       ids.push(id);
     }
   }
}
```

❶   Here, we don't want to be restrictive regarding the type of the fake ID for new entities and
     therefore use the == operator, which only tests the value and not the type. Both the number -1
     and string "-1" are recognized as new.

When the RefsHandler is notified of incoming entity data, the related entries in the missing references
object have to be deleted. If an order is complete, the above completeOrder function is called. If all
orders are complete, the 'loading ready' event is published.

Listing 12.11. RefsHandler function to register incoming entities

```
function resolveMissing(entityName, id) {
   let idString, orderId, orderMissing, ids, pos;
   let count = 0;

   for (idString in _missingData) {
     count++;

     orderMissing = _missingData[idString];
     if (typeof orderMissing[entityName] !== "undefined") {
       ids = orderMissing[entityName] ;
       pos = ids.indexOf(id);
       if (pos > -1) {
         ids.splice(pos, 1);

         if (ids.length === 0) {
           delete orderMissing[entityName];
           if (!orderMissing.hasOwnProperty("address") &&    No more missing address or product?
              !orderMissing.hasOwnProperty("product")) {
             orderId = parseInt(idString.substring(5));
             completeOrder(orderId);                          The order is completely loaded

             delete _missingData[idString];
             count--;
           }
         }
       }
     }
   }
}
```

```
    if (count === 0) {                                    No more incomplete orders?
        oui5lib.event.publishReadyEvent("orders");        Publish 'loading' 'ready' event
    }
}
```

In case of an error, we want to be able to reset the missing data object to start anew. Here is the method:

```
function clearMissingData() {
    _missingData = {};
}
refsHandler.clearMissingData = clearMissingData;
```

Having taken care of these 'private' functions, we can now move on to the 'public' functions. Because these functions can be tested, we proceed with test specifications. The 'private' functions will be tested indirectly thought the functions using them.

The setup for the following test specifications is more complex. First, we add the orders data to the collection object and initiate spies for the Loader functions to load addresses and products and for the publishReadyEvent function of the oui5lib.event namespace. Before each specification we prepare a clear scenario by emptying the addresses and products collection and resetting the spies for new expectations.

```
describe("Namespace oum.do.RefsHandler", function() {
    beforeAll(function() {
        oum.do.orders.addData(oum.fixture.ordersData);

        spyOn(oui5lib.event, "publishReadyEvent");        Initiate spies
        spyOn(oum.do.Loader, "loadAddresses");
        spyOn(oum.do.Loader, "loadProducts");
    });
    beforeEach(function() {
        oum.do.addresses.resetData();                     Empty address data
        oum.do.products.resetData();                      Empty products data

        oui5lib.event.publishReadyEvent.calls.reset();    Reset spies
        oum.do.Loader.loadAddresses.calls.reset();
        oum.do.Loader.loadProducts.calls.reset();
        oum.do.RefsHandler.clearMissingData();            Reset missing data object
    });
});
```

Our first test specification expects that calling the RefsHandler processOrderReferences function with orders data will result in two calls of Loader functions. One of the calls requests the array of collected address IDs. The other call requests the referenced array of product ISBNs.

```
it ("should call the Loader to fetch referenced product and address data of orders", function() {
    oum.do.RefsHandler.processOrderReferences(oum.fixture.ordersData);

    expect(oum.do.Loader.loadAddresses.calls.count()).toEqual(1);
    expect(oum.do.Loader.loadAddresses)
        .toHaveBeenCalledWith([ 1, 2, 3]);

    expect(oum.do.Loader.loadProducts.calls.count()).toEqual(1);
    expect(oum.do.Loader.loadProducts)
        .toHaveBeenCalledWith([ "0394718747", "0889610356", "1859847390"]);
});
```

The next specification first adds all referenced addresses and products to the collections, so that the test orders are found completely loaded and the related events are published for each of the two test orders and one for all processed orders. Additionally, we expect the `procAddresses` function of the orders collection object to be called for each order.

```
it ("should add address names to orders and publish events", function() {
    oum.do.addresses.addData(oum.fixture.addressesData);
    oum.do.products.addData(oum.fixture.productsData);

    spyOn(oum.do.orders, "procAddresses");

    oum.do.RefsHandler.processOrderReferences(oum.fixture.ordersData);

    expect(oum.do.orders.procAddresses.calls.count()).toEqual(2);

    expect(oui5lib.event.publishReadyEvent.calls.count()).toEqual(3);
    expect(oui5lib.event.publishReadyEvent)
        .toHaveBeenCalledWith({ entity: "order", id: 1 });
    expect(oui5lib.event.publishReadyEvent)
        .toHaveBeenCalledWith({ entity: "order", id: 2 });
    expect(oui5lib.event.publishReadyEvent)
        .toHaveBeenCalledWith("orders");
});
```

To fulfill the expectations stated above, the following `processOrderReferences` function loops through all the orders collecting referenced IDs not yet loaded and adding them as missing data. If there are any such addresses or products after going through the orders, the `Loader` is called to load the missing data.

```
function processOrderReferences(orders) {
    const addressesToLoad = [];
    const productsToLoad = [];

    const addressTypes = oum.do.orders.getAddressTypes();
    let isOrderComplete, addressId;

    orders.forEach(function(order) {                                    Loop the orders
        isOrderComplete = true;

        addressTypes.forEach(function(addressType) {                    Handle address references
            addressId = order[addressType + "AddressId"];
            if (addressId !== null && !oum.do.addresses.isItemLoaded(addressId)) {
                isOrderComplete = false;

                if (addressesToLoad.indexOf(addressId) === -1) {
                    addressesToLoad.push(addressId);                    Address has to be loaded
                    addToMissing(order.id, "address", addressId);
                }
            }
        });

        const orderLines = order.items;
        orderLines.forEach(function(orderLine) {                        Handle product references
            const productId = orderLine.productId;
            if (!oum.do.products.isItemLoaded(productId)) {
                isOrderComplete = false;
```

```
                if (productsToLoad.indexOf(productId) === -1) {
                    productsToLoad.push(productId);                          Product has to be loaded
                    addToMissing(order.id, "product", productId);
                }
            }
        });

        if (isOrderComplete) {
            completeOrder(order.id); ❶
        }
    });

    if (addressesToLoad.length > 0) {
        oum.do.Loader.loadAddresses(addressesToLoad);                        Call Loader for addresses
    }
    if (productsToLoad.length > 0) {
        oum.do.Loader.loadProducts(productsToLoad);                          Call Loader for products
    }
    if (addressesToLoad.length === 0 && productsToLoad.length === 0) {
        oui5lib.event.publishReadyEvent("orders");                           All orders are complete
    }

}
refsHandler.processOrderReferences = processOrderReferences;
```

❶   If all referenced addresses and products are already loaded, the above `completeOrder` function
    is called.

After collecting the addresses and products not yet loaded, the above `processOrderReferences` function
calls the `Loader` to request the missing addresses and products asynchronously. In case of a successful
response, the Loader's `handleSuccessfulResponse` function is called to add the incoming data to the
entity collections. In order to resolve the missing references, the `RefsHandler` has to be notified by
the Loader about the data having become available. So, we will need to add another specification
of the Loader:

```
it ("should notify the RefsHandler of incoming data", function() {
    spyOn(oum.do.RefsHandler, "handleDataLoaded");

    const responseObject = {
        result: true,
        value: oum.fixture.addressesData
    };
    const requestInfo = { entity: "address" };
    loader.handleSuccessfulResponse(responseObject, requestInfo);

    expect(oum.do.RefsHandler.handleDataLoaded.calls.count()).toEqual(1);
    expect(oum.do.RefsHandler.handleDataLoaded)
        .toHaveBeenCalledWith("address", oum.fixture.addressesData);
});
```

It only requires a small change to the `handleSuccessfulResponse` function (see Listing 12.6, "Loader
function to handle the successful response") to meet the above expectation:

```
function handleSuccessfulResponse(responseObject, requestInfo) {
   const entity = requestInfo.entity;
   if (responseObject.result) {
      ...

      oum.do.RefsHandler.handleDataLoaded(entity, data);
   } else {
      oui5lib.logger.error("Data service reports error");
   }
}
```

After testing that the handleDataLoaded function is indeed being called by the Loader, we can now add
our expectations for the RefHandler handleDataLoaded function. The following unit test calls the function
directly. We expect it to publish one event for each completed order and another one when all order
references have been loaded.

```
it ("should publish events when order references are resolved", function() {
   oum.do.RefsHandler.processOrderReferences(oum.fixture.ordersData);

   spyOn(oui5lib.event, "publishReadyEvent");

   oum.do.RefsHandler.handleDataLoaded("address",
                                       [ { id: 1 }, { id: 2 }, { id: 3 } ]);
   oum.do.RefsHandler.handleDataLoaded("product",
                                       [ { isbn: "0394718747" },{ isbn: "0889610356" } ]);

   expect(oui5lib.event.publishReadyEvent.calls.count()).toEqual(1);
   expect(oui5lib.event.publishReadyEvent)
      .toHaveBeenCalledWith({ entity: "order", id: "1" });       First order is complete

   oum.do.RefsHandler.handleDataLoaded("product",
                                       [ { isbn: "1859847390" } ]);
   expect(oui5lib.event.publishReadyEvent.calls.count()).toEqual(3);
   expect(oui5lib.event.publishReadyEvent)
      .toHaveBeenCalledWith({ entity: "order", id: "2" });       Second order is complete

   expect(oui5lib.event.publishReadyEvent)
      .toHaveBeenCalledWith("orders");                           All orders are ready
});
```

The handleDataLoaded function loops through the incoming data and calls the resolveMissing function
to clear the related entry from the missing references (see Listing 12.11, "RefsHandler function to
register incoming entities").

```
function handleDataLoaded(entityName, data) {
   data.forEach(function(item) {
      switch(entityName) {
      case "address":
         resolveMissing(entityName, item.id);
         break;
      case "product":
         resolveMissing(entityName, item.isbn);
         break;
      case "status":
         updateOrderStatuses();
         break;
      default:
```

```
        oui5lib.logger.warn("Unknown entity: " + entityName);
    }
  });
}
refsHandler.handleDataLoaded = handleDataLoaded;
```

The RefsHandler won't do anything, until we actually refer the handling of the order references to it. Upon a successful response, the Loader calls the addData function of the related collection with the incoming data.

The following test specification adds orders data to the collection, like the Loader. As a result we expect that the processOrderReferences function of the oum.do.RefsHandler is being called once.

```
it ("should call function to handle referenced addresses and products", function() {
    spyOn(oum.do.RefsHandler, "processOrderReferences");
    oum.do.orders.addData(oum.fixture.ordersData, true);

    expect(oum.do.RefsHandler.processOrderReferences.calls.count()).toEqual(1);
});
```

The expected functionality is implemented by adding code to the orders collection object (see Listing 12.2, "A basic orders collection object"). We add a listener function to the collection objects dataChanged event with the addDataChangedListener function.

```
function processReferences() {
    oum.do.RefsHandler.processOrderReferences(this.getData());
}
orders.addDataChangedListener(processReferences, orders);
```

Fortunately, all the above-mentioned specifications succeed and we see an all green SpecRunner result:

```
11 specs, 0 failures                                        finished in 0.088s


    Domain Objects
      should load orders into the orders collection object
      should load an order into the orders collection object

    Orders collection object
      should add address names to the order data
      should call function to handle referenced addresses and products

    Order entity object
      should have functions to get the billing and shipping addresses
      should get referenced address entity objects

    Address entity object
      should return the name for an Address

    Namespace oum.do.RefsHandler
      should call the Loader to fetch referenced product and address data of orders
      should add address names to orders and publish events
      should publish events when order references are resolved

    Namespace oum.do.Loader
      should notify the RefsHandler of incoming data
```

12.5. Further processing of incoming data

The incoming order data need to be processed further. Date strings needs to be parsed into a JavaScript Date. The order total must be calculated and added to the record. Accordingly, we add expectations for the orders collection object.

```
it ("should convert date string to Date object", function() {
   const order = oum.do.orders.getItem(1);
   expect(order.orderDate instanceof Date).toBe(true);
});

it ("should calculate and add the orderTotal ", function() {
   const order = oum.do.orders.getItem(1);
   expect(typeof order.orderTotal).toEqual("string");
   expect(order.orderTotal).toEqual("29.50");
});
```

After the order data are either added or updated to the collection, the procData function is called, which we registered with the registerProcFunction function (see Listing 12.2, "A basic orders collection object"). To meet the specifications, we add some more code to the procData function of the orders collection object.

Listing 12.12. Process incoming order data

```
function calculateOrderTotal(orderLines) {
   let total = 0.00;
   orderLines.forEach(function(orderLine) {
      const quantity = orderLine.quantity;
      const price = orderLine.unitPrice;
      total += quantity * price;
   });
   return total.toFixed(2);
}

function getDateFromString(dateString, dateFormat) {
   if (oui5lib.util.isUI5Env()) {
      const oDateFormat = sap.ui.core.format.DateFormat.getDateTimeInstance({
         pattern: dateFormat
      });
      return oDateFormat.parse(dateStr, false, true);
   } else {
      return new Date(dateString);
   }
}

function procData(ordersData) {
   const orderDateSpec = oui5lib.mapping.getEntityAttributeSpec("order",
                                                   "orderDate");
   orders.forEach(function(order) {
      const orderDateString = order.orderDate;
      if (typeof orderDateSpec.dateFormat === "string") {
         order.orderDate = getDateFromString(orderDateString,
                                       orderDateSpec.dateFormat);
      } else {
         order.orderDate = new Date(orderDateString);
      }
```

```
      order.total = calculateOrderTotal(order.items);
   }
}
orders.registerProcFunction(procData);
```
Register function to process added data

12.6. Adding logic to the entity object

If we follow this procedure to incrementally add specifications of and features to our data objects, we will arrive at a state of reasonable confidence that the objects actually do what we expect.

The application will have to list the sales order lines in the user interface. Instead of just the product ID, unit price and quantity, the order line will also need the product name and line total. Instead of putting the logic into some model formatter function, we add it to the Order entity object, where we will add a function named getOrderLines, which returns the order lines. To prepare the scenario, we add the required product data to the products collection.

 The following expectations for the function could be split into several specifications for a more fine-grained unit testing approach, but the author decided against it in favor of a more compact read.

```
it ("should process and return the enriched order lines", function() {
   oum.do.products.addData(oum.fixture.productsData, true);

   const order = new oum.do.Order(1);
   const orderLines = order.getOrderLines();

   orderLines.forEach(function(orderLine) {
      expect(typeof orderLine.productName).toBe("string");
      expect(typeof orderLine.lineTotal).toBe("string");
   });

   expect(orderLines.length).toEqual(2);
   expect(orderLines[0].quantity).toEqual(2);
   expect(orderLines[0].unitPrice).toEqual("4.80");
   expect(orderLines[0].lineTotal).toEqual("9.60");

   expect(orderLines[1].quantity).toEqual(1);
   expect(orderLines[1].unitPrice).toEqual("19.90");
   expect(orderLines[1].lineTotal).toEqual("19.90");
});
```

The getOrderLines function loops through the order lines and checks if the referenced product data are loaded. Then it adds the product name to the order line. The unit price is originally a float value, which is being converted into a string to avoid any complications with UI controls. Finally, the line total is calculated and the lineTotal property added.

Listing 12.13. Prepare and return the order lines

```
function getOrderLines() {
   const orderLines = this.getProperty("items");
   orderLines.forEach(function(orderLine) {
      if (oum.do.products.isItemLoaded(orderLine.productId)) {
         const product = new oum.do.Product(orderLine.productId);
         orderLine.productName = product.getName();
      }
```
Add product name

```
      const unitPrice = item.unitPrice;
      if (typeof unitPrice === "number") {
         const total = unitPrice * orderLine.quantity;          Compute line total

         orderLine.unitPrice = unitPrice.toFixed(2);            Add unit price
         orderLine.lineTotal = total.toFixed(2);               Add line total
      }
   });
   return orderLines;
}
Order.prototype.getOrderLines = getOrderLines;
```

The user interface will provide the ability to change the order line quantity, to add a new order line
and delete an existing one. All these functions need to retrieve a particular order line by its key, the
product ID. And after any change of order lines we need to recalulate the order total. We add the
required functions to the order entity object.

Listing 12.14. Get an order line by the product ID

```
const listHelper = oui5lib.lib.listHelper;

function getOrderLine(productId) {
   const orderLine = this.getOrderLines();
   return listHelper.getItemByKey(orderLine, "productId", productId);
}

function setOrderTotal() {
   const orderLines = this.getOrderLines();
   const total = oum.do.orders.calculateOrderTotal(orderLines);  ❶
   this.setProperty("total", total);
   return total;
}

Order.prototype.getOrderLine = getOrderLine;
Order.prototype.setOrderTotal = setOrderTotal;
```

❶   See Listing 12.12, "Process incoming order data".

The expectations for the changeOrderLineQuantity function are testing the 'before' state mainly for
readability, because the original data are a test fixture. We expect that besides updating the quantity,
the line total and order total are also recalculated.

```
it ("should change the order line quantity and update related totals", function() {
   const order = new oum.do.Order(1);
   let orderLine = order.getOrderLine("0394718747");

   expect(orderLine.quantity).toEqual(2);                       Before updating the quantity
   expect(orderLine.lineTotal).toEqual("9.60");
   expect(order.getProperty("total")).toEqual("29.50");

   const success = order.changeOrderLineQuantity("0394718747", "1");
   expect(success).toBe(true);

   expect(orderLine.quantity).toEqual(1);                       After updating the quantity
   expect(orderLine.lineTotal).toEqual("4.80");
   expect(order.getProperty("total")).toEqual("24.70");
});
```

Our function first makes sure, that the given parameters are valid. Consequently, we check if the productId references an order line and the quantity parameter can be parsed into a number. After that the rest is simple math and updating of properties.

Listing 12.15. Update the quantity of an order line and recalculate totals

```
function updateOrderLineQuantity(productId, quantity) {
    const orderLine = this.getOrderLine(productId);
    if (orderLine === null || isNaN(parseInt(quantity))) {
        return false;
    }

    orderLine.quantity = parseInt(quantity);
    const unitPrice = parseFloat(orderLine.unitPrice);
    if (typeof unitPrice === "number") {
        let total = unitPrice * orderLine.quantity;
        orderLine.lineTotal = total.toFixed(2);
    }
    this.setOrderTotal();
    return true;
}
Order.prototype.changeOrderLineQuantity = updateOrderLineQuantity;
```

The expectations for removing an order line are straightforward. We pass a product ID and the order line should be gone. Again, we expect the order total to be recalulated.

```
it ("should remove an order line and recalulate the order total", function() {
    const order = new oum.do.Order(1);
    const orderLines = order.getOrderLines();

    expect(orderLines.length).toEqual(2);                        Before removing an order line
    expect(order.getProperty("total")).toEqual("29.50");

    const removedLine = order.removeOrderLine("0394718747");
    expect(typeof removedLine === "object").toBe(true);

    expect(orderLines.length).toEqual(1);                        After removing an order line
    expect(order.getProperty("total")).toEqual("19.90");
});
```

With the listHelper, it just takes a few lines of code to fulfill the above-stated expectations. If no order line exists for the given product, nothing happens.

Listing 12.16. Remove an order line by the product ID and recalculate order total

```
function removeOrderLine(productId) {
    let removedLine;
    if (this.getOrderLine(productId) !== null) {
        const orderLines = this.getOrderLines();
        removedLine = listHelper.removeByKey(orderLines, "productId", productId);
        if (removedLine !== null) {
            this.setOrderTotal();
        }
    }
    return removedLine;
}
Order.prototype.removeOrderLine = removeOrderLine;
```

To test the function to add an order line, we will formulate two specifications. One, to ensure that an order line is only added if there is none for the given product. And the other to test the functionality for adding an order line.

```
it ("should not add another order line for a product already ordered", function() {
    const order = new oum.do.Order(1);
    const orderLines = order.getOrderLines();

    order.addOrderLine("0394718747", 3);

    expect(orderLines.length).toEqual(2);
    expect(order.getProperty("total")).toEqual("29.50");
});

it ("should add a new order line and recalulate the order total", function() {
    const order = new oum.do.Order(1);
    const orderLines = order.getOrderLines();

    order.addOrderLine("0521560241", 1);

    expect(orderLines.length).toEqual(3);
    expect(order.getProperty("total")).toEqual("134.50");
});
```

To begin with, our function tests the given parameters. Product data need to available in the products collection to get the current sales price. And the quantity must be a number.

Listing 12.17. Add an order line with the given product ID

```
function addOrderLine(productId, quantity) {
    if (!oum.do.products.isItemLoaded(productId) || isNaN(quantity)) {
        return;
    }

    if (this.getOrderLine(productId) === null) {
        const product = new oum.do.Product(productId);
        const orderLine = {
            "productId": productId,
            "quantity": quantity,
            "unitPrice": product.getProperty("salesPrice")
        };
        const orderLines = this.getOrderLines();
        orderLines.push(orderLine);

        this.setOrderTotal();
    }
}
Order.prototype.addOrderLine = addOrderLine;
```

12.7. Summary

In this chapter, we looked at constructing custom entity collections and item objects and how to test their basic functionality. After that, we gradually added 'domain logic' to the objects, expressed in test specifications and plain JavaScript.

By separating the domain logic into easily testable objects, we went a long way to allow our controllers to focus on preparing views and handling user events.

Chapter 13. Validation

In this chapter we will look at the issues of client-side user input validation. Let us begin by clarifying what we want to achieve:

1. Any user input control has to be validated upon leaving the input field. In case the input value is not valid, the control has to visually indicate an error and also show a related message informing the user about the failed expectations. Once the input value is corrected, the control will indicate success and the message be removed.

2. When the form is submitted, the whole record has to be validated and a list of errors and warnings shown to the user. All controls with invalid values should behave like described under item 1.

How do we actually implement the validating steps? Are the means offered by UI5 sufficient or should we rather come up with our own solution?

We have already looked at examples of input validation in Section 9.5, "Validation UI5 Style". There are various model types included in UI5 with a wealth of constraints to validate a value. And custom types are not too complicated to create (see Listing 9.16, "Basic custom type: Email").

The functionality to use types comes from the `sap.ui.base.ManagedObject` as an option to the `bindProperty` function binding info. That means validation happens on the control level, which leaves out certain use cases we need to cover:

• If an input isn't focused, or the input value is left unchanged, validation will not be triggered.

• If the form is submitted, we have to validate the whole record and not just individual inputs.

When the user submits a form, the connected controller gets the form model and then we want to validate the model data. Unfortunately, the models have no data validation function. Instead, we could go through all the form controls to get their value state and the related message.

```
> nameInput.getValueState()
< "Error"
> nameInput.getValueStateText()
< "Enter a value with at least 3 characters"
> |
```

But even that approach is insufficient, because it only works for validated inputs. So, we would first have to programmatically trigger validation for each of the form controls allowing user input. It should be possible to write such a functionality, but it seems odd to me. Why go through the user interface controls to validate the data we already have?

Can we, at least, use the UI5 types separately and use their implementation of constraints and related i18n error messages? Let's look at an example:

Listing 13.1. Use UI5 type to validate a value

```
const stringType = new sap.ui.model.type.String({},
                            { minLength: 3, maxLength: 20 });

try {
   stringType.validateValue("hi");
} catch(e) {
   const name = e.name;                          ValidateException
   const message = e.message;                    Enter a value with at least 3 characters
   const violatedConstraints = e.violatedConstraints;   ["minLength"]
}
```

Ok. That works. Anyway, to validate some value against a number of contraints isn't much of a programming effort. That alone doesn't justify using the UI5 types. But what about the messages? The
message texts are meant for the user. Sending messages to the user is a different story to input validation, which we will look at somewhere else (see Listing 16.12, "Open message box with validation
errors "). If we want to use the messages, we can find them in the `sap.ui.core` messagebundles:

```
sap.ui.getCore().getLibraryResourceBundle().getText("String.MinLength");
```

The evaluation of the UI5 means to validate user input shows them insufficient of performing all the
necessary validation steps, at least if we don't want to rely on the server-side to do the validation and
return error messages. To me, sending a form to the server for validation is not acceptable. Surely,
the server always has to validate anyway, but the client application should provide more immediate
feedback, telling the user what is wrong and how to fix it. Validation is a task for both sides. Bearing
this in mind, we can not save ourselves the time and effort to design and implement a custom solution
- at least not with a clear conscience.

13.1. Extending the mapping

An important topic to add to the mappings is validity. The question is how to do it. The first step
seems obvious. Because it is impossible to express validity with a single term, we will need an array:

```
{
    "name": "firstname",
    "validate": []
}
```

To normalize the `validate` property of the entity attribute specifications, we make sure to always have
an array. If an attribute is `required`, we add "required" to the array of validation terms. If there is
nothing to validate we leave the property `undefined`.

```
function setEntityAttributeDefaults(attributeSpec) {
    let tests = [];
    if (typeof attributeSpec.validate !== "undefined" &&
        attributeSpec.validate instanceof Array) {
        tests = attributeSpec.validate;
    }
    if (attributeSpec.required) {
        tests.push("required");
    }
    if (tests.length > 0) {
        attributeSpec.validate = tests;
    }
}
```

A value may not be defined, of primitive types undefined or null, or an empty string. All these, are regarded as having no value. We need a function to test if a string variable has a value. This is a function not only useful for validation. Therefore, we add it to the oui5lib.util namespace:

```
function isBlank(value) {
    if (typeof value === "undefined" || value === null) {
        return true;
    }
    if (typeof value === "object") {
        throw new TypeError("The given value is not a string");
    }
    if (typeof value === "string") {
        for (let i = 0; i < value.length; i++) {
            let c = value.charAt(i);
            if (c != " " && c != "\n" && c != "\t") {
                return false;
            }
        }
    }
    return true;
}
util.isBlank = isBlank;
```

Apart from being "required", what list of terms do we use for our validate array?

13.1.1. Validation terms and related validation functions

For the list of validation terms let us look at the constraints provided by the various UI5 model types:

- String: minLength/maxLength (int), search (RegExp), startsWith/startsWithIgnoreCase, endsWith/endsWithIgnoreCase, contains, equals (all string)
- Integer: minimum/ maximum (int)
- Currency: minimum/ maximum (float)
- Float: minimum/ maximum (float)
- Date: minimum/ maximum (Date | string)
- Time: none
- DateTime: none
- Boolean: none

What does it mean for our mapping? The minLength, maxLength, minimum and maximum constraints all require an integer or float value. We can simply append the number to the constraint name like this:

```
{
    "name": "firstname",
    "validate": [
        "minLength_2",
        "maxLength_40"
    ]
},{
    "name": "quantity",
    "validate": [
        "minimum_1",
        "maximum_10"
    ]
},{
    "name": "sum",
    "validate": [
        "maximum_99.9"
    ]
}
```

Assuming a type of string, the length, minLength and maxLength constraints are easily evaluated:

```
function verifyLength(value, number) {
    if (value.length !== number) {
        return false;
    }
    return true;
}
function minLength(value, number) {
    if (value.length < number) {
        return false;
    }
    return true;
}
function maxLength(value, number) {
    if (value.length > number) {
        return false;
    }
    return true;
}
```

The minimum and maximum constraints hardly require more effort. If the given value is not a number, we return false. A string is first being parsed and then evaluated:

```
function min(value, number) {
    value = getFloatValue(value);
    if (value) {
        if (value >= number) {
            return true;
        }
    }
    return false;
}
```

```
function max(value, number) {
   value = getFloatValue(value);
   if (value) {
      if (value <= number) {
         return true;
      }
   }
   return false;
}

function getFloatValue(value) {
   if (isNaN(value)) {
      return false;
   }
   if (typeof value === "string") {
      value = parseFloat(value);
   }
   return value;
}
```

The Date minimum/ maximum is a moving target because the earth travels around the sun and the moon around the earth. We usually have constraints like "in the past", "today", "in the future" or "within 1 to 10 days from now", which could be expressed like this:

```
{
   "name": "orderDate",
   "type": "Date",
   "validate": [
      "past"
   ]
},{
   "name": "shippingDate",
   "type": "Date",
   "validate": [
      "today"
   ]
},{
   "name": "deliveryDate",
   "type": "Date",
   "validate": [
      "minFuture_1",
      "maxFuture_4"
   ]
}
```

To validate the today, past and future constraints, we assume to have an instance of Date.

```
function isFuture(value) {
   const now = new Date();
   return (now.getTime() < value.getTime());
}

function isPast(value) {
   const now = new Date();
   return (now.getTime() > value.getTime());
}
```

```
function isToday(value) {
   const now = new Date();
   return (now.getFullYear() === value.getFullYear() &&
           now.getMonth() === value.getMonth() &&
           now.getDate() == value.getDate());
}
```

The UI5 `String` type has several more constraints which we may want to cover. The "equals" constraint is easily expressed:

```
{
   "name": "errorGroup",
   "default": "PM911"
}
```

The remaining string constraints (startsWith/startsWithIgnoreCase, endsWith/endsWithIgnoreCase, contains) can all be covered by a regular expression (search).

Let us look at a simple regular expression for a phone number: /^0{2}[1-9][\d]*$/.

Regular expression don't tell anyone but programmers what they might mean. And more complex regular expressions are practically unreadable for humans, like this one to match a valid email address: /[a-z0-9!#$%&'*+/=?^_`{|}~-]+(?:\.[a-z0-9!#$%&'*+/=?^_`{|}~-]+)*@(?:[a-z0-9](?:[a-z0-9-]*[a-z0-9])?\.)+[a-z0-9](?:[a-z0-9-]*[a-z0-9])?/

Clearly, we don't want to put regular expressions in the mapping files, because they are not very informative. We had better use named constraints in the mapping, like "email" or "phone".

```
{
   "name": "emailAddress",
   "validate": [
      "email"
   ]
},{
   "name": "phoneNumber",
   "validate": [
      "phone"
   ]
}
```

Here, we assume that we get the related regular expressions from our `oui5lib.configuration`:

```
function custom(fnme, value) {
   let regex;

   switch(fnme) {
   case "email":
      regex = configuration.getEmailRegex();
      break;
   case "phone":
      regex = configuration.getPhoneRegex();
      break;
   }
   return regex.test(value);
}
```

Further useful constraints using a regular expression are "noNumbers", "numbersOnly" or "hasLetters". Here are example mapping entries:

```
{
    "name": "lastname",
    "validate": [
        "noNumbers",
        "minLength_2",
        "maxLength_40"
    ]
},{
    "name": "errorCode",
    "validate": [
        "numbersOnly"
    ]
},{
    "name": "description",
    "validate": [
        "containsLetters"
    ]
}
```

For the `containsLetters`, `numbersOnly` and `noNumber` constraints we use regular expressions:

```
function hasLetters(value) {
    const regex = /[A-Za-z]+/;
    return regex.test(value);
}
function numbersOnly(value) {
    const regex = /^[\d]+$/;
    return regex.test(value);
}
function noNumbers(value) {
    const regex = /^[^\d]+$/;
    return regex.test(value);
}
```

At this point, we have our list of validation terms, which seem expressive enough to allow most participants to make sense of them. And we have the related test functions. We can now put it all together.

13.2. Custom functions for validation

For validation issues, we use the obvious namespace `oui5lib.validation`. The `isValid` function takes a value to be validated and an array of constraints to pass. It loops through the validation terms and calls the related tests. It will return `true` if all the tests pass, otherwise `false`.

Listing 13.2. Namespace oui5lib.validation

```
(function(configuration, util) {
    const validation = oui5lib.namespace("validation");

    function isValid(value, tests) {
        if ((tests.indexOf("required") > -1)) {            It a value required?
            if ((typeof value === "string") && util.isBlank(value)) {
                return false;
            }
        }

        let valid = true;
        if (tests instanceof Array && tests.length > 0) {    Are there any tests?
```

```
    tests.forEach(function(test) {
        const match = test.match(/([a-zA-Z]+)_(\d+)/);        Is this a test term with a number?
        let number = null;
        if (match !== null && match.length === 3) {
            test = match[1];
            number = parseInt(match[2]);                       We got the test term and number
        }

        if (value instanceof Date) {                           The value is a Date instance
            switch (test) {
            case "future":
                if (!isFuture(value)) {
                    valid = false;
                }
                break;
            case "past":
                ...
            case "today":
                ...
            }
            return valid;
        }

        switch (test) {                                        The value is a string or number
        case "length":
            if (!verifyLength(value, number)) {
                valid = false;
            }
            break;
        case "minLength":
            ...
        case "maxLength":
            ...
        case "minimum":
            ...
        case "maximum":
            ...
        case "numbersOnly":
            ...
        case "noNumbers":
            ...
        case "containsLetters":
            ...
        case "email":
        case "phone":
            if (!(util.isBlank(value))) {
                if (!custom(test, value)) {
                    valid = false;
                }
            }
            break;
        }
    });
}
return valid;
}
validation.isValid = isValid;
```

```
    // all the above test functions go in here
    ...
}(oui5lib.configuration, oui5lib.util));
```

Validating a value is useful for a single form field or property value, but we also want to be able to validate a whole entity record. When a form is submitted we want to simply get the data from the bound model and validate them against our entity attribute specificatons of the mapping.

In order to work, the model data property path has to match the related entity attribute specification name. This may seem as an unpleasant restriction, but using the same names for the same things will greatly improve the readability of the code[1].

To get a value for an entity attribute name, we first try to get it from the data object. If the given data object doesn't have such a property, we use the default property value of the attribute specification instead if that is defined. If no value can be found, null is returned:

Listing 13.3. Function to get the value of the entity attribute

```
function getAttributeValue(data, attributeSpec) {
    const attributeName = attributeSpec.name;
    let attributeValue = null;
    if (typeof data[attributeName] !== "undefined") {
        attributeValue = data[attributeName];
    } else if (typeof attributeSpec.default !== "undefined") {
        attributeValue = attributeSpec.default;
    }
    return attributeValue;
}
```

On top of telling us if the data are valid, we also want to know what is wrong. And if there are multiple errors we want to know about all of them. Therefore, the function has to return an array of errors. If it is empty, everything is fine. Otherwise, we expect a list of strings about errors found.

The error strings are meant to be further processed to communicate them to the user. At least, we have to set the valueState of the related form field controls to visually highlight the errors. We may also want to show a list of messages. To be able to do that, the error string has to include the entity attribute name and the reason of the error. We have several possible error reasons:

- *missing* - A required value is not given.
- *wrongType* - The given value is not of the specified type.
- *notAllowed* - The given value is not in the list of allowed values.
- *invalid* - The given value did not validate against the specified constraints.

Let us formalize our expectations. As an example entity, we use a simple user and specify the attributes.

```
const userAttributeSpecs = [
    {
        "name": "name",
        "required": true,
        "type": "string",
        "validate": [ "hasLetters" ]
    },
```

---

[1]If, for whatever reasons, we have to or want to use different names, an intermediate transformation of the model data is required.

```
    {
        "name": "email",
        "required": false,
        "type": "email",
        "validate": [ "email" ]
    },{
        "name": "emailValidated",
        "required": true,
        "default": false,
        "type": "boolean"
    },{
        "name": "role",
        "required": true,
        "type": "string",
        "allowedValues": [ "developer", "user", "administrator" ]
    }
];
```

Using the above entity attribute specifications, we can formulate our expectations of how the validate-function should work.

Listing 13.4. Specify expectations for the function to validate data

```
it("should validate data against entity attribute specifications", function() {
    let userData = {};
    let msgs = oui5lib.validation.validateData(userData, userAttributeSpecs);

    expect(msgs.length).toEqual(2);
    expect(msgs[0]).toEqual("missing:name");
    expect(msgs[1]).toEqual("missing:role");

    userData = {
        name: "123",
        email: "anyhost.name",
        emailValidated: "false",
        role: "guest"
    };
    msgs = oui5lib.validation.validateData(userData, userAttributeSpecs);

    expect(msgs.length).toEqual(4);
    expect(msgs[0]).toEqual("invalid:name");
    expect(msgs[1]).toEqual("invalid:email");
    expect(msgs[2]).toEqual("wrongType:emailValidated");
    expect(msgs[3]).toEqual("notAllowed:role");

    userData = {
        name: "Carst Heinrigs",
        email: "oui5lib@cahein.de",
        role: "developer"
    };
    msgs = oui5lib.validation.validateData(userData, userAttributeSpecs);

    expect(msgs.length).toEqual(0);
});
```

After specifying our expectations, we will follow up with an implementation.

An entity attribute specification can set the property allowedValues. The following function tests if a value is allowed:

```
function isValueAllowed(allowedValues, value) {
   if (allowedValues.indexOf(value) === -1) {
      return false;
   }
   return true;
}
```

Our function to test the correct type just handles a few basic types. It returns false if the value has the specified type. Remember that the default type is "string".

```
function hasWrongType(type, value) {
   switch(type) {
   case "string":
   case "email":
   case "phone":
      if (typeof value !== "string") { return true; }
      break;
   case "int":
      if (typeof value === "string") {
         if (parseInt(value)) { value = parseInt(value); }
      }
      if (typeof value !== "number") { return true; }
      break;
   case "boolean":
      if (typeof value !== "boolean") {
         if (!(value instanceof Boolean)) { return true; }
      }
      break;
   case "Date":
      if (!(value instanceof Date)) { return true; }
      break;
   }
   return false;
}
```

The mapping can have a type "array". The related value can either be an array of strings or an array of objects. The following function handles both cases. If it finds another level of attribute specifications, it issues a recursive call of the validateData function we are going to present next. It detects two kinds of errors: a value which is not allowed, and a missing value if the given data are not an array while a value is specified as required.

```
function handleArray(data, attributeSpec, _msgs) {
   if (data instanceof Array && data.length > 0) {
      if (typeof attributeSpec.arrayItem !== "undefined") {        Is it an Array of objects?
         const arraySpecs = attributeSpec.arrayItem;
         data.forEach(function(item) {
            validateData(item, arraySpecs, false);
         });
      } else {                                                      An Array of strings
         if (typeof attributeSpec.allowedValues !== "undefined") {
            const allowedValues = attributeSpec.allowedValues;
            data.forEach(function(value) {
               if (!isValueAllowed(allowedValues, value)) {
                  _msgs.push("notAllowed:" + attributeSpec.name + ":" + value);
               }
            });
         }
      }
   }
```

```
      } else {
        if (attributeSpec.required) {
          _msgs.push("missing:" + attributeSpec.name);
        }
      }
    }
}
```

Finally, we come to the function to make the expectations of Listing 13.4, "Specify expectations for the function to validate data" pass. Because it may be called recursively it has a parameter `newValidation` to continue a running validation. The value defaults to `true` which means it clears the array of error messages and begins a new validation.

Listing 13.5. Validate data against the entity attribute specifications

```
let _msgs;

function validateData(data, attributeSpecs, newValidation) {
    if (typeof newValidation !== "boolean") { newValidation = true; }
    if (newValidation) { _msgs = []; }

    for (let i = 0, s = attributeSpecs.length; i < s; i++) {
        const attributeSpec = attributeSpecs[i];
        const attributeName = attributeSpec.name;

        switch (attributeSpec.type) {
        case "array":
            handleArray(data[attributeName], attributeSpec, _msgs);
            continue;
        case "object":
            if (typeof data[attributeName] === "object") {
                validateData(data[attributeName], attributeSpec.objectItem, false); ❶
            } else {
                if (attributeSpec.required) {
                    _msgs.push("missing:" + attributeName);
                }
            }
            continue;
        }

        const attributeValue = getAttributeValue();   ❷

        if (attributeSpec.required) {                              Is a value required?
            if (attributeValue === null ||
                (typeof attributeValue === "string" && util.isBlank(attributeValue))) {
                _msgs.push("missing:" + attributeName);           A required value is missing
                continue;
            }
        }

        if (attributeSpec.type || attributeValue !== null) {      Is a type specified?
            if (hasWrongType(attributeSpec.type, attributeValue)) {
                _msgs.push("wrongType:" + attributeName);         Value is a wrong type
                continue;
            }
        }

        if (attributeSpec.validate !== undefined &&               Are there validation constraints?
            attributeSpec.validate instanceof Array) {
```

```
        if (!isValid(attributeValue, attributeSpec.validate)) {
            _msgs.push("invalid:" + attributeName);
            continue;
        }
    }

    if (typeof attributeSpec.allowedValues !== "undefined") {
        const allowedValues = attributeSpec.allowedValues;
        if (!isValueAllowed(allowedValues, attributeValue)) {
            _msgs.push("notAllowed:" + attributeName);
            continue;
        }
    }
  }
}
return _msgs;
}
validation.validateData = validateData;
```

Some constraint is violated

Are allowed values specified?

The value is not allowed

❶   Both an array of objects and the properties of an object need to be validated as well. This is done by calling this function recursively to handle each following level.

❷   See Listing 13.3, "Function to get the value of the entity attribute".

13.3. Summary

In this chapter we looked into the means offered by UI5 to validate user input and found them deficient. We introduced validation terms to be used in the mapping to describe the validity of a property and provided functions to perform the related validation of given values against the specifications.

Upon getting errors we need to process them to inform the user. This is a user interface issue we will cover in the following chapters. Apart from showing a list of messages (see Chapter 6, *Events and Messages*), we also need to set the valueState of the related controls. To be able to do that we need the ID of the control. This leads us to the next chapter: the construction of form field controls.

Chapter 14. Form Control Generation

Constructing form field controls is tedious. Given the wealth of properties and events, we can only expect inconsistencies to spread throughout the application. For this, it makes no difference if we use XML or JS fragments and views. It just feels like going back to the old times, in which we were repeating similar code too many times.

A standard way of getting away from repeating code is employing functions with parameters. It will also help to use conventions to get rid of some possible but not essential parameters.

UI5 provides too many form element controls to cover completely here. I have therefore limited the selection to a small number of form controls from the `sap.m` namespace, which I found most useful to have generated:

- Standard text input controls: `Input`, `Textarea`, `MaskInput`.
- Boolean choices: `CheckBox`, `Switch`.
- Single and multi-select lists: `Select`, `ComboBox`, `MultiComboBox`
- Specialized controls for date and time: `DatePicker`, `DateTimePicker`, `TimePicker`.

What information do we need, in order to generate a form element and the related label? Instead of trying to include all properties, associations, aggregations and events, we had better try to focus on the more important ones and leave it up to the developer to further customize the control. The selected controls have some things in common:

- All inherit the aggregation `tooltip` from the `Element`.
- All have an association `ariaLabelledBy`.
- Most have a property `width` (excluding the Switch).
- Most have a property `valueState` (excluding the Switch) and a related `valueStateText` (excluding the Switch and CheckBox).

There is a subgroup of these controls which require an array of `sap.ui.core.Item` objects as a list of options (see `Select` and `ComboBoxBase`). This means we need a model and property paths for the list of "key: value" pairs to be able construct these controls.

The figure below shows selected controls with important keys and a hint what values they require. 'Entity Model property' refers to the model property binding. 'Enum' refers to an Enumeration.

Figure 14.1. Overview of important form field controls

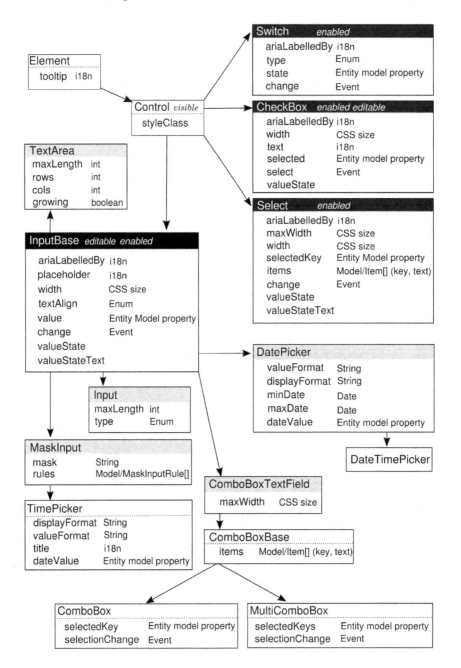

14.1. Mapping and model binding

We split the information for the mapping into two sections. The keys for the language specific texts of more general use: `label`, `tooltip`, `placeholder` and an error message text, which is shown to explain `invalid` input go into the `i18n` section. The control-specific information goes into the `ui5` section.

Let us begin by describing a simple `sap.m.Input` field for the `exampleEntity` attribute `first_name`.

```
{
    "description": "Example entity definition",
    "primaryKey": "id",
    "entity": [
        {
            "name": "id"
        },
        {
            "name": "first_name",                                 Attribute name and model property path
            "required": true,                                     The Label indicates that input is required
            "validate": [
                "hasLetters", "minLength_3", "maxLength_20"       Attach validation of constraints
            ],
            "ui5": {
                "control": "sap.m.Input"
            },
            "i18n": {
                "label": "exEntity.firstName.label",              I18n key for Label text
                "placeholder": "exEntity.firstName.placeholder",  I18n key for the Input placeholder
                "tooltip": "exEntity.firstName.tooltip",
                "invalid": "exEntity.firstName.invalid"
            }
        }
    ]
}
```

Adhering to the MVC pattern, we probably ought to construct form controls in the view. But on the other hand, we don't want to litter the views by adding programming logic. Therefore, we will use the controller to provide functions to add controls to a form.

Because the functionality we provide will be useful for most controllers dealing with a form, we begin by defining a `oui5lib.controller.FormController` extending the `oui5lib.controller.BaseController`:

```
sap.ui.define([
    "oui5lib/controller/BaseController"
], function(oController) {
    "use strict";

    const FormController = oController.extend("oui5lib.controller.FormController", {

    });
    return FormController;
});
```

At this point, I will assume that we have a model, which holds the entity data to be edited. It should be bound to the form and given the name of the entity:

```
form.setModel(entityModel, "entityName");
```

Each entity attribute specification has a unique name (in the above example: "id", "first_name") which we use to bind data from a model to the related form element control property according to the following convention:

```
"{entityName>/attributeName}"
```

 The controls are constructed using the entity attribute specifications, whereby the entity attribute name of the mapping is expected to be the same as the related model property path.

We will also use this combo (entityName and propertyPath) to construct the IDs for the controls:

```
getControlId: function(entityName, propertyPath) {
    return this.getView().createId(entityName + "_" + propertyPath);
}
```

14.2. Common properties

We have certain common properties for a number of controls. Only the tooltip property and the ariaLabelledBy association are available for all controls.

The ariaLabelledBy is problematic to generalize because it is an association to a control, for example an InvisibleText, which we don't want to add to the form. Where else to put it? The problem can be solved with another convention like a control ID to which to add all the ARIA references. But that seems too much convention at this point.

We also leave out the handling of the visible, editable and enabled properties because these are best used to implement form field permissions (see Section 5.2, "Properties to implement user permissions").

For all remaining common properties, the code first checks if it has been specified for the entity attribute and then it tests if the related function is available for the form field control.

Listing 14.1. Set common control properties

```
setCommons: function(attributeSpec, element) {
    if (typeof attributeSpec.i18n.tooltip === "string") {            Element
        if (typeof element.setTooltip === "function") {
            element.setTooltip(
                oui5lib.util.getI18nText(attributeSpec.i18n.tooltip)
            );
        }
    }

    if (typeof attributeSpec.ui5.width === "string") {               InputBase, CheckBox, Select
        const width = attributeSpec.ui5.width;
        if (sap.ui.core.CSSSize.isValid(width) &&                    Validate CSS size value
            typeof element.setWidth === "function") {
            element.setWidth(width);
        }
    }

    if (typeof attributeSpec.i18n.invalid === "string") {            InputBase, Select
        if (typeof element.setValueStateText === "function") { ❶
            element.setValueStateText(
```

```
                  oui5lib.util.getI18nText(attributeSpec.i18n.invalid)
          );
      }
  }

  if (typeof attributeSpec.ui5.maxWidth === "string") {          ComboBoxBase, Select
      const maxWidth = attributeSpec.ui5.maxWidth;
      if (sap.ui.core.CSSSize.isValid(maxWidth) &&               Validate CSS size value
         typeof element.setMaxWidth === "function") {
         element.setMaxWidth(maxWidth);
      }
  }

  if (typeof attributeSpec.i18n.placeholder === "string") {      InputBase
      if (typeof element.setPlaceholder === "function") {
         element.setPlaceholder(
             oui5lib.util.getI18nText(attributeSpec.i18n.placeholder)
         );
      }
  }

  if (typeof attributeSpec.ui5.maxLength === "number") {         Input, TextArea
      if (typeof element.setMaxLength === "function") {
         element.setMaxLength(attributeSpec.ui5.maxLength);
      }
  }
}
```

❶ Most of the selected controls have a `valueStateText` property. This is a text shown below the control when the `valueState` is set to `Warning` or `Error` (see Section 6.3, "Value state messages"). To prepare the control, we use the `i18n.invalid` value from the attribute specification.

The related function to set the `valueState` of a control seems more generally useful and not just limited to the `FormController`. We therefore add it to the new namespace `oui5lib.ui`.

Listing 14.2. Namespace oui5lib.ui

```
(function() {
   /** @namespace oui5lib.ui */
   const ui = oui5lib.namespace("ui");

   function setControlValueState(control, isValid) {
      if (typeof control === "undefined") {
         return;
      }
      if (typeof control.setValueState === "function") {
         if (isValid) {
            control.setValueState("None");
         } else {
            control.setValueState("Error");
         }
      }
   }
   ui.setControlValueState = setControlValueState;
}());
```

We have now covered common properties of the selected controls. Some other issue common to all controls is the status of the form data. Were the data changed or not? When the user leaves the form, we need to know if any changes were made to oblige the user to confirm that these changes will be discarded. It is also useful to know if an empty form is submitted, because in that case we have nothing to post to the server.

Listing 14.3. FormController record changed status

```
_recordChanged: false,

setRecordChanged: function() {
   this._recordChanged = true;
},
resetRecordChanged: function() {
   this._recordChanged = false;
},
wasRecordChanged: function() {
   return this._recordChanged;
}
```

 We will only know whether the current record was changed if all controls allowing modification of the data call the setRecordChanged function, in case of the related event.

14.3. Construct Input

All controls extending the InputBase have a change event to which we attach field level validation. We get the value of the input with the getValue function. We need to save this (the controller) to a variable (line 2), because in case of a change event the attached function (lines 4 to 11) will have this set to the input field, but we also need the controller to be able to set the record to changed (line 4).

```
1 attachChange: function(inputBase, constraints) {
2     const controller = this;
3     inputBase.attachChange(function() {
4         controller.setRecordChanged();
5
6         if (oui5lib.validation.isValid(inputBase.getValue(), constraints)) {
7             oui5lib.ui.setControlValueState(inputBase, true);
8         } else {
9             oui5lib.ui.setControlValueState(inputBase, false);
10            this.focus();
11        }
12    });
13 }
```

At this point, we have everything prepared to construct the sap.m.Input.

Listing 14.4. FormController: Construct Input

```
_availableInputTypes: ["Email", "Number", "Password", "Tel", "Text", "Url"],

getInput: function(entityName, propertyPath) {
    const attributeSpec = oui5lib.mapping.getEntityAttributeSpec(entityName, propertyPath); ❶
    if (attributeSpec === null) {
       return null;
    }
```

```
const controlId = this.getControlId(entityName, propertyPath);
const input = new sap.m.Input(controlId, {
    value: "{" + entityName + ">/" + propertyPath + "}"
});

this.setCommons(attributeSpec, input);
this.attachChange(input, attributeSpec.validate);

if (typeof attributeSpec.ui5.type === "string") { ❷
    const inputType = attributeSpec.ui5.type;
    if (this._availableInputTypes.indexOf(inputType) > -1) {
        input.setType(inputType);
    }
}
return input;
}
```

❶   All controls we construct with the help of the `FormController` get the required information from
the mapping with the `oui5lib.mapping.getEntityAttributeSpec` function. If the entity mapping file
cannot be found (HTTP 404 error) or the attribute `name` does not exist, the function returns `null`.

❷   The type property is specific to the Input. It is responsible for setting the type attribute of the
HTML `<input>`. The default is 'Text'.

The code to construct a `TextArea` and `MaskInput` is very similar to the `Input`, but there are a few control-specific properties we need to address.

The `TextArea` has properties to specify the size of the input area - `rows`, `cols` and `growing` (see Section 9.4.4, "TextArea"). And the `MaskInput` requires a `mask` to be set (see Section 9.4.3, "MaskInput").

14.4. Elements with option lists

Another group of controls needs a list of options to choose from (the `ComboBox`, `MultiComboBox` and
`Select`). For these controls we need to add some properties to the entity attribute specification:

```
{
    "name": "location",
    "ui5": {
        "control": "sap.m.ComboBox",
        "itemsModel": "locations",      The model name
        "itemKey": "key",               The Item key
        "itemText": "text",             The Item text
        "sortBy": "text",
        "sortOrder": "ASC"
    },
    "i18n": {
        "label" : "exEntity.location",
        "placeholder": "exEntity.location.placeholder",
        "invalid": "validation.required.selection"
    }
}
```

Luckily, all these controls require the same type of control for their `items` aggregation (the
`sap.ui.core.Item`). We can construct it using the above-mentioned entity attribute `itemsModel`, `itemKey`
and `itemText` properties:

```
getItemTemplate: function(attributeSpec) {
   const modelName = attributeSpec.ui5.itemsModel;
   const key = attributeSpec.ui5.itemKey;
   const text = attributeSpec.ui5.itemText;

   const itemTemplate = new sap.ui.core.Item({
      key: "{" + modelName + ">" + key + "}",
      text: "{" + modelName + ">" + text + "}"
   });
   return itemTemplate;
}
```

Normally, we will also want the options to be sorted. For this, we will need to construct a Sorter based upon the sortBy and sortOrder properties of the mapping:

```
getSorter: function(attributeSpec) {
   const oSorter= [];
   if (typeof attributeSpec.ui5.sortBy === "string") {
      const sortBy = attributeSpec.ui5.sortBy;

      let sortOrder;
      if (typeof attributeSpec.ui5.sortOrder === "string") {
         switch(attributeSpec.ui5.sortOrder) {
         case "ASC":
            sortOrder = false;
            break;
         case "DESC":
            sortOrder = true;
            break;
         default:
            sortOrder = false;
         }
      }
      oSorter.push(new sap.ui.model.Sorter(sortBy, sortOrder));
   }
   return oSorter;
}
```

The Item template and the Sorter would be useless without binding them to the items aggregation of a related control. The itemsModel property from the attribute specification is used for the model property path.

```
bindItemTemplate: function(attributeSpec, control) {
   const modelName = attributeSpec.ui5.itemsModel;
   const itemTemplate = this.getItemTemplate(attributeSpec);
   const oSorter= this.getSorter(attributeSpec);

   control.bindAggregation("items", modelName + ">/", itemTemplate, oSorter);
}
```

As an example, we will look at the function to construct a sap.m.ComboBox. If an item is selected, both the selectionChange and change events are triggered. Whatever can be selected is expected to be a valid value. We will, therefore, attach a function to the selectionChange event (re)setting the valueState to None.

The change event is also triggered when the user types something in the input field without selecting one of the items. This makes it the appropriate event to attach a function to mark the record changed and to optionally check if the inserted value is matching any of the items.

Listing 14.5. FormController: Construct ComboBox

```
 1 getComboBox: function(entityName, propertyPath) {
 2    const attributeSpec = mapping.getEntityAttributeSpec(entityName, propertyPath);
 3    if (attributeSpec === null) {
 4       return null;
 5    }
 6
 7    const controller = this;
 8    const controlId = this.getControlId(entityName, propertyPath);
 9    const comboBox = new sap.m.ComboBox(controlId, {
10       selectedKey: "{" + entityName + ">/" + propertyPath + "}",
11       selectionChange: function(oEvent) {
12          comboBox.setValueState("None");
13       },
14       change: function() {
15          controller.setRecordChanged();
16          const onlyItems = attributeSpec.ui5.onlyItems;
17          if (typeof onlyItems === "boolean" && onlyItems) {
18             oui5lib.ui.checkComboBox(comboBox); ❶
19          }
20       }
21    });
22    this.setCommons(attributeSpec, comboBox);
23
24    this.bindItemTemplate(attributeSpec, comboBox);
25
26    return comboBox;
27 }
```

❶   In Section 9.4.5, "ComboBox and MultiComboBox", we already mentioned the behavior of
the ComboBox allowing the insertion of a text value without selecting one of the items . This is
a feature, but sometimes this is not what we want. To add the related check to the change event
we set the entity attribute property onlyItems of the 'ui5' section of the manifest totrue.

The Select control only has the change event, and for the MultiComboBox we only use the selectionChange
event. Otherwise, these controls are constructed like the ComboBox.

14.5. Date and Time

The DatePicker, DateTimePicker and TimePicker are special because they handle the control value both
as a string and a Date instance in parallel. The valueFormat is used to parse a string into a Date and
also to format a Date into a string. Because this issue is independent from the locale conventions,
I recommend overwriting the UI5 default using a short format pattern from the current locale and
instead use the component-wide default "date", "time" and "dateTime" patterns for the valueFormat.

On the other hand, the displayFormat should show the date and time strings according to the current
locale conventions. Instead of setting a pattern, we had better just set a format style ("short", "medium", "long", "full") and let UI5 get the related pattern from the LocaleData. The default is to show
the "medium" format.

```
setDateFormats: function(attributeSpec, control, type) {
    let valuePattern = oui5lib.configuration.getDateTimeValuePattern(type); ❶
    if (attributeSpec.ui5.valueFormat) {
        valuePattern = attributeSpec.ui5.valueFormat;
    }
    control.setValueFormat(valuePattern);

    if (attributeSpec.ui5.displayFormat) {
        control.setDisplayFormat(attributeSpec.ui5.displayFormat);
    }
}
```

❶   The configuration uses the following default patterns:
    * date: yyyy-MM-dd,
    * time: HH:mm:ss,
    * dateTime: yyyy-MM-dd HH:mm:ss.

These default patterns can be overwritten with the help of properties in the oui5lib.json configuration file under defaultFormats.

For more information, see java.text.SimpleDateFormat [https://docs.oracle.com/javase/9/docs/
api/java/text/SimpleDateFormat.html].

The DatePicker allows the user both to insert an invalid date string, as well as a different date string
than the Date value it returns. To check these situations, we add a function to the oui5lib.ui namespace:

```
function checkDatePicker(datePicker) {
    const dateValue = datePicker.getDateValue();

    const value = datePicker.getValue();
    const oDate = new Date(value);
    if (oDate == "Invalid Date") {
        datePicker.setValueStateText(oui5lib.util.getI18nText("date.invalid"));
        datePicker.setValueState("Error");
        return false;
    } else if (!(oDate.getFullYear() === dateValue.getFullYear() &&
                 oDate.getMonth() === dateValue.getMonth() &&
                 oDate.getDate() === dateValue.getDate())) {
        datePicker.setValueStateText(
            oui5lib.util.getI18nText("date.unequal") + " " + dateValue.toString()
        );
        datePicker.setValueState("Warning");
        return false;
    }
    datePicker.setValueState("None");
    return true;
}
ui.checkDatePicker = checkDatePicker;
```

We use the function above for the change event of the DatePicker and only set the record to changed
if the inserted value is valid. Otherwise, its valueState is set to either "Error" (not a valid date) or
"Warning" (the date string parses into a different date than the Date we get from the getDateValue
function).

Listing 14.6. FormController: Construct DatePicker

```
 1 getDatePicker: function(entityName, propertyPath) {
 2    const attributeSpec = mapping.getEntityAttributeSpec(entityName, propertyPath);
 3    if (attributeSpec === null) {
 4       return null;
 5    }
 6
 7    const controller = this;
 8    const controlId = this.getControlId(entityName, propertyPath);
 9    const datePicker = new sap.m.DatePicker(controlId, {
10       dateValue : "{" + entityName + ">/" + propertyPath + "}",
11       change: function() {
12          if (oui5lib.ui.checkDatePicker(datePicker)) {
13             datePicker.setValueState("None");
14             controller.setRecordChanged();
15          }
16       }
17    });
18    this.setCommons(attributeSpec, datePicker);
19    this.setDateFormats(attributeSpec, datePicker, "date");
20
21    return datePicker;
22 }
```

The functions to construct the DateTimePicker and TimePicker look very similar. Yet the TimePicker doesn't need an extra check since it does well at preventing the user from inserting an invalid time.

We can further improve the construction of the DatePicker and DateTimePicker by using their minDate and maxDate properties both requiring a Date object. For this, we will add an attribute specification boolean property future. If true, the minDate property is set. If false, the maxDate is set instead.

```
setDateConstraints: function(attributeSpec, control) {
   if (typeof attributeSpec.ui5.future === "boolean") {
      const currentDate = new Date();
      if (attributeSpec.ui5.future) {
         if (control instanceof sap.m.DatePicker) {
            currentDate.setHours(0);
            currentDate.setMinutes(0);
            currentDate.setSeconds(0);
         }
         control.setMinDate(currentDate);
      } else {
         if (control instanceof sap.m.DatePicker) {
            currentDate.setHours(23);
            currentDate.setMinutes(59);
            currentDate.setSeconds(59);
         }
         control.setMaxDate(currentDate);
      }
   }
}
```

 For the DatePicker, we set the time either to the first or last second of the day. For the Date-TimePicker, we can simply take the current date and time.

14.6. Boolean elements

The CheckBox and Switch are the simplest of our selected controls. We bind the boolean value from the model and attach a handler to register that the record was changed. Finally, we set the common properties like we did for all the other controls.

```
getCheckBox: function(entityName, propertyPath) {
    const attributeSpec = mapping.getEntityAttributeSpec(entityName, propertyPath);
    if (attributeSpec === null) {
        return null;
    }
    const controller = this;
    const controlId = this.getControlId(entityName, propertyPath);
    const checkBox = new sap.m.CheckBox(controlId, {
        selected: "{" + entityName + ">/" + propertyPath + "}",
        select: function() {
            controller.setRecordChanged();
        }
    });
    this.setCommons(attributeSpec, checkBox);
    return checkBox;
}
```

14.7. Add form element to a Form or SimpleForm

The FormController should not just construct controls, but also add them to a given form. Before we have a look at that, we will need to take care of the Label. We don't always want to add a label for each form element. Sometimes, we want a row with a label and multiple form elements.

As a convention, the SimpleForm adds a new row to the form if a Label is added to its content aggregation. To keep the use of our function flexible, we will use an optional boolean parameter addLabel, which defaults to true. The following function will only return a Label, if both the parameter addLabel is true and the attribute specification has a i18n.label property. Otherwise, it will return null.

Listing 14.7. FormController: Construct Label

```
getLabel: function(addLabel, attributeSpec, labelFor) {
    if (typeof addLabel !== "boolean" || addLabel) {
        if (attributeSpec.i18n.label) {
            const label = new sap.m.Label({
                text: "{i18n>" + attributeSpec.i18n.label + "}",
                labelFor: labelFor
            });
            if (attributeSpec.required) {
                label.setRequired(true);
            }
            return label;
        }
    }
    return null;
}
```

We can now move on to the function adding a form element to a form. It handles both implementations of a form. It will only add a label, if the above getLabel function returned one.

Listing 14.8. Add Control to Form or SimpleForm

```
addToForm: function(formControl, label, element) {
   if (formControl === null) {
      return;
   }
   if (formControl instanceof sap.ui.layout.form.SimpleForm)        This is a SimpleForm
      if (label !== null) {
         formControl.addContent(label);
      }
      formControl.addContent(element);
   }

   if (formControl instanceof sap.ui.layout.form.FormContainer) {    This is a Form
      const oFormElement = new sap.ui.layout.form.FormElement();
      if (label !== null) {
         oFormElement.setLabel(label);
      }
      oFormElement.addField(element);
      formControl.addFormElement(oFormElement);
   }
}
```

So far, we have implemented functions to construct form element controls and return them. For each of these controls, we will have to add another function to literally add the control to the form. The following example gets the Input (see Listing 14.4, "FormController: Construct Input") and the related Label (Listing 14.7, "FormController: Construct Label") to add both to the form.

```
addInput: function(form, entityName, propertyPath, addLabel) {
   const input = this.getInput(entityName, propertyPath);
   if (input === null) {
      return null;
   }
   const attributeSpec = oui5lib.mapping.getEntityAttributeSpec(entityName,
                                                   propertyPath);
   const label = this.getLabel(addLabel, attributeSpec, input);

   this.addToForm(form, label, input);
   return input;
}
```

 The form parameter accepts either a SimpleForm or a FormContainer. The propertyPath parameter is a string pointing to both the entity attribute name and the model property path.

If we want to add more than one input field to a row, we again have to consider the two different types of forms. It is easy for the SimpleForm, because the SimpleForm will only start a new row if a Label is added to the content.

Using the FormController, adding label and inputs to the SimpleForm only takes a few lines of code in the related view.

```
const firstNameInput = oController.addInput(simpleForm, "exampleEntity", "first_name");
firstNameInput.setMaxLength(20);

oController.addInput(simpleForm, "exampleEntity", "last_name", false);
```

Example form

                    *Name:

For a `FormContainer`, the above code will not work, because we have to add the second form element ('last_name') to the `FormElement` `fields` aggregation. For this, therefore, we need to have another function, specifically for this case. It will add the given element to the last row of the `FormContainer`.

```
addToLastFormElement: function(formContainer, element) {
    if (!(formContainer instanceof sap.ui.layout.form.FormContainer)) {
        return false;
    }
    const formElements = formContainer.getFormElements();
    const formRow = formElements[formElements.length - 1];
    return formRow.addField(element);
}
```

With this function in place, we are now ready to add a label and two form fields to the current last row (`FormElement`) of a `FormContainer`. Analog to the above SimpleForm example, we will have to write:

```
const firstNameInput = oController.addInput(formContainer, "exampleEntity", "first_name");
firstNameInput.setMaxLength(20);

const lastNameInput = oController.getInput("exampleEntity", "last_name");
oController.addToLastFormElement(formContainer, input);
```

We will see more examples of how to use the FormController in the next part of the book, which is about building an example application.

14.8. Summary

The chapter began with an overview of important form controls and their properties. It moved on to look into mapping entries used by a form controller. Step by step, we learned how to generate selected form controls from the mapping. After constructing the form controls, the chapter closed with the issue of adding these controls to a form.

Part III. Building an Example Application

In this chapter, I will try to bring together all the aspects we covered before by building an example application to query, list, create and edit orders. The example application is designed to show the reader solutions for common problems of developing with UI5. For this, we can omit certain parts like payments and shipments and only prepare the handling of particular aspects, like the order status.

We will use the data objects presented in Chapter 12, *Custom data objects*. They greatly simplify UI5 development by allowing us to exclusively focus on the user interface aspects. If you don't want to use separate data objects, the business/domain logic needs to be written either into custom models or the controllers.

Likewise, request handling, form control generation and user input validation are supported by using the code we went through in Chapter 11, *Request Handling*, Chapter 14, *Form Control Generation* and Chapter 13, *Validation*. If you didn't read the second part of the book, you won't know what is going on behind the scenes but should nevertheless be able to make use of the ideas and code presented in the following chapters.

The code presented here is nearly complete, although heavily fragmented. If unsure, you can always find the complete code among the online resources for the book: Code-ExampleApp [https://github.com/cahein/ui5guide/tree/edition_1/Code-ExampleApp].

If you are actually planning to develop a less than trivial application with UI5, this part of the book should be most useful to study carefully.

Table of Contents

Chapter 15. Beginning application development

Our starting point is the template component from the oui5lib project. It is basically the same as the one we built in Chapter 2, *Building a basic responsive Web Application*. At the time of writing, the main difference between these templates is that the one from the oui5lib project has two custom namespaces to separate generally useful code (namespace `oui5lib`) from application specific code (namespace `oum`).

To get the template component, please visit the oui5lib project [https://github.com/cahein/oui5lib]. You can either copy the required files from the `examples/ComponentTemplate` folder, or have the component template generated. You will find the instructions on how to do this in the `templates/README.md`.

For our example application, the `sap-ui-bootstrap` script tag in the `index.html` is expected to have the following entries:

```
data-sap-ui-libs="sap.m, sap.ui.layout"          Namespace sap.ui.layout is required for forms
data-sap-ui-bindingSyntax="complex"
data-sap-ui-resourceroots='{
    "oum": ".",
    "oum.do": "./domainObjects",                 Resource root for the custom data objects
    "oui5lib": "./oui5lib"
}'
```

For the domain data, we are going to use the mappings and custom data objects introduced in Chapter 12, *Custom data objects*. You will find the required files among the online resources for this book at Code-DomainObjects [https://github.com/cahein/ui5manual/tree/edition_1/Code-Domain-Objects]. Make sure to have the `mappingDirectory` property set in the `oui5lib.json`, and that the mapping files can indeed be found there. Likewise, the custom data collection and entity objects are expected to be found by UI5 with the help of the resource root entry for `oum.do`.

Furthermore, we will use the `Loader` (Listing 11.8, "Namespace oum.do.Loader: loading domain data") and `RefsHandler` (Section 12.4, "Handle referenced data") to load domain data into the collection objects.

We load most required code early by adding the following to the `lib/init.js`, which will be executed upon entering the component:

```
sap.ui.require([
    "oum/do/RefsHandler",
    "oum/do/Loader",
    "oum/do/orders",
    "oum/do/Order",
    "oum/do/addresses",
    "oum/do/Address",
    "oum/do/products",
    "oum/do/Product"
], function() {
    oui5lib.logger.info("Loader is ready");
});
```

We don't include the `oum.do.statuses` and `oum.do.countries` collection objects, because they are designed to request their data upon being loaded. We will require them only when needed.

The application is now prepared. Our development environment is being completed by starting the mock-server, which is a small ruby application built with the help of Sinatra. You need to have the sinatra and logger gems installed to be able to start the server. You can download the code from the online resources at Code-ExampleApp/MockServer [https://github.com/cahein/ui5manual/tree/edition_1/Code-ExampleApp/MockServer].

```
cahein@nobux:~/projects/book/Code-ExampleApp/MockServer$ ruby main.rb
== Sinatra (v2.0.3) has taken the stage on 3000 for development with backup from Thin
Thin web server (v1.7.2 codename Bachmanity)
Maximum connections set to 1024
Listening on 0.0.0.0:3000, CTRL+C to stop
```

 If you don't want to, or can't use the mock-server provided by the author, but want to run the example application, you can either use a `sap.ui.core.util.MockServer`, or use the approach explained in Section 11.2.3, "Prepare environments" and used in Section 11.3.1, "Setup for testing".

15.1. Manifest

A good point to start developing is the application manifest, which provides basic information about the application we will build. Because we plan to use the `Router` to navigate to the application views, we will add three routes to the manifest, one route for the orders list and two routes for order details. The order route has an optional `id` parameter and gets an array of targets for the order navigation and the overview. The order address route requires an `id` (the order ID) and a `type` ('billing' or 'shipping' address) parameter.

```
{
    "pattern": "orders",
    "name": "ordersList",
    "target": "ordersList"
},{
    "pattern": "order/:id:",                    Optional parameter: Order id
    "name": "order",
    "target": ["orderOverview", "orderNav"]
},{
    "pattern": "order/{id}/address/{type}",     Mandatory parameters: Order id and Address type
    "name": "orderAddress",
    "target": ["orderAddress", "orderNav"]
}
```

The routes above refer to four targets, three of them for the `SplitApp`. We have to add these targets to the targets section of the manifest. Because of the default configuration (see Listing 2.5, "Routing section of the manifest") the 'ordersList' target just needs a view name. The other targets need to also specify the `parent`, `controlId` and `controlAggregation`.

```
"ordersList": {
   "viewName": "orders"
},
"orderNav": {
   "parent": "splitApp",
   "viewName": "orderNavigation",
   "controlId": "oumSplitApp",
   "controlAggregation": "masterPages"
},
"orderOverview": {
   "parent": "splitApp",
   "viewName": "order",
   "controlId": "oumSplitApp",
   "controlAggregation": "detailPages"
},
"orderAddress": {
   "parent": "splitApp",
   "viewName": "orderAddress",
   "controlId": "oumSplitApp",
   "controlAggregation": "detailPages"
}
```

After editing the manifest, we want to add two tiles to the entry page. One to navigate to a view to query and list orders, and another to create a new order. This is done by adding entries to the config.json entryPoints (see Listing 2.28, "Add Tiles to Page"). As always, we won't want to forget to add the related keys to the i18n property files.

```
"entryPoints": [
   {
      "header" : "{i18n>tiles.orders.header}",
      "footer" : "{i18n>tiles.orders.footer}",
      "tooltip" : "{i18n>orders.tooltip}",
      "icon" : "sap-icon://my-sales-order",
      "iconText" : "{i18n>tiles.orders.iconText}",
      "routeName" : "ordersList"
   },
   {
      "header" : "{i18n>tiles.order.header}",
      "footer" : "{i18n>tiles.order.footer}",
      "tooltip" : "{i18n>order.tooltip}",
      "icon" : "sap-icon://my-sales-order",
      "iconText" : "{i18n>tiles.order.iconText}",
      "routeName" : "order"
   }
   ...
]
```

So far, we have gone through the preparatory steps to get our application up and running.

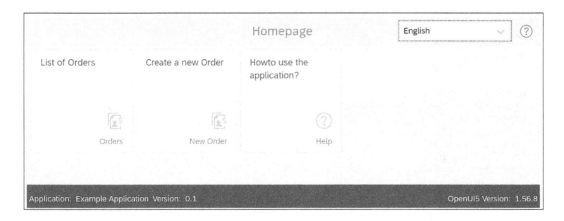

15.2. Common issues

Before we get to the orders view, there are some things to consider which concern all views and controllers of our application.

15.2.1. Non-disruptive message for the receiving view

Frequently, we want to exit one view and have the next view display a message, giving the user a non-disruptive feedback message about some action. For example, after saving an order, we navigate to the orders list and want to show a message that the order has been successfully saved.

We can't simply use the MessageToast, because it disappears as soon as the navigation happens, regardless of how long we set its duration property. We could defer navigation using the JavaScript setTimeout function, but that would confuse the application flow.

We could get the receiving view by its ID and add a message to its content. But we want to keep each view/controller code separate from other views and also don't want to begin worrying about view IDs.

We could add optional parameters to the route patterns, in effect carrying a one-time message as URL-appended hash string. But that would run contrary to our efforts to make the URLs bookmarkable.

A feasible way would be to publish an event on the component level. Each view could subscribe to messages addressed to itself. But at what stage do we remove the received message or messages? That looks like a lot of complication for a simple thing. After all, we just want to hand a message to the next view.

All these approaches are not satisfying to me. My preferred solution entails reserving a custom property for a message object, so oum.message for the purpose of our example. The route matched handlers can check if there is a message and act upon it. Afterwards, the message is immediately deleted.

Again, it helps to normalize things through convention. Here, we assume that every view has a sap.m.VBox container for messages. The VBox is a specialized sap.m.FlexBox. To minimalize the code to show such a message, we need a common function. You might wonder, where to add it? It seems too much convention for the general oui5lib library because how to present a message seems a question of application design. Instead, the function goes into the oum.lib.ui namespace.

```
(function() {
    const ui = oum.namespace("lib.ui");                    Namespace oum.lib.ui

    function handleMessage(messagesContainer) {
        if (typeof messagesContainer.removeAllItems === "function" && ❶
            typeof messagesContainer.addItem === "function") {
            messagesContainer.removeAllItems();            Clear current messages

            if (typeof oum.message !== "undefined") {
                messagesContainer.addItem(                 Add message
                    new sap.m.MessageStrip({
                        text: oum.message.text,
                        type: oum.message.type,
                        showIcon: true
                    })
                );
            }
        }
        delete oum.message;                                Delete message object
    }
    ui.handleMessage = handleMessage;                      Add function to namespace
}());
```

❶   To be most flexible regarding the given `messagesContainer` object, we test the availability of
     the functions we will use. This way, the given container could be a `sap.m.FlexBox` or one of its
     subclasses (`VBox`, `HBox`).

Now, we only need to have the connected controllers attach a handler function to the route pattern
matched event and call the `handleMessage` function. We will soon get to an example (Listing 15.3,
"Initial orders controller").

15.2.2. Request failure events

The other issue concerns the request failure events. When a request is sent, the application usually
has to visually indicate that it is waiting for a response. In UI5 this is done using the `busy` property
inherited by every subclass of `sap.ui.core.Control`. Often the `View` is set to busy, or some content control
like a `List` or `Form`.

Using the `oui5lib.request` functions means to handle request failure events separately from the current
view and controller (see Listing 11.1, "Namespace oui5lib.request"). If such an error occurs, we need
to be able to unset the `busy` state and display some useful error message. And because it is quite a
long way to get the current view from the component, and even longer to get a particular control set
to busy, it is much easier to set and unset the busy state of the `UIComponent` root control. We add such
a function to the `oum.lib.ui` namespace.

```
function setBusy(isBusy, delay) {
   if (typeof delay !== "number") {
      delay = 300;                                            Default delay in milliseconds
   }
   const component = oui5lib.configuration.getComponent();
   const rootControl = component.getRootControl();
   if (isBusy) {
      rootControl.setBusyIndicatorDelay(delay).setBusy(true);
   } else {
      rootControl.setBusy(false);
   }
}
ui.setBusy = setBusy;
```

The request failure event handler function primarily has to take care of generating an informative error message to be presented to the user. Of course, it may also try to post to some server to send a notification about the error to responsible system administrators. There is no general way of dealing with these errors.

```
(function() {
    const eventHandlers = oum.namespace("lib.eventHandlers");          Namespace oum.lib.eventHandlers

    function handleRequestFailure(channelId, eventId, eventData) { ❶
        oui5lib.logger.error("request error: " + eventId);
        const xhr = eventData.xhrObj;

        let msg = "";

        switch(eventId) {
        case "error":
            msg = oui5lib.util.getI18nText("request.error", [
                eventData.entity
            ]);
            break;
        case "status":
            msg = oui5lib.util.getI18nText("request.status", [
                xhr.status, eventData.entity, eventData.request
            ]);
            break;
        case "timeout":
            msg = oui5lib.util.getI18nText("request.timeout", [
                eventData.entity
            ]);
            break;
        }

        oui5lib.messages.showErrorMessage(msg);
        oum.lib.ui.setBusy(false);                                     Unset busy state
    }
    eventHandlers.handleRequestFailure = handleRequestFailure;         Add function to namespace
}());
```

❶   The channelId is always "xhr". The eventId matches the related XMLHttpRequest events (error, status and timeout). The eventData object has further properties helping us to investigate the error (entity, request, requestParameters, and the XMLHttpRequest object xhrObj).

After adding both the "oum/lib/ui" and "oum/lib/eventHandlers" as dependencies to the Component.js we are ready to subscribe to the request failure events. Because these events concern the whole component, the best place to do this is in the Component.onInit function.

```
const eventBus = this.getEventBus();
eventBus.subscribe("xhr", "status", oum.lib.eventHandlers.handleRequestFailure);
eventBus.subscribe("xhr", "error", oum.lib.eventHandlers.handleRequestFailure);
eventBus.subscribe("xhr", "timeout", oum.lib.eventHandlers.handleRequestFailure);
```

15.3. First view: A List of Orders

For the example orders view we use the sap.m.Page to be loaded into the App root control. Let us begin with the landmarks to clarify the structure of the orders view we are going to construct.

```
const landmarkInfo = new sap.m.PageAccessibleLandmarkInfo({
    rootLabel: "Query and list orders",
    headerRole: "Navigation",
    headerLabel: "Navigate home, back and to the help page",
    subHeaderRole: "Search",
    subHeaderLabel: "Filter orders field and toggle order form button",
    contentLabel: "The query form and the list of orders",
    footerRole: "None"
});
```

The orders view header provides basic navigation buttons. For this, we will use the customHeader aggregation. The header is a good candidate for a fragment because we can reuse it for the order and orderAddress views, which we will construct in the following chapters.

Our header Bar has a BackButton on the left side, a Title in the middle and both a HomeButton and HelpButton on the right side. Initially, the title property text remains empty because it depends upon the route.

Listing 15.1. Fragment returning a Bar with Back and Home navigation

```
sap.ui.jsfragment("oum.fragment.NavigationHeader", {
    createContent: function(oController) {
        const headerTitle = new sap.m.Title(oController.getView().createId("pageTitle"), {
            level: "H2", titleStyle: "H4"
        });
        const headerBar = new sap.m.Bar({
            contentLeft: [
                sap.ui.jsfragment("oui5lib.fragment.BackButton", oController)
            ],
            contentMiddle: [ headerTitle ],
            contentRight: [
                sap.ui.jsfragment("oui5lib.fragment.HomeButton", oController),
                sap.ui.jsfragment("oum.fragment.HelpButton")
            ]
        });
        return headerBar;
    }
});
```

Here is a screenshot of our NavigationHeader fragment:

<

The initial orders view connects to a controller with the same name (orders). It has the NavigationHeader fragment set to the customHeader aggregation. For now, the only content is a container for messages.

Listing 15.2. Initial orders view

```
sap.ui.jsview("oum.view.orders", {
   getControllerName : function() {
      return "oum.controller.orders";
   },

   createContent : function(oController) {
      return new sap.m.Page({
         landmarkInfo: landmarkInfo,
         customHeader: sap.ui.jsfragment("oui5lib.fragment.NavigationHeader", oController),
         content: [
            new sap.m.VBox(this.createId("messagesContainer"))
         ]
      });
   }
});
```

We prepare the initial orders controller to extend the oui5lib.controller.BaseController (see Listing 2.29, "A custom BaseController"), and declare our Loader, and the order and status collection objects as dependencies.

Listing 15.3. Initial orders controller

```
sap.ui.define([
   "oui5lib/controller/BaseController",
   "oum/do/Loader",
   "oum/do/orders",
   "oum/do/statuses",
   "oum/lib/ui"
], function(Controller, Loader, orders, statuses, ui) {
   "use strict";

   const ordersController = Controller.extend("oum.controller.orders", {
      onInit: function() {
         this.getRouter().getRoute("ordersList").attachPatternMatched(
            this._onRouteMatched, this);
         }
      },
      _onRouteMatched: function() {
         const messagesContainer = this.getView().byId("messagesContainer");
         ui.handleMessage(messagesContainer);                              Any message for the view?

         this.setHeaderTitle();
      },
      setHeaderTitle: function() {
         const pageTitle = this.getView().byId("pageTitle");
         pageTitle.setText(oui5lib.util.getI18nText("ordersPage.title"));
      }
   );
   return ordersController;
});
```

Successively, we are going to add functionality to the controller. For now, we want to return to the orders view.

15.3.1. Preparing the item template

We use a `sap.m.List` with an `sap.m.ObjectListItem` as item template to present the orders data. The list item needs to show the customer name, the order total and currency, the order date and status. If needed, we can add further properties later. The list item `type` is set to `Active`, which means that the `press` event will be triggered when the item is pressed.

```
1 const itemTemplate = new sap.m.ObjectListItem({
2    title: "{billingName}",
3    number: "{total}",
4    numberUnit: "{currency}",
5    type: "Active",                              Enumeration sap.m.ListType
6    press: function(oEvent) {
7        oController.showOrderDetails(oEvent);    Controller function to navigate to the order
8    }
9 });
```

 Here, the model paths (lines 2 to 4) don't have a model name because we will set the orders model directly to the `List`, thereby minimizing the potential of any clashes with other models.

The `showOrderDetails` function needs the order ID to navigate to the order details. To avoid having to go through the binding context to get the order data and the ID property (see Listing 8.3, "How to get the item data from a ListBase event"), it is easier to add the order ID to the list template `customData` aggregation.

```
const itemData = new sap.ui.core.CustomData({ key: "orderId" });
itemData.bindProperty("value", "id");

itemTemplate.addCustomData(itemData);
```

With the `CustomData` added, writing the controller `showOrderDetails` function to navigate to the order details is straightforward:

```
showOrderDetails: function(oEvent) {
    const item = oEvent.getSource();
    const orderId = item.data("orderId");          Get custom data by key

    this.info("navigate to detail view of order: " + orderId);
    this.getRouter().vNavTo("order", { id: orderId });
}
```

In addition to the billing customer name and order total, the order item also needs to show the order status and date. Let us begin with the order status.

We want certain order statuses to be visually highlighted to draw attention to it. The `sap.m.ObjectStatus` control provides colorization of values depending upon the `ValueState`. And the `ObjectListItem` has two aggregations for an `ObjectStatus` (`firstStatus` and `secondStatus`), both positioned on the right side of the item. For the example code, see Listing 8.1, "Construct an ObjectListItem".

As `text`, we show the language specific `statusText` being added in Listing 12.3, "A statuses collection object". As `state`, we use the `valueState` property assumed to be available in the status data.

15.3.1.1. Displaying the order date

The original incoming order date value is a string carried as JSON, which we convert into a JavaScript `Date` instance (see Listing 12.12, "Process incoming order data"). To display the date, we now need to format the date object back into a string. Because the string expression of date and time is regionally different, we want to format the date depending upon the chosen language.

A Date object is formatted into a string using date patterns. As a default, we use the date formats of the current sap.ui.core.Locale.

The following getDateTimeDisplayPattern function returns the format pattern for the current Locale. It requires two parameters. A type, which can be 'dateTime', 'date' or 'time'. And a style, which can be 'short', 'medium', 'long' or 'full'. Because it is a generally useful function, we add it to the oui5lib.configuration namespace.

Listing 15.4. Function to get date/time pattern

```
/**
 * @param {string} type Possible values: "dateTime", "date", "time".
 * @param {string} style Possible values: "short", "medium", "long", "full".
 */
function getDateTimeDisplayPattern(type, style) {
   const ui5Locale = new sap.ui.core.Locale(getCurrentLanguage());
   const ui5LocaleData = new sap.ui.core.LocaleData(ui5Locale);

   switch (type) {
   case "dateTime": {
      let pattern = ui5LocaleData.getDateTimePattern(style);        'en' long: "{1} 'at' {0}"
      pattern = pattern.replace("{1}", ui5LocaleData.getDatePattern(style));
      pattern = pattern.replace("{0}", ui5LocaleData.getTimePattern(style));
      return pattern;
   }
   case "date":
      return ui5LocaleData.getDatePattern(style);                   'en' long: "MMMM d, y"
   case "time":
      return ui5LocaleData.getTimePattern(style);                   'en' long: "h:mm:ss a z"
   default:
      return undefined;
   }
}
configuration.getDateTimeDisplayPattern = getDateTimeDisplayPattern;
```

To add the order date to the item template attributes aggregation, we use an sap.m.ObjectAttribute. This is one of the cases where the path/formatter notation comes in handy (see Section 7.7.2, "Formatting values for display").

```
const dateAttr = new sap.m.ObjectAttribute({
   title: "{i18n>order.orderDate}",
   text: {
      path: "orderDate",
      formatter: function(dateObject) {
         return oController.formatOrderDate(dateObject);
      }
   }
});
itemTemplate.addAttribute(dateAttr);
```

Our custom formatter function (formatOrderDate) needs to be added to the connected orders.controller.js. It will be called for every order line. To save unnecessary computing steps, we want to store the date display pattern as a controller property.

Here, we have a device dependency issue because the various date format styles result in strings of different length. Longer strings are usually easier to identify, but not fitting when the visible space is limited. We, therefore, want to use a different style for different screen widths.

UI5 collects information about the used device, the browser and the operating system under the namespace `sap.ui.Device`. It also provides handlers for related events, like resizing or changing the orientation of the display. In this case, we want to attach a function to the event that the available visible width changes.

```
onInit: function() {
    ...

    const mediaRangeSets = sap.ui.Device.media.RANGESETS.SAP_STANDARD;

    sap.ui.Device.media.attachHandler(
        this._handleMediaWidthChanged, this, mediaRangeSets);
    this._handleMediaWidthChanged(
        sap.ui.Device.media.getCurrentRange(mediaRangeSets));
}

handleMediaSizeChanged: function(mParams) {
    let style;

    switch(mParams.name) {
    case "Phone":
        style = "short";
        break;
    case "Tablet":
        style = "medium";
        break;
    default:
        style = "long";
    }

    this._dateTimeDisplayPattern = oui5lib.configuration        Store 'dateTime' display pattern
        .getDateTimeDisplayPattern("dateTime", style);
    this._dateDisplayPattern = oui5lib.configuration            Store 'date' display pattern
        .getDateTimeDisplayPattern("date", style);

    const ordersList = this.getView().byId("ordersList"); ❶
    const model = ordersList.getModel();
    if (model !== undefined) {
        model.updateBindings(true);
    }
}
```

❶ At this point, we haven't constructed the `ordersList` control and also haven't provided a model for it yet. We will get to these steps next. For now, it is important to understand that after updating the pattern we need to update the related model bindings to reflect that change.

After solving the issue of the date format pattern, the custom formatter function has just a few lines. We use the static class `sap.ui.core.format.DateFormat` to do the actual formatting.

```
formatOrderDate: function(dateObject) {
    const oDateFormat = sap.ui.core.format.DateFormat.getDateTimeInstance({
        pattern: this._dateTimeDisplayPattern          Use the stored 'dateTime' display pattern
    });
    return oDateFormat.format(dateObject);
}
```

15.3.2. Construct the list and query orders data

Our list item template is now prepared, so that we can construct the List and bind the model path to
its items aggregation. We also add a Sorter to sort the orders by the order date.

Because we are going to set the orders model to the List, we want to be able to conveniently access
the control in the controller by an ID. As usual, we let the view create the control ID to avoid any
ID duplication.

```
const oSorter= [];
oSorter.push(new sap.ui.model.Sorter("orderDate", true));        Default sort order

const ordersList = new sap.m.List(this.createId("ordersList"), {
    headerText: "{i18n>ordersPage.list.headerText}",
    growing: true
});
ordersList.bindAggregation("items", {
    path: "/",
    template: itemTemplate,
    sorter: oSorter
});
```

Moving to the controller parts, we need to query orders data and handle the related events. For this, we
will use the queryOrders function of our custom Loader (see Listing 11.8, "Namespace oum.do.Loader:
loading domain data").

The query parameters object is provided by a getQueryData function. We initially set the startDate to
60 days back and limit the statuses to 'active' orders most likely needing attention and handling.

Listing 15.5. Query Orders

```
 1 getQueryData: function() {
 2     if (this._queryData === undefined) {
 3         const startDate = new Date();
 4         startDate.setDate(startDate.getDate() - 60);          Start 60 days ago
 5         this._queryData = {
 6             "startDate": startDate,
 7             "endDate": null,
 8             "statuses": [ "pending", "processing", "payment_overdue" ]
 9         };
10     }
11     return this._queryData;
12 },
13
14 queryOrders: function() {
15     ui.setBusy(true);                                          Show busy indicator
16     orders.resetData();                                        Clear orders collection
17     Loader.queryOrders(this.getQueryData());                   Call the oum.do.Loader
18 }
```

In case of a successful response to our `queryOrders` request, we expect an event about the orders query result being available. It will either come from the `Loader` when there are no orders matching the query parameters, or from the `RefsHandler` publishing a 'loading ready' event when all requested orders are fully loaded and processed, including the related addresses and products. Therefore, we want to subscribe to the event and attach the `_handleLoaded` to it.

The `_handleLoaded` function is responsible for setting the orders model to the list. We get the model from the orders collection. It is always the same model holding whatever collection data we have. The order model is set for the list once (line 17) and otherwise calls the models `updateBindings` function to refresh the view (line 19).

Listing 15.6. Controller subscribing to 'loading ready' events

```
 1 onInit: function() {
 2    ...
 3
 4    const eventBus = sap.ui.getCore().getEventBus();
 5    eventBus.subscribe("loading", "ready", this._handleLoaded, this);
 6
 7    this.queryOrders();
 8 },
 9
10 _handleLoaded: function(channel, event, eventData) {
11    if (typeof eventData === "string") {
12       switch (eventData) {
13       case "orders": {
14          const ordersList = this.getView().byId("ordersList");
15          const model = ordersList.getModel();
16          if (model === undefined) {
17             ordersList.setModel(orders.getModel());
18          } else {
19             model.updateBindings();
20          }
21          ui.setBusy(false);                          Unset busy state
22          break;
23       }
24    }
25 }
```

After adding the orders list to the `Page content` aggregation, we can reload the `orders` route and should now see the list of orders. Here, it is a simulated phone in portrait mode with a short date format.

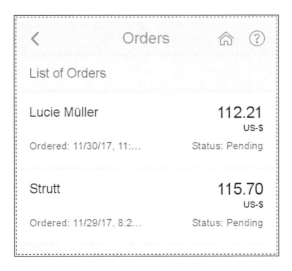

15.3.3. Adding a page sub-header toolbar

There are at least two things missing in this view. One is a search input field to find particular orders in the list. The other is to show information about the currently used query parameters.

For the search, we will use the SearchField control. Here, we will use the liveChange event. It needs to be used with care because it is repeatedly triggered with each change of the value in the input field. But it is a nice feature for the user to see an immediate result. However, if the list is too long, this can result in unacceptable user interface delays.

```
const searchField = new sap.m.SearchField({
   width: "150px",
   showSearchButton: false,
   tooltip: "{i18n>ordersPage.searchField.tooltip}",
   liveChange: function(oEvent) {
      oController.searchOrders(oEvent);
   }
});
```

The searchOrders controller function first gets the search string. If it is shorter than three characters, we set the string so that the filter will match all list entries. For simplicity, we only use one Filter matching all entries where the billing address name contains the given search string. For more detailed information on how to use filters, see Section 8.6, "Filtering and Searching".

```
searchOrders: function(oEvent) {
   let searchString = oEvent.getParameter("newValue");
   if (searchString.length < 3) {
      searchString = "";
   }

   const filterArray = [
      new sap.ui.model.Filter("billingName", "Contains", searchString)
   ];

   const ordersList = this.getView().byId("ordersList");
   ordersList.getBinding("items").filter(filterArray);
}
```

After taking care of providing a search input field, we are now getting to the presentation of current query parameters. To show the query parameters, we will use a simple sap.m.Text control. Initially, the text is empty.

```
const queryText = new sap.m.Text(this.createId("queryText"));
```

When the query results come in, we want to show a text explaining the used query parameters. The following function generates such a text and sets it to the text property of the Text control.

```
setQueryText: function() {
    const oDateFormat = sap.ui.core.format.DateFormat.getDateTimeInstance({
        pattern: this._dateDisplayPattern                    Use the stored 'date' display pattern
    });

    const queryData = this.getQueryData();                   See Listing 15.5, "Query Orders"
    const startDateString = oDateFormat.format(queryData.startDate);

    let endDateString;
    if (queryData.endDate === null) {
        endDateString = oui5lib.util.getI18nText("common.now");
    } else {
        endDateString = oDateFormat.format(queryData.endDate);
    }

    let statusText = "";
    const selectedStatuses = queryData.statuses;
    for (let i = 0, s = selectedStatuses.length; i < s; i++) {
        if (i > 0) {
            statusText += ", ";
        }
        statusText += oui5lib.util.getI18nText("orderStatus." + selectedStatuses[i]);
    }

    const queryText = oui5lib.util.getI18nText("ordersPage.queryText", ❶
                                        [startDateString, endDateString, statusText]);

    const queryTextControl = this.getView().byId("queryText");
    queryTextControl.setText(queryText);
}
```

❶ In this case, our i18n resource property value uses placeholders: 'Orders from {0} until {1}. \nStatuses: {2}'. Our utility function Listing 6.8, "Utitily function to get I18n resource property" will take care of replacing the '{n}' placeholders.

Whenever we receive a 'loading ready' event for orders, the query text has to be updated. Therefore, we want to add the function call to the _handleLoaded function of Listing 15.6, "Controller subscribing to 'loading ready' events".

```
_handleLoaded: function(channel, event, eventData) {
    if (typeof eventData === "string") {
        switch (eventData) {
        case "orders": {
            ...
            this.setQueryText();
            break;
        }
    }
}
```

But where can we add the controls? Unfortunately, the content of the List headerToolbar and info-
Toolbar aggregations disappear out of view when the list is scrolled down far enough. This is not
what we want here because refining the query should not require scrolling up. Luckily, the content
of the Page subHeader aggregation always remains on top of the page. Therefore, we prefer to add the
query controls to this aggregation. Regardless of our choice, all the above mentioned aggregations
accept an OverflowToolbar.

```
const queryToolbar = new sap.m.OverflowToolbar({
    content: [ searchField, queryText ]
});
```

At this point, the orders Page control should look like this:

```
return new sap.m.Page({
    landmarkInfo: landmarkInfo,
    customHeader: headerBar,
    showSubHeader: true,
    subHeader: queryToolbar,
    content: [
        new sap.m.VBox(this.createId("messagesContainer")),
        ordersList
    ]
});
```

15.3.4. Query Form

On top of listing the orders, the interface needs to allow the user to modify the predefined query
parameters and request orders matching the updated query. For this, we are going to construct a query
form.

For the start and end dates, we use the DatePicker control.

```
const startDate = new sap.m.DatePicker({
    dateValue: "{/startDate}",
    width: "200px"
});
const endDate = new sap.m.DatePicker({
    dateValue: "{/endDate}",
    width: "200px"
});
```

More difficult is the choice of the control for the order statuses. A `MultiComboBox` is just an input field. If several entries are selected, the input field will not be wide enough to display all selected statuses. A `SelectDialog` is well suited for a long list which requires search functionality but not needed for the relatively short list of statuses. A `List` with `mode` "MultiSelect" seems most appropriate.

```
const statusList = new sap.m.List(this.createId("statusList"), {
   mode: "MultiSelect"                               Enumeration sap.m.ListMode
});
const statusItem = new sap.m.StandardListItem({
   title: "{statuses>statusText}",
   selected: "{statuses>selected}"                   Boolean value
});
statusList.bindAggregation("items", {
   path: "statuses>/",                               Bind 'statuses' model
   template: statusItem
});
```

Which model should we use for the `List`? The `oum.do.statuses` collection object (see Listing 12.3, "A statuses collection object") is already prepared to have a language-specific property `statusText`. For the status list, we need to add a boolean property `selected` to indicate which statuses are selected.

Listing 15.7. Set Model to Status List

```
setStatusesModel: function() {
   const selectedStatuses = this.getQueryData().statuses;    Get the currently selected statuses

   const statusData = statuses.getData();                    Get all statuses from the collection object
   statusData.forEach(function(statusItem) {
      if (selectedStatuses.indexOf(statusItem.status) > -1) {
         statusItem.selected = true;
      } else {
         statusItem.selected = false;
      }
   });

   const statusList = this.getView().byId("statusList");
   statusList.setModel(statuses.getModel(), "statuses");     Set the 'statuses' model for the List
}
```

We also need a `Button` to submit the query.

```
const submitButton = new sap.m.Button({
   width: "140px",
   text: "{i18n>ordersPage.query.submit}",
   tooltip: "{i18n>ordersPage.query.submit.tooltip}",
   press: function() {
      oController.submitQueryForm();
   }
});
```

At this point, we have prepared all the pieces for the query form. Instead of the `SimpleForm`, we will use the `Form` with two `FormContainer` controls. We put the dates in one container and the statuses in another. This way, the form will adjust better to different screen sizes because the statuses are always kept together in a `FormContainer`. If the width permits, both containers are displayed side by side. If not, the statuses container will appear below the dates container.

```
const datesContainer = new sap.ui.layout.form.FormContainer({
    formElements: [
        new sap.ui.layout.form.FormElement({
            label: "{i18n>orders.query.startDate.label}",
            fields: [ startDate ]                              DatePicker for the start date
        }),
        new sap.ui.layout.form.FormElement({
            label: "{i18n>orders.query.endDate.label}",
            fields: [ endDate ]                                DatePicker for the end date
        })
    ]
});

const statusContainer = new sap.ui.layout.form.FormContainer({
    formElements: [
        new sap.ui.layout.form.FormElement({
            label: "{i18n>orders.query.status}",
            fields: [ statusList ]                             Multi-select list of statuses
        }),
        new sap.ui.layout.form.FormElement({
            label: "{i18n>orders.query.actions}",
            fields: [ submitButton ]                           Submit button
        })
    ]
});
```

Now, we construct the Form with the containers above. The ID is set to conveniently access the control in the controller. The query form is a good example of content for a fragment. Not mainly for reusability, but to separate the related code from the other view code. So, we will wrap all the view code belonging to the query form into a fragment.

```
sap.ui.jsfragment("oum.fragment.OrdersQueryForm", {
    createContent: function (oController) {
        ...

        const queryForm = new sap.ui.layout.form.Form(this.createId("queryForm"), {
            editable: true,
            visible: false,                                    Initially invisible
            layout: [
                new sap.ui.layout.form.ResponsiveGridLayout({
                    labelSpanL: 3, columnsL: 3,
                    labelSpanM: 2, columnsM: 2
                })
            ],
            formContainers: [ datesContainer, statusContainer ],
            toolbar: new sap.m.Toolbar({
                content: [
                    new sap.m.Title({
                        text: "{i18n>orders.queryForm.title}"
                    }),
                    submitButton.clone() ❶
                ]
            })
        });
        return queryForm;
    }
});
```

❶ We have already added a submit button at the end of the statuses list. This is convenient when the user changes the statuses, but may require unnecessary scrolling if he or she only wants to change the query dates. Thus, we will add the button again at the top of the query form.

As a highly attentive reader, you will surely have noticed that the form above is set to be invisible. Why is that? To answer that, we will need to think about another question. How do we integrate the form into the user interface? We could open the orders query form in a Dialog or even in another Page. Here, we are going to add it to the orders list page and show/hide it with a button. This is why it is initially hidden.

To show/hide the form, we add a Button to the OverflowToolbar to be used as the Page subHeader.

```
const queryToolbar = new sap.m.OverflowToolbar({
   content: [
      searchField, queryText,
      new sap.m.ToolbarSpacer(),
      new sap.m.Button(this.createId("toggleFormButton"), {
         icon: "sap-icon://hide",
         text: "{i18n>orders.queryForm.button.open}",
         press: function() {
            oController.toggleQueryForm();
         }
      })
   ]
});
```

The attached controller function not only toggles the visibility of the query form. It also changes the icon and text properties of the Button accordingly. And when the form is shown, we also scroll to the top to ensure that it is always visible.

```
toggleQueryForm: function() {
   const button = this.getView().byId("toggleFormButton");
   const queryForm = this.getView().byId("queryForm");

   if (queryForm.getVisible()) {
      queryForm.setVisible(false);
      button.setIcon("sap-icon://hide");
      button.setText(oui5lib.util.getI18nText("queryForm.button.open"));
   }
   else {
      queryForm.setVisible(true);
      button.setIcon("sap-icon://show");
      button.setText(oui5lib.util.getI18nText("queryForm.button.close"));

      const page = this.getView().getContent()[0];
      page.scrollTo(0);
   }
}
```

So far, we have written the function to set the statuses model to the status list (see Listing 15.7, "Set Model to Status List") but haven't actually called it. We also haven't provided a model for the order query start and end dates of the query form.

When the view is initialized, we don't know if the statuses object is already initialized or not. If the statuses are already loaded, we can set the model in the controller onInit function.

```
onInit: function() {
   ...

   if (statuses.isInitialized()) {
      this.setStatusesModel();
   }
   const queryForm = this.getView().byId("queryForm");
   queryForm.setModel(
      new sap.ui.model.json.JSONModel(this.getQueryData())      See Listing 15.5, "Query Orders"
   );
}
```

If the statuses are not yet loaded upon initialization of the controller, we use the 'loading ready' event
published by the statuses collection object (see Listing 12.3, "A statuses collection object").

```
_handleLoaded: function(channel, event, eventData) {
   if (typeof eventData === "string") {
      switch (eventData) {
      case "orders":
         ...
         break;
      case "statuses":
         this.setStatusesModel();                              See Listing 15.7, "Set Model to Status List"
         break;
      }
   }
}
```

Our final orders Page is constructed like this:

```
return new sap.m.Page({
   landmarkInfo: landmarkInfo,
   customHeader: headerBar,
   showSubHeader: true,
   subHeader: queryToolbar,
   content: [
      new sap.m.VBox(this.createId("messagesContainer")),
      sap.ui.jsfragment("oum.fragment.OrdersQueryForm", oController),
      ordersList
   ]
});
```

We haven't yet provided the submitQueryForm function attached to the press event of our submit query Button.

To run the actual query, we need to prepare the parameters for the queryOrders request, which we specified in Listing 10.3, "Example mapping: specify order requests". Due to the TwoWay binding of the JSONModel set to the query form, the start and end date values are updated by the form controls. But the statuses need to be processed. We first get the 'statuses' model from the status list and collect all selected statuses into an array. This array is then set to the statuses property of the query parameters.

After preparing the query parameters, we call the function to query the orders (see Listing 15.5, "Query Orders"). If the requests run successfully, the 'loading ready' event will be published for the orders to be handled by the _handleLoaded function (see Listing 15.6, "Controller subscribing to 'loading ready' events").

```
submitQueryForm: function() {
   const statusList = this.getView().byId("statusList");
   const statusData = statusList.getModel("statuses").getData();

   const selectedStatuses = [];
   statusData.forEach(function(statusItem) {
      if (statusItem.selected) {
         selectedStatuses.push(statusItem.status);        The item is selected
      }
   });
   this.getQueryData().statuses = selectedStatuses;        Set statuses parameter

   this.queryOrders();
   this.toggleQueryForm(); ❶
}
```

❶   After querying the orders, we hide the query form to make space for the results.

The orders view is now complete and we can move on to the order detail views, to be navigated to by clicking on a list item triggering the above showOrderDetails function.

15.4. Summary

In this chapter, we started to develop an example application. After preparing the initial UIComponent, we began with the manifest and proceeded to clarify application-wide concerns regarding messages to the user and the handling of request related events.

Then, we constructed the orders view as a list of items and learned how to use the 'loading ready' events to update the list model. We further added a query form to allow the user to change the query parameters and update the orders list. We went back and forth between view and controller code to add controls to the view and to handle events in the controller.

Chapter 16. Edit Order page

In Chapter 15, *Beginning application development*, we developed the application to the point where it presents a list of orders and gives the user tools to find a particular order. Upon selecting an order, we now want to add a view or views to see the details and allow editing of the selected order.

An order has several different aspects, like a list of line items, billing and shipping addresses, payments and shippings. Instead of one large view with all the related information, we will create a view which displays basic order information and provides means to edit the order lines (this chapter). Another view is to edit or create addresses (next chapter). For real-life purposes, you would probably need other views, like payment and shipment views, but that is outside the scope of this example application.

To edit or create an order, we use a `SplitApp`. It has `masterPages` and `detailPages`. For the `masterPages` aggregation, we have an `orderNavigation` view. Like the name suggests, its function is to navigate to the order detail views. For our example application, we just have two such views: an `order` view for an overview and editing capabilities for the order lines, and an `orderAddress` view to edit the billing and shipping addresses.

16.1. Order details navigation

The `orderNavigation` view `content` is a short `List` of items for navigation. The List `mode` is set to `SingleSelectMaster`, meaning that the whole item is selectable and the selected item is highlighted.

Listing 16.1. Master view: navigation to order details

```
sap.ui.jsview("oum.view.orderNavigation", {
   getControllerName : function() {
      return "oum.controller.orderNavigation";
   },

   createContent : function(oController) {
      const orderSections = new sap.m.List(this.createId("orderSections"), {
         mode: "SingleSelectMaster",                          Enumeration sap.m.ListMode
         selectionChange: function (oEvent) {
            oController.navigate(oEvent);
         }
      });

      const overview = new sap.m.StandardListItem({           Order Overview item
         icon: "sap-icon://sales-order",
         title: "{i18n>orderNav.overview}",
         tooltip: "{i18n>orderNav.overview.tooltip}",
         info: "{common>/info}", ❶
         infoState: "{common>/infoState}"                     Enumeration sap.ui.core.ValueState
      });
      overview.data("routeName", "order");                    Add route name
      orderSections.addItem(overview);
```

```
        const billingAddress = new sap.m.StandardListItem({          Billing Address item
            icon: "sap-icon://addresses",
            title: "{i18n>address.billing}",
            tooltip: "{i18n>address.billing.tooltip}"
        });
        billingAddress.data("routeName", "orderAddress");           Add route name
        billingAddress.data("addressType", "billing");             Add address type
        orderSections.addItem(billingAddress);

        const shippingAddress = new sap.m.StandardListItem({         Shipping Address item
            icon: "sap-icon://addresses",
            title: "{i18n>address.shipping}",
            tooltip: "{i18n>address.shipping.tooltip}",
            visible: "{common>/hideShippingAddress}" ❷
        });
        shippingAddress.data("routeName", "orderAddress");          Add route name
        shippingAddress.data("addressType", "shipping");           Add address type
        orderSections.addItem(shippingAddress);

        return new sap.m.Page({
            content: [ orderSections ]
        });
    }
});
```

❶   If the user changes the order, we want to add a short text next to the item title to inform the
     user of unsaved changes. The info property is for the text and the infoState property is for
     the highlighting. We will look more closely at this issue in Section 16.3.2, "Indicate pending
     changes".
❷   If the billing address is the same as the shipping address, we want to hide the shipping address
     list item.

Initially, the view has no title because we want to set the title according to the route parameters. Also
depending upon the requested route is the selection of one of the list items. The connected controller
has to take care of these issues.

Because the controller needs to react to multiple routes, we attach a handler function to the routePat-
ternMatched event of the Router (line 9) and then act only upon the route names of the related order
detail views (line 15).

Listing 16.2. Order details navigation controller

```
 1 sap.ui.define([
 2    "oui5lib/controller/BaseController",
 3    "oum/do/statuses"
 4 ], function(Controller) {
 5    "use strict";
 6
 7    const orderNavController = Controller.extend("oum.controller.orderNavigation", {
 8       onInit: function() {
 9          this.getRouter().attachRoutePatternMatched(this._onRouteMatched, this);
10       },
11       _onRouteMatched: function(oEvent) {
12          const params = oEvent.getParameters();
13          const routeName = params.name;
14
```

```
15          if (routeName === "order" || routeName === "orderAddress") {
16              const orderId = params.arguments.id;
17
18              let pageTitle = "";
19              if (orderId  === undefined || orderId == "-1") { ❶
20                  this.orderId = "-1";
21                  pageTitle = oui5lib.util.getI18nText("orderNav.pageTitle.newOrder");
22              } else {
23                  this.orderId = orderId;
24                  pageTitle = oui5lib.util.getI18nText("orderNav.pageTitle.Order", orderId);
25              }
26              this.debug("current orderId: " + this.orderId);
27
28              const page = this.getView().getContent()[0];        The Page is the only content item
29              page.setTitle(pageTitle);                           Set Page title
30
31              this.selectListItem(routeName, params);             Call function to select list item
32          }
33      },
34
35      selectListItem: function(routeName, params) {
36          const sectionList = this.getView().byId("orderSections");
37          const sectionItems = sectionList.getItems();            Get all list items
38
39          let selectedItem = null;
40
41          switch(routeName) {
42          case "order":                                           Route 'order'
43              selectedItem = sectionItems[0];
44              break;
45          case "orderAddress": {                                  Route 'orderAddress'
46              const addressType = params.arguments.type;
47              if (addressType === "billing") {                    Type 'billing'
48                  selectedItem = sectionItems[1];
49              } else if (addressType === "shipping") {            Type 'shipping'
50                  selectedItem = sectionItems[2];
51              }
52              break;
53          }
54          }
55          if (selectedItem === null) {
56              this.getRouter().navTo("noRoute");
57              return;
58          }
59          sectionList.setSelectedItem(selectedItem, true);        Select the matching item
60      }
61  });
62  return orderNavController;
63 });
```

❶   To be able to recognize a new order which is currently being edited, but hasn't been saved yet, we use the fake ID -1 or "-1".

We attached the navigate function to the selectionChange event of the order navigation list (Listing 16.1, "Master view: navigation to order details"). The selected item gives us the routeName and, if needed, the addressType. Depending upon the route parameters, the _onRouteMatched function above sets the orderId property (lines 20 and 23), which we need for navigation.

Listing 16.3. Controller function to navigate to the order detail routes

```
navigate: function(oEvent) {
   if (sap.ui.Device.system.phone) { ❶
      return;
   }

   const list = oEvent.getSource();
   const selectedItem = list.getSelectedItem();

   const routeName = selectedItem.data("routeName");        Get the route name
   this.info("navigate to " + routeName);

   switch(routeName) {
   case "orderAddress": {
      const addressType = selectedItem.data("addressType");   Get the address type
      this.getRouter().vNavTo("orderAddress", {
         id: this.orderId,
         type: addressType
      });
      break;
   }
   case "order":
      this.getRouter().vNavTo("order", {
         id: this.orderId
      });
      break;
   default:
      this.getRouter().navTo("noRoute");
   }
}
```

❶ When used with a phone, the SplitApp has only one NavContainer instead of two. Because of this behavior, our targets for a SplitApp with masterPages and detailPages won't work. This is why, in our manifest, we don't claim that the application will work on phones. As a workaround, we would have to add special routes and targets for phones.

The basic orderNavigation view is now functional and we can move on to the order detail views.

16.2. Order detail views: common fragments and controller

The order detail views use the NavigationHeader fragment (see Listing 15.1, "Fragment returning a Bar with Back and Home navigation") for the customHeader aggregation. They will also share the same footer, which we will therefore implement as fragments.

The footer Bar has two buttons on the right side: One to save the order and the second to cancel any changes. We will get to the attached saveRecord and cancel functions towards the end of this chapter.

Listing 16.4. Fragment returning a Bar with a Save and Cancel button

```
sap.ui.jsfragment ("oum.fragment.CancelAndSaveBar", {
   createContent: function(oController) {                    Requires a controller
      const btnSave = new sap.m.Button({
         icon: "sap-icon://save",
         tooltip: "{i18n>button.save.tooltip}",
         press: function() {
            oController.saveRecord();
         }
      });
      const btnCancel = new sap.m.Button({
         icon: "sap-icon://sys-cancel",
         tooltip: "{i18n>button.cancel.tooltip}",
         press: function() {
            oController.cancel();
         }
      });
      const bar = new sap.m.Bar({
         contentRight: [ btnSave, btnCancel ]
      });
      return bar;
   }
});
```

Let us specify the landmarks to clarify the structure of the Page. The only content at this stage is a container for messages.

Listing 16.5. Initial order view

```
sap.ui.jsview("oum.view.order", {
   getControllerName : function() {
      return "oum.controller.order";
   },
   createContent : function(oController) {
      const landmarkInfo = new sap.m.PageAccessibleLandmarkInfo({
         rootLabel: "Order overview. Edit order lines.",
         headerRole: "Navigation",
         headerLabel: "Navigate home, back and to the help page",
         contentRole: "Main",
         contentLabel: "Basic order infos with table of line items",
         footerRole: "Complementary",
         footerLabel: "Save the order or cancel"
      });

      return new sap.m.Page({
         landmarkInfo: landmarkInfo,
         customHeader: sap.ui.jsfragment("oum.fragment.NavigationHeader", oController),
         content: [
            new sap.m.VBox(this.createId("messagesContainer"))
         ],
         footer: sap.ui.jsfragment("oum.fragment.CancelAndSaveBar", oController)
      });
   }
});
```

The order detail views are handling different aspects of the same order. It will help to have them extend a common controller. For example, all order detail views need a function to get and set the currently edited order. Adding a variable to the master view controller or the SplitApp seems to complicate the issue unnecessarily. Instead, we store the currently edited order as variable `oum.do.editedOrder`. In this way, we can always access the object easily, independent from any particular controller.

Regarding the `prepareEditedOrder` function, we need to remember that the views and controllers remain in the state they were left before. The previously edited order could still be set as the currently edited order and therefore our code needs to check if the currently edited order is the same as the one requested by the route. Otherwise, we will replace it with the requested order using cloned data to ensure that the user can't change the order entity data without explicitly submitting the changes.

Listing 16.6. Common controller for order detail controllers to extend

```
sap.ui.define([
    "oui5lib/controller/FormController"
], function(Controller) {
    "use strict";

    const orderBaseController = Controller.extend("oum.controller.OrderBaseController", {
        setEditedOrder: function(order) {
            oum.do.editedOrder = order;
        },
        getEditedOrder: function(orderId) {
            return oum.do.editedOrder;
        },

        prepareEditedOrder: function(orderId) {
            if (orderId === undefined) {
                return;
            }
            let order = this.getEditedOrder();
            if (order === undefined || order.id !== orderId) {
                if (orderId == "-1") {
                    order = new oum.do.Order();              Start a new Order
                } else {
                    order = new oum.do.Order(orderId, true);  Use cloned data
                }
                if (order instanceof oum.do.Order) {
                    this.setEditedOrder(order);               Set current edited Order
                }
            }
        }
    });
    return orderBaseController;
});
```

16.3. Order overview

The `order` view can be accessed directly by navigating to its route. It may have an `id` parameter to edit an existing order or none to create a new order. On top of an order model holding the currently edited order data, the order view also needs a statuses model for a list of available statuses. Since the route may be requested as an entry point into the application, we cannot count on any required data to be available.

The order data may already have been loaded, for example if the view is entered from the orders list. Otherwise, the order data will have to be requested. The same is true for the status data, which are requested once the statuses collection object is loaded. Let's prepare the controller to handle these different scenarios in its onInit function.

Listing 16.7. Initial order controller

```
 1 sap.ui.define([
 2    "oum/controller/OrderBaseController",
 3    "oum/do/orders",
 4    "oum/do/Order",
 5    "oum/do/products",
 6    "oum/do/statuses",
 7    "oum/lib/ui"
 8 ], function(oController, orders, Order, products, statuses, ui) {
 9    "use strict";
10
11    const orderController = oController.extend("oum.controller.order", {
12       onInit: function() {
13          const eventBus = sap.ui.getCore().getEventBus();
14          eventBus.subscribe("loading", "ready", this._handleLoaded, this);
15
16          this.getRouter().getRoute("order")
17             .attachPatternMatched(this._onRouteMatched, this);
18
19          if (statuses.isInitialized()) {
20             this.setStatusesModel();
21          }
22       }
23    });
24    return orderController;
25 });
```

When the 'order' route pattern is matched, the _onRouteMatched function is being called (lines 16 and 17). If the route has no id parameter, a new Order is created. The case of an id value "-1" is a new order. All other cases are existing orders.

Again, we have to set the Title text property of the header, because it is provided by a fragment and every page using it needs to set its own.

```
_onRouteMatched: function(oEvent) {
   this.debug("order overview");

   const messagesContainer = this.getView().byId("messagesContainer");
   ui.handleMessage(messagesContainer);                    Display message, if there is one

   let orderId = oEvent.getParameter("arguments").id;
   let order = null;
   if (typeof orderId === "undefined") {
      this.setEditedOrder(undefined); ❶
      orderId = "-1";
   }
   if (orderId !== "-1") {
      this.info("edit order: " + orderId);
      order = new Order(orderId);                          Get an existing Order
   }
   this.orderId = orderId;
```

```
    if (order === null || !order.isLoading()) {        The Order is new or already loaded
        this.setOrderModels();
    }

    this.setHeaderTitle();
},

setHeaderTitle: function() {
    const pageTitle = this.getView().byId("pageTitle");
    pageTitle.setText(oui5lib.util.getI18nText("order.overview.pageTitle"));
}
```

❶   To start a new order, the route is requested without id parameter. We, therefore, have to clear any
     previously edited order. To continue editing a new order the route id parameter would be "-1".

The above _onRouteMatched function covers the cases of a new order and an existing order already
available from the orders collection object. The case, where an existing order has to be requested, is
handled with the help of the 'loading ready' event, to which the controller subscribes (see Listing 16.7,
"Initial order controller" line 14).

```
_handleLoaded: function(channel, eventId, eventData) {
    if (typeof eventData === "object") {
        if (eventData.entity === "order" &&
            eventData.id == this.orderId) {
            this.setOrderModels();                The order has been loaded
        }
    } else {
        if (eventData === "statuses") {
            this.setStatusesModel();              The status data have been loaded
        }
    }
}
```

We have now completed the preliminary work for setting up the controller to react to its route being
requested, getting the required data and setting the text property of the NavigationHeader Title. Before
we get to the setOrderModels and setStatusesModel functions, we need to think about the structure of
the user interface controls.

For a compact overview of the currently edited order, a SimpleForm seems most fitting. The orderDate
and total are just shown, but can't be edited. We refer the editing of the addresses to a separate
orderAddress view, but show the billing and shipping address names. Furthermore, next to the billing
address we put a CheckBox indicating if the billing address is also the shipping address. Because the
checkbox will also be used for the address view, we implement it as a fragment.

We use two models to configure the CheckBox. One model named state, which holds status-related
properties of the order (editable, statusChangeable, saved). Another model named common, which holds
properties shared by all the order views (shiptoBillingAddress/hideShippingAddress, info/infoState). We
will revisit the issue of setting/updating and using these models a couple of times.

```
sap.ui.jsfragment("oum.fragment.ShiptoBillingAddressCheckBox", {
   createContent: function (oController) {
      const view = oController.getView();
      const checkBox = new sap.m.CheckBox({
         editable: "{state>/editable}",                    Can the order still be edited?
         selected: "{common>/shiptoBillingAddress}",       Is the billing address used as shipping address?
         text: "{i18n>order.shiptoBilling}",
         tooltip: "{i18n>order.shiptoBilling.tooltip}",
         select: function(oEvent) {
            oController.handleShiptoBilling(oEvent);
         }
      });
      return checkBox;
   }
});
```

Having prepared the fragment for the checkbox, we are ready to construct the order overview form. A real-world application would have to implement a more or less sophisticated logic of order states, allowing manual changes from one status to only a set of others statuses triggering related mandatory actions. For simplicity, we just assume that the status automatically changes depending upon the fulfillment flow of the order. Hence, we will disable the status control but nevertheless use a Select control with our statuses, and also employ a model to set the enabled property of the control.

We use the FormController to add the Input fields specified in the mapping. The details are explained in Chapter 10, *Entity specifications: Mapping* and particularly Chapter 14, *Form Control Generation*. But example entity attribute specifications may help at this point to follow the flow of our current example.

```
{
   "name": "billingName",
   "ui5": {
      "control": "sap.m.Input"
      "width": "200px"
   },
   "i18n": {
      "label": "address.billing",
      "tooltip": "address.billing.tooltip"
   }
},{
   "name": "status",
   "default": "new",
   "referenceTo": "status.status",
   "ui5": {
      "control" : "sap.m.Select",
      "itemsModel": "statuses",
      "itemKey": "status",
      "itemText": "statusText"
   },
   "i18n": {
      "label": "order.status.label",
      "tooltip": "order.status.tooltip"
   }
}
```

With the mapping (order.json) in place and the FormController extending the connected controller, we can greatly simplify the construction of controls.

We use the 'state' model to configure some of the form controls.

- DateTimePicker: The control will not be visible for a 'new' order because the date will only be set when the order is being submitted.
- CheckBox: The assigned addresses may only be changed until the order reaches a certain status.
- Select: Manual editing of the order status is disabled.

Listing 16.8. Form showing basic order information

```
 1 const form = new sap.ui.layout.form.SimpleForm(this.createId("orderForm"), {
 2    editable: true,
 3    layout: "ResponsiveGridLayout",
 4    labelSpanM: 3, labelSpanL: 2
 5 });
 6
 7 const orderDate = oController.addDateTimePicker(form, "order", "orderDate");
 8 orderDate.setEditable(false);
 9 orderDate.bindProperty("visible", "state>/saved")
10
11 let input = oController.addInput(form, "order", "billingName");
12 input.setEditable(false);
13
14 const shiptoBillingAddressCheckBox = sap.ui.jsfragment(
15    "oum.fragment.ShiptoBillingAddressCheckBox", oController
16 );
17 form.addContent(shiptoBillingAddressCheckBox);
18
19 input = oController.addInput(form, "order", "shippingName");
20 input.setEditable(false);
21 input.bindProperty("visible", "common>/hideShippingAddress");
22
23 const select = oController.addSelect(form, "order", "status");
24 select.bindProperty("enabled", "state>/statusChangeable");
25
26 input = oController.addInput(form, "order", "total");
27 input.setEditable(false);
```

Having constructed the view, let us get back to the controller. By convention, when we use the FormController to construct controls, the SimpleForm expects a model named order to bind the order data. For this, we use the setOrderModels function called either from the above _onRouteMatched or _handleLoaded functions.

We can be sure, that the setOrderModels function will only be called when the required order data are available. First, we prepare and get the Order entity object to be edited (lines 2 and 3). The Order object is then used to set the order model for the form (line 10), or to update the model data (line 12). Lastly, we take care of preparing and setting the 'state' model (lines 14 to 23).

Listing 16.9. Set order model for the form

```
 1 setOrderModels: function() {
 2    this.prepareEditedOrder(this.orderId);
 3    const order = this.getEditedOrder();
 4    if (!(order instanceof oum.do.Order)) {          This should never happen ;-)
 5        throw new TypeError("Need an oum.do.Order to edit");
 6    }
 7    const orderForm = this.getView().byId("orderForm");    Get SimpleForm control
 8    const orderModel = orderForm.getModel("order");
 9    if (orderModel === undefined) {
10        orderForm.setModel(order.getModel(), "order");     Set order model
11    } else {
12        orderModel.setData(order.getData());               Update model data
13    }
14    let editable = false;
15    if (order.isNew() === "new" || order.getProperty("status") === "pending") {
16        editable = true;
17    }
18    const orderStateModel = new sap.ui.model.json.JSONModel({
19        editable: editable,
20        statusChangeable: false,
21        saved: !order.isNew()
22    });
23    this.getView().setModel(orderStateModel, "state");
24 }
```

So far, our status `Select` control has no options. The mapping entry for the 'status' specifies an `itemsModel` 'statuses'. The FormController uses this value as model name to bind the `items` aggregation of the control. To set the model for the `Select`, we use the statuses collection object.

```
setStatusesModel: function() {
   const statusSelect = this.getView().byId("order_status"); ❶
   statusSelect.setModel(statuses.getModel(), "statuses"); ❷
}
```

❶ By convention, the FormController lets the `sap.ui.core.mvc.View` object create the control ID as 'entityName_propertyPath', in this case 'order_status'.

❷ For our example application, we will just show how to use a `Select` control to edit the status. But we don't want to look more deeply into the issue of order statuses and will, therefore, simply use all statuses here.

16.3.1. Common Model

Having set the 'order', 'statuses' and 'state' models, we are left with the task to set the 'common' model. As the name of the model indicates, this is a model common to multiple order views. For example, the /hideShippingAddress model path is used to show/hide both the shipping address list item of the order navigation list and the input field for the shipping address of the order form. The value depends upon the order. Here is the relevant function from the `Order` entity object:

```
function shiptoBillingAddress() {
   return this.getProperty("billingAddressId") === this.getProperty("shippingAddressId");
}
```

The smallest common scope for this model is the `SplitApp` and its values are derived from the currently edited `Order` entity object. The best place to set the model is the `setEditedOrder` function of the `OrderBaseController` (see Listing 16.6, "Common controller for order detail controllers to extend").

```
 1 setEditedOrder: function(order) {
 2    oum.do.editedOrder = order;              Store the order entity object
 3    this.setCommonModel();                   Set/update the common model
 4    this.setOrderNotSaved(false);            There are no pending changes
 5 },
 6 getEditedOrder: function() { ... },
 7 prepareEditedOrder: function() { ... },
 8
 9 setCommonModel: function() {
10    const splitApp = this.getView().getParent().getParent(); ❶
11    let model = splitApp.getModel("common");
12    if (model === undefined) {
13       model = new sap.ui.model.json.JSONModel();
14       splitApp.setModel(model, "common");
15    }
16    const currentOrder = this.getEditedOrder();
17    if (currentOrder instanceof oum.do.Order) {
18       model.setProperty("/shiptoBillingAddress",
19                         currentOrder.shiptoBillingAddress());
20       model.setProperty("/hideShippingAddress",
21                         !currentOrder.shiptoBillingAddress());
22    }
23 },
24 getCommonModel: function() {
25    const splitApp = this.getView().getParent().getParent();
26    return splitApp.getModel("common");
27 }
```

❶   The parent of the view is the `NavContainer` whose parent is the `SplitApp`.

16.3.2. Indicate pending changes

If any changes were made to the order which need to be saved to make them permanent, we want to visually indicate that to the user. We use the `StandardListItem` properties `info` and `infoState` to show a colored text next to the navigation list item. These properties are set in Listing 16.1, "Master view: navigation to order details", referring to paths of the 'common' model. Initially, these paths are undefined and the default values apply, which means there is no text and the `ValueState` is "None".

In the previous code listing, an `Order` entity object is assigned to `oum.do.editedOrder` (line 2). At this point, it can't have been edited and we therefore have to reset the 'record changed' status of the `FormController`, and also the related properties of the 'common' model. For this, we call the `setOrder-NotSaved` function with a boolean parameter value (line 4). Here is the function:

```
setOrderNotSaved: function(bool) {
    const model = this.getCommonModel();
    if (bool) {
        this.setRecordChanged();                                        Set record changed

        model.setProperty("/info", oui5lib.util.getI18nText("common.notSaved"));
        model.setProperty("/infoState", "Warning");
    } else {
        this.resetRecordChanged();                                      Reset record changed

        model.setProperty("/info", "");
        model.setProperty("/infoState", "None");
    }
}
```

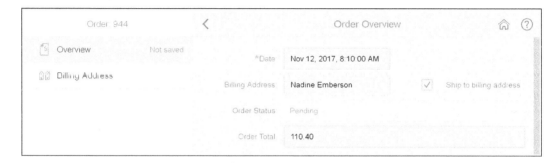

16.3.3. Ship to billing address?

Currently, what can the user do if he wants to work on the order? The only available action is to toggle the 'Ship to billing address' checkbox, if the order status permits it. This seems trivial, at first, but is actually quite tricky to implement.

We begin with the function setting the billing address as the shipping address. When done, we will show a notification to the user, update the 'common' model and mark the order as 'Not saved'.

```
setBillingAsShippingAddress: function(order) {
    order.setProperty("shippingAddressId",
                    order.getProperty("billingAddressId"));
    order.setProperty("shippingName",
                    order.getProperty("billingName"));

    oui5lib.messages.showNotification(
        oui5lib.util.getI18nText("order.shippingAddress.copyBilling"));

    this.setCommonModel();
    this.setOrderNotSaved(true);
}
```

Having taken care of this, we have to think about the flow of user interaction. If the checkbox state is changed, the handleShiptoBilling function is called. There are a few cases to consider:

• If there are no addresses (lines 5 and 6), the checkbox is checked. Before setting the shipping address as different from the billing address, we first expect a billing address. We notify the user (lines 7 and 8) and revert the checkbox state (line 9).

- If both addresses are different and the user wants to use the billing address also as the shipping address, the current shipping address would eventually be overwritten. We will, therefore, ask the user for confirmation, to avoid any unwelcome surprises (lines 15 to 18).

- If the addresses are the same and the user wants to add a different shipping address, we will simply reset the shipping address (lines 23 and 24), set a warning message for the receiving view that the shipping address has been cleared (lines 29 to 32) and navigate to the shipping address view (lines 33 to 36).

```
1 handleShiptoBilling: function(oEvent) {
2     const shiptoBilling = oEvent.getParameter("selected");
3
4     const currentOrder = this.getEditedOrder();
5     if (currentOrder.getProperty("billingAddressId") === null &&
6         currentOrder.getProperty("shippingAddressId") === null) {
7         oui5lib.messages.showNotification(                           An order without addresses
8             oui5lib.util.getI18nText("order.billingAddress.first"));
9         this.toggleShiptoBilling();
10         return;
11     }
12
13     if (shiptoBilling) {
14         if (currentOrder.getProperty("shippingAddressId") !== null) {
15             oui5lib.messages.confirmDelete(                          Let the user confirm
16                 oui5lib.util.getI18nText("order.shippingAddress.overwrite?"),
17                 this.handleShiptoBillingConfirmed.bind(this)        Callback function binds 'this'
18             );
19         } else {
20             this.setBillingAsShippingAddress(currentOrder);
21         }
22     } else {
23         currentOrder.setProperty("shippingAddressId", null);        Clear shipping address
24         currentOrder.setProperty("shippingName", "");
25
26         this.setCommonModel();
27         this.setOrderNotSaved(true);
28
29         oum.message = {
30             text: oui5lib.util.getI18nText("order.shippingAddress.cleared"),
31             type: "Warning"
32         };
33         this.getRouter().vNavTo("orderAddress", {
34             id: currentOrder.id,
35             type: "shipping"
36         });
37     }
38 },
39
40 toggleShiptoBilling: function() {
41     const model = this.getCommonModel();
42     const shiptoBillingAddress = model.getProperty("/shiptoBillingAddress");
43
44     model.setProperty("/shiptoBillingAddress", !shiptoBillingAddress);
45     model.setProperty("/hideShippingAddress", shiptoBillingAddress);
46 }
```

The `oui5lib.messages.confirmDelete` function was given the callback `handleShiptoBillingConfirmed` function to process the user decision (line 17). If the deletion is confirmed, we set the billing as the shipping address. Otherwise, the checkbox is reset to the previous state.

```
handleShiptoBillingConfirmed: function(action) {
    if (action === "DELETE") {
        this.setBillingAsShippingAddress(this.getEditedOrder());    Set billing as shipping address
    } else {
        this.toggleShiptoBilling();                                 Revert the change of the checkbox state
    }
}
```

This completes the ship to billing address functionality. We constructed the `CheckBox` as a fragment to be able to use it for both the order overview and address views. By adding all the related functions to the `OrderBaseController`, we ensure that the fragment will work with the connected controllers, if they indeed extend the `OrderBaseController`.

16.4. Edit Order lines

For the order lines, we will use a table with five columns (product id, product name, quantity, unit price and line total). Let us begin with the row template, which has to be of type `ColumnListItem`. The quantity column is an `Input` control allowing convenient editing of the ordered quantity if the order has an editable status.

```
const rowTemplate = new sap.m.ColumnListItem({
    cells : [
        new sap.m.Text({ text: "{orderLines>productId}" }),
        new sap.m.Text({ text: "{orderLines>productName}" }),
        new sap.m.Input({                                   Use Input control for the quantity
            value: "{orderLines>quantity}",
            type: "Number",
            editable: "{state>/editable}",                  Only editable with certain statuses
            change: function(oEvent) {
                oController.handleLineQuantityChanged(oEvent);
            }
        }),
        new sap.m.Text({ text: "{orderLines>unitPrice}" }),
        new sap.m.Text({ text: "{orderLines>lineTotal}" })
    ]
});
```

 The `ColumnListItem` `cells` aggregation should match the `Table` `columns` aggregation.

The `Table` mode is set to `Delete` to allow the deletion of an order line. If the visible space is insufficient, the product name and line total will 'pop-in'. Pop-in means that a column is removed from the table and the property instead be placed below the table row. After the next listing we will look at screenshots illustrating the feature.

Listing 16.10. Order items table

```
const orderLinesTable = new sap.m.Table(this.createId("orderLinesTable"), {
    headerText: "{i18n>order.itemsList.header}",
    mode: "Delete",
    delete: function(oEvent) {
        oController.deleteOrderLine(oEvent);
    },
    alternateRowColors: true,
    columns: [
        new sap.m.Column({
            width: "100px",
            header: new sap.m.Label({ text: "{i18n>orderLine.columnHeader.product.id}" })
        }),
        new sap.m.Column({
            minScreenWidth: "Tablet", demandPopin: true,
            header: new sap.m.Label({ text: "{i18n>orderLine.columnHeader.product.title}" })
        }),
        new sap.m.Column({
            width: "80px",
            header: new sap.m.Label({ text: "{i18n>orderLine.columnHeader.quantity}" })
        }),
        new sap.m.Column({
            width: "80px", hAlign: "End",
            header: new sap.m.Label({ text: "{i18n>orderLine.columnHeader.product.price}" })
        }),
        new sap.m.Column({
            minScreenWidth: "Tablet", demandPopin: true, popinDisplay: "Inline",
            width: "80px", hAlign: "End",
            header: new sap.m.Label({ text: "{i18n>orderLine.columnHeader.total}" })
        })
    ]
});

orderLinesTable.bindAggregation("items", {
    path: "orderLines>/",
    template: rowTemplate
});
```

The `Table` binds a model named `orderLines` to its `items` aggregation. We provide that model by appending a few lines to the `setOrderModels` function (see Listing 16.9, "Set order model for the form").

```
const orderLinesTable = this.getView().byId("orderLinesTable");      Get the order lines table
const orderLinesModel = new sap.ui.model.json.JSONModel(
    order.getOrderLines()
);
orderLinesTable.setModel(orderLinesModel, "orderLines");

if (editable) {
    orderLinesTable.setMode("Delete");                               The order is still editable
} else {
    orderLinesTable.setMode("None");                                 The order is in fulfillment
}
```

The complete order `Page` is now constructed like this:

```
return new sap.m.Page({
   landmarkInfo: landmarkInfo,
   customHeader: sap.ui.jsfragment("oum.fragment.NavigationHeader", oController),
   content: [
      new sap.m.VBox(this.createId("messagesContainer")),
      form, orderLinesTable
   ],
   footer: sap.ui.jsfragment("oum.fragment.CancelAndSaveBar", oController)
});
```

Order lines table with mode 'None'

Ordered items:					
Product ID	Product Title		Quantity	Unit Price	Total
0862329264	From feast to famine :		1	17.49	17.49
0816513724	American Indians & national parks /		1	5.95	5.95

Order lines table with pop-in and mode 'Delete'

Ordered items:			
Product ID	Quantity	Unit Price	
0312749104	3	17.00	⊗
Product Title:			
The Soviet Union and revolutionary Iran /			
Total: 51.00			
0803247222	2	24.90	⊗
Product Title:			
The roots of dependency :			
Total: 49.80			

Having prepared the table, we will now implement the required functionality. Changing the order line quantity, adding or deleting an order line will all trigger a recalculation of the order total. It requires a model refresh to update the order total in the form and the order lines in the table.

```
updateModelBindings: function() {
   const orderForm = this.getView().byId("orderForm");
   const orderModel = orderForm.getModel("order");
   orderModel.refresh();

   const orderLinesTable = this.getView().byId("orderLinesTable");
   const orderLinesModel = orderLinesTable.getModel("orderLines");
   orderLinesModel.refresh();
}
```

After changing the order data, we want to refresh the view to reflect the changes, display a 'Not saved' warning and mark the record changed. We combine the related function calls in the `handleOrderChanged` function.

```
handleOrderChanged: function() {
   this.updateModelBindings();
   this.setOrderNotSaved(true);
}
```

When the user changes the quantity or presses the delete icon, we need to get the related order line data. The simplest way is through the binding context.

```
getLineData: function(control) {
   const bindingContext = control.getBindingContext("orderLines");
   const orderLinesModel = bindingContext.getModel("orderLines");
   return orderLinesModel.getProperty(bindingContext.getPath());
}
```

Now, we have everything prepared to actually work on the order lines.

16.4.1. Changing the line quantity

After changing the quantity in the `Input`, the `handleLineQuantityChanged` function is called with the event object. The functionality to actually change the quantity of an order line is delegated to the `Order` entity object (see Listing 12.15, "Update the quantity of an order line and recalculate totals"). The controller only needs to take care of calling the function.

```
handleLineQuantityChanged: function(oEvent) {
   const input = oEvent.getSource();
   const lineData = this.getLineData(input);

   this.getEditedOrder().changeOrderLineQuantity(lineData.productId,
                                                 lineData.quantity);
   this.handleOrderChanged();
}
```

16.4.2. Removing an item

Constructing our `Table`, we attached the `deleteOrderLine` function to the `delete` event. As a precaution, we will first ask the user for confirmation. Only when confirmed, the `removeOrderLine` function (see Listing 12.16, "Remove an order line by the product ID and recalculate order total") of the `Order` entity object is called to actually remove the order line.

```
deleteOrderLine: function(oEvent) {
   const selectedItem = oEvent.getParameter("listItem");
   const lineData = this.getLineData(selectedItem);

   oui5lib.messages.confirmDelete(
      oui5lib.util.getI18nText("order.deleteItem.confirm"),
      this.confirmedDeleteOrderLine.bind(this, lineData.productId)     Callback function binding 'this'
   );
},
confirmedDeleteOrderLine: function(productId, action) {
   if (action === "DELETE") {
      this.getEditedOrder().removeOrderLine(productId);
      this.handleOrderChanged();
   }
}
}
```

16.4.3. Adding an item

Besides deleting order items and changing the ordered quantity, we also need a way to add an order item. For this, the user needs to find the right product. Depending on the number of active products available, finding products is a serious user interface challenge. A select dialog may be a good choice, offering a query interface by SKU or name. Another way might be to first go through the product catalog categories, until a reasonable number of products is left to load. Anyway, this issue has the potential to significantly slow down the user interface. Client-side filtering or sorting of an incomplete list of products does not make sense here. Therefore, in a productive environment, any query must check the result count and require the user to further specify the query if there are too many records.

We start by adding a button to open the dialog. To achieve this, we construct the Button as content of a Toolbar and set it to the infoToolbar aggregation of the order lines Table.

```
orderLinesTable.setInfoToolbar(
   new sap.m.Toolbar({
      content: [
         new sap.m.Button({
            enabled: "{state>/editable}",
            text: "{i18n>order.addItem}",
            tooltip: "{i18n>order.addItem.tooltip}",
            press: function() {
               oController.openProductDialog();
            }
         })
      ]
   })
);
```

The following listing show how to construct the dialog control. This time, the fragment is implemented as XML, simply because it is small and easy enough. The SelectProductDialog fragment uses a StandardListItem for the items aggregation of the SelectDialog control. The products here are books. The item displays the ISBN, author and title.

Listing 16.11. SelectProductDialog fragment

```xml
<?xml version="1.0" encoding="UTF-8"?>
<core:FragmentDefinition
    xmlns="sap.m"
    xmlns:core="sap.ui.core">

  <SelectDialog
      title="{i18n>product.find}"
      confirm="handleProductSelected"        A product is selected
      search="queryProducts"                  Query products
      items="{/}"
      >

    <StandardListItem
        title="{isbn}: {author}" ❶
        description="{title/a}{title/b}"
        />
  </SelectDialog>
</core:FragmentDefinition>
```

❶   This syntax only works if the data-sap-ui-bindingSyntax parameter is set to 'complex'. See Listing 2.1, "sap-ui-bootstrap".

The openProductDialog function loads the fragment and adds it to the dependents aggregation. As dependent object, it inherits the i18n model and also gets destroyed together with the view or through
the destroyDependents function. After setting a model without data for the SelectDialog, the dialog is
opened and a reference saved.

```javascript
openProductDialog: function() {
    const selectProductDialog = sap.ui.xmlfragment("oum.fragment.SelectProductDialog", this);
    this.getView().addDependent(selectProductDialog);

    selectProductDialog.setModel(new sap.ui.model.json.JSONModel());
    selectProductDialog.open();

    this.productDialog = selectProductDialog;
}
```

We attached the queryProducts function to the search event of the SelectDialog. To conveniently query
products, we add an entry to the product.json mapping. The request requires a query string.

```json
"request": {
    "queryProducts": {
        "pathname": "queryProducts",
        "method": "GET",
        "parameters": [
            { "name": "query", "required": true }
        ]
    }
}
```

We don't want to run the query with a string shorter than 3 characters. In case, the user tries to
do this, we send a message, using the noDataText property of the SelectDialog. The actual request
is asynchronous. This time, we don't use our Loader but use the oui5lib.request.sendMappingRequest
directly. The reason is, that the response is only relevant for the current view and we don't want to

have all the queried products added to the products collection, which might otherwise grow too big
and slow down the application.

```
queryProducts: function(oEvent) {
   const queryString = oEvent.getParameter("value");
   if (queryString.length > 2) {
      this.productDialog.setBusy(true);

      oui5lib.request.sendMappingRequest(
         "product", "queryProducts",
         { query: queryString },
         this.handleQueriedProducts.bind(this)
      );
   } else {
      this.productDialog.setNoDataText(
         oui5lib.util.getI18nText("selectDialog.minQueryLength", [ "3" ])
      );
   }
}
```

The callback function for the asynchronous request takes the queried product data and excludes
those already among the currently selected products. With the remaining products, we update the
SelectDialog model.

```
handleQueriedProducts: function(responseObject, requestProps) {
   this.productDialog.setBusy(false);

   if (responseObject.result) {
      const orderLines = this.getEditedOrder().getOrderLines();        Get current order lines
      const productIds = [];
      orderLines.forEach(function(line) {
         productIds.push(line.productId);
      });

      const data = responseObject.value;
      const products = [];
      data.forEach(function(product) {
         if (productIds.indexOf(product.isbn) === -1) {
            products.push(product);
         }
      });
      const model = this.productDialog.getModel();
      model.setData(products);                                         Update the dialog model data

      if (products.length === 0) {                                     No matching products?
         this.productDialog.setNoDataText(
            oui5lib.util.getI18nText(
               "list.noMatchingData",
               [ requestProps.entity, requestProps.requestParameters.query ]
            )
         );
      }
   } else {
      this.productDialog.close();
      oui5lib.messages.showErrorMessage(
         oui5lib.util.getI18nText("query.result.error", [ requestProps.entity ]));
   }
}
```

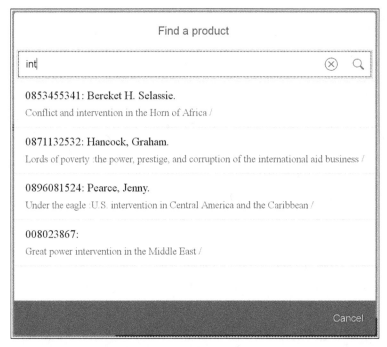

Only if the user selects a product from the list do we add it to the products collection, to have all referenced data for the order stored in client memory. Again, we see how the Order entity object hides the logic of adding an order line. We only need to call the addOrderLine function of the Order entity object (see Listing 12.17, "Add an order line with the given product ID"). In this way, the controller code remains concise and focused.

```
handleProductSelected: function(oEvent) {
    const selectedItem = oEvent.getParameter("selectedItem");
    const bindingContext = selectedItem.getBindingContext();
    const productsModel = bindingContext.getModel();
    const productData = productsModel.getProperty(bindingContext.getPath());

    products.addItem(productData);                              Add product data to the products collection

    this.getEditedOrder().addOrderLine(productData.isbn, 1);    Add new order line
    this.handleOrderChanged();
}
```

16.5. Save and Cancel, Back and Home

The footer fragment (see Listing 16.4, "Fragment returning a Bar with a Save and Cancel button") adds two buttons to save the order or cancel editing. The related handler functions (saveRecord and cancel) need to be implemented.

Saving the order means to first validate the order data against the mapping specifications. We covered the issue in Chapter 13, *Validation*. If the validation returns any errors, we display an error message to the user and stop further processing.

If the data are invalid, we have to generate the error message based upon the format of validation errors returned by the oui5lib.validation.validateData function (see Listing 13.4, "Specify expectations for the function to validate data"). This is a complementary step of validation concerning the user interface and, therefore, we will add a showValidationErrors function to the oui5lib.ui namespace.

Listing 16.12. Open message box with validation errors

```
function showValidationErrors(errors) {
    let msgs = [], error;
    errors.forEach(function(errorStr) {
        error = errorStr.split(":");
        msgs.push(oui5lib.util.getI18nText("validation." + error[0])
                + ": " + error[1]);
    });
    let msgText = oui5lib.util.getI18nText("validation.fix-errors") + "\n\n";
    for (let i = 0, s = msgs.length; i < s; i++) {
        msgText += msgs[i] + "\n";
    }
    oui5lib.messages.showErrorMessage(msgText);
}
oui5lib.ui.showValidationErrors = showValidationErrors;
```

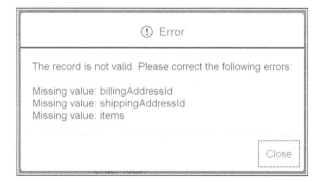

If the order data are validated successfully, we are ready to submit the order. The saveOrder request is configured in the order mapping (see Listing 10.3, "Example mapping: specify order requests"). The order data are sent as JSON.

```
saveOrder: function(orderData) {
    ui.setBusy(true);

    oui5lib.request.sendMappingRequest(
        "order", "saveOrder",
        { "orderString": JSON.stringify(orderData) },
        this.orderSaved.bind(this)
    );
}
```

Upon a successful response, the orderSaved function will be called. If the response result is false, we show a generic error message. Of course, in case the response is designed to provide an error message or messages from the server, these should be added as well.

If the order was successfully saved, we add or update the order data in the orders collection. At this point, we have completed the saving procedure. After setting a feedback message, we can navigate to the orders list and finally reset the order view.

```
orderSaved: function(responseObject) {
  ui.setBusy(false);

  if (!responseObject.result) {                        Was there an error?
    oui5lib.messages.showErrorMessage(
       oui5lib.util.getI18nText("order.saved.error"));
    return;
  }

  const orderData = responseObject.value; ❶
  orders.addData(orderData);                           Add order to the collection

  oum.message = {
     text: oui5lib.util.getI18nText("order.saved.success"),
     type: "Success"
  };
  this.getRouter().vNavTo("ordersList");
  this.resetView();
}
```

❶   Because the order gets its date and status from the server-side, we expect the order data to be included in the response.

Resetting the order view means to clear the models and destroy the objects in the dependents aggregation of the view, which, in this case, is only the SelectProductDialog.

Listing 16.13. Reset order view

```
resetView: function() {
  this.resetRecordChanged();
  this.setEditedOrder(undefined);

  const orderForm = this.getView().byId("orderForm");
  orderForm.setModel(null, "order");

  const orderLinesTable = this.getView().byId("orderLinesTable");
  orderLinesTable.setModel(null, "orderLines");

  this.getView().setModel(null, "state");
  this.getView().destroyDependents();
}
```

With all the required pieces prepared, we can lastly implement the saveRecord event handler function, which we attached to the save-button press event. Before we call the function to request saving the order, the order data are sanitized by deleting all properties which where added only to accommodate the user interface requirements.

Listing 16.14. Controller function to save an order

```
saveRecord: function() {
   const orderData = this.getEditedOrder().getData();
   if (orderData.status === "new") {                              A new order?
      orderData.orderDate = new Date();                           The 'orderDate' is required
   }

   const orderSpecs = oui5lib.mapping.getEntityAttributeSpecs("order");
   const errors = oui5lib.validation.validateData(orderData, orderSpecs);   Validate order data
   if (errors.length > 0) {                                       Errors found?
      oui5lib.ui.showValidationErrors(errors);
      return;
   }
   // The order seems valid
   delete orderData.billingName;                                  Sanitize order data
   delete orderData.shippingName;
   delete orderData.total;
   delete orderData.statusText;
   delete orderData.valueState;

   const orderLines = orderData.items;
   orderLines.forEach(function(orderLine) {
      delete orderLine.productName;
      delete orderLine.lineTotal;
   });

   this.saveOrder(orderData);
}
```

That being taken care of, we have to implement the cancel event handler function, which we attached to the press event of the cancel-button. What does canceling mean? While saving seems unambiguous, canceling is hardly as clear. Does it mean to 'go back'? But what happens if there is no previous application history? Should we then always navigate to the orders list view? Whatever we do has to be communicated and decided for every project and then implemented consistently.

There is another question. Should we discard any changes without asking? This doesn't seem right. Let us look more closely at the issue of unsaved changes.

16.5.1. Handle pending changes

How do we know that the record has been edited? Unfortunately, the 'client' models don't tell us. We could compare the original and the current data objects. This seems a reasonable idea, but we would have to strictly distinguish between changes caused by user action and those done by the controller to drive the user interface.

Instead, we will use a different approach here. Every time the record is modified due to user action, we set a status property to mark the record changed. By extending the oui5lib.controller.FormController, we can get some help to achieve that. By design, all form controls generated by the FormController call the setRecordChanged function when the user changes something. We can use the function anywhere in the controller, like we did in the setOrderNotSaved function of the OrderBaseController.

Leaving aside those user actions our application doesn't control, like using the browser back button or reloading the current page, we have to take care of the 'Home', 'Back' and 'Help' buttons to have

the user confirm discarding unsaved changes. As an example, let us take a look at the enhanced
HomeButton fragment.

Listing 16.15. HomeButton fragment checking for unsaved changes

```
sap.ui.jsfragment("oui5lib.fragment.HomeButton", {
    createContent: function(oController) {
        const btn =  new sap.m.Button({
            icon: "sap-icon://home",
            tooltip: "{i18n>button.home.tooltip}",
            press: function () {
                if (oController && typeof oController.wasRecordChanged === "function" &&
                    oController.wasRecordChanged()) {

                    oui5lib.messages.confirmUnsavedChanges( ❶
                        oController.handleUnsavedChanges.bind(oController), "home");
                } else {
                    const router = oui5lib.util.getRouter();
                    router.vNavTo("home");
                }
            }
        });
        return btn;
    }
});
```

❶   See Listing 6.10, "Function to ask the user to confirm discarding unsaved changes". We add
the navto parameter "home" to allow the handleUnsavedChanges function to perform the requested
navigation.

When the onClose event of the MessageBox is triggered, the handleUnsavedChanges function is called. Because this concerns all our order detail views, we add the function to the common OrderBaseController.
If the user doesn't confirm, nothing happens. If he or she gives the OK to discard unsaved changes,
the function either navigates to the given navto parameter value and resets the view, or reverts any
changes.

Listing 16.16. OrderBaseController function to handle unsaved changes

```
handleUnsavedChanges: function(action, navto) {
    if (action === "OK") {
        if (typeof navto === "string") {
            switch(navto) {
            case "home":
                this.getRouter().vNavTo("home");
                break;
            case "back":
                this.getRouter().navBack();
                break;
            default:
                this.getRouter().vNavTo(navto);
            }
            this.resetView();
            return;
        }
        this.revertChanges();
    }
}
```

While the general procedure is common for all detail views, the resetView (see Listing 16.13, "Reset order view") and revertChanges functions must be implemented for every particular controller because each view is structured differently.

We are now left with implementing the revertChanges function. Since we used cloned data for the Order entity object (see Listing 16.9, "Set order model for the form"), we can now conveniently construct the original Order entity and update the models.

```
revertChanges: function() {
    this.resetRecordChanged();

    const originalOrder = new Order(this.orderId, true);
    this.setEditedOrder(originalOrder);
    this.setOrderModels();
}
```

Keeping the problem of unsaved changes in mind, we need to revisit the navigate function of the orderNavigation.controller.js (see Listing 16.3, "Controller function to navigate to the order detail routes". It also needs to check for unsaved changes. Let us now take care of that by adding a was-RecordChanged function to the controller.

If the edited order is newly created, we just mark the list item 'Not saved'. The reason is simply that a new order hasn't been saved and may be invalid and therefore not savable. For all already saved orders, we check if there are pending changes. We get the currently relevant order detail controller through the SplitApp.

```
wasRecordChanged: function() {
    if (oum.do.editedOrder.isNew()) {
        return false;
    }
    const splitApp = this.getView().getParent().getParent();
    const detailView = splitApp.getCurrentDetailPage();
    const detailController = detailView.getController();
    if (typeof detailController.wasRecordChanged === "function" &&
        detailController.wasRecordChanged()) {

        oui5lib.messages.confirmUnsavedChanges(
            detailController.handleUnsavedChanges.bind(detailController));
        return true;
    }
    return false;
}
```

To complete the issue, a small addition to the navigate function plugs the remaining hole.

```
navigate: function(oEvent) {
    const list = oEvent.getSource();
    const selectedItem = list.getSelectedItem();

    if (this.wasRecordChanged()) {
        list.setSelectedItem(selectedItem, false);
        return;
    }
    ...
}
```

We have now done what we can to make the user either save pending changes or actively discard them.

16.6. Summary

This was likely the most complicated chapter owing to some complicated issues requiring your close attention.

We began with the view providing navigation to the order detail views, to be loaded into the master-Pages aggregation of the SplitApp.

We proceeded with fragments and controller code common to all the order detail views. Our initial detail view was the order overview. We constructed a form for basic order information and implemented the feature to use the billing address as the shipping address. Next, we constructed a table for the order lines and went through the code to change the quantity, delete an order line, and add another. Adding a new order line required us to give the user a convenient tool to query and find the product to be added to the cart.

Next, we went through the steps to validate the order and send it to the server for saving. To round up this chapter, we presented the reader with a procedure to handle the issue of pending changes.

Chapter 17. Edit Address view

The view to edit addresses is used for both the billing and shipping address. Much of the code we went through for the order view is very similar here. If you ask me, this is a good thing because it shows the potential to improve productivity through code generators.

Like the order view, the address view uses the `NavigationHeader` and `CancelAndSaveBar` fragments. The related landmark labels for the header and footer are also identical. This indicates potential for normalization either using a fragment returning the common `Page` layout, or through the approach presented in Section 4.2.5.1, "Using a common layout view". But for two views, it doesn't matter much to normalize a few lines of duplicated code.

Listing 17.1. Initial order address view

```
sap.ui.jsview("oum.view.orderAddress", {
    getControllerName : function() {
        return "oum.controller.orderAddress";
    },

    createContent : function(oController) {
        const landmarkInfo = new sap.m.PageAccessibleLandmarkInfo({
            rootLabel: "Edit or add new order address",
            headerRole: "Navigation",
            headerLabel: "Navigate home, back and to the help page",
            contentRole: "Main",
            contentLabel: "Form to edit the address. Includes an address search",
            footerRole: "Complementary",
            footerLabel: "Save the address or cancel"
        });

        return new sap.m.Page({
            landmarkInfo: landmarkInfo,
            customHeader: sap.ui.jsfragment("oum.fragment.NavigationHeader", oController),
            content: [
                new sap.m.VBox(this.createId("messagesContainer")),
                sap.ui.jsfragment("oum.fragment.ShiptoBillingAddressCheckBox", oController) ❶
            ],
            footer : sap.ui.jsfragment("oum.fragment.CancelAndSaveBar", oController)
        });
    }
});
```

❶   Like the order overview controller, the order address controller extends the `OrderBaseController`. It contains all the code making the `ShiptoBillingAddressCheckBox` work. Therefore, the fragment will continue to work as expected.

The `FormController` functions need the specifications of the mapping to construct the form controls. Because it is crucial to understand how this works, we start form construction with an excerpt of the `address.json` mapping file. Without these metadata, we would have to code all form controls 'manually'.

```
{
    "description": "Specify Address",
    "primaryKey": "id",
    "entity": [
        {
            "name": "id",
            "type": "int"
        },{
            "name": "firstname",
            "required": true,
            "validate": [ "hasLetters", "minLength_3", "maxLength_40" ],
            "ui5": {
                "control": "sap.m.Input"
            },
            "i18n": {
                "label": "address.firstName",
                "tooltip": "address.firstName.tooltip",
                "invalid": "address.firstName.invalid"
            }
        },

        ...

        {
            "name": "countryCode",
            "required": true,
            "ui5": {
                "control": "sap.m.Select",
                "itemsModel": "countries",
                "itemKey": "code",
                "itemText": "country",
                "sortBy": "country"
            },
            "i18n": {
                "label": "address.country",
                "tooltip": "address.country.tooltip",
                "invalid": "address.country.required"
            }
        },{
            "name": "phone",
            "validate": [ "phone" ],
            "ui5": {
                "control": "sap.m.Input",
                "type": "Number"
            },
            "i18n": {
                "label": "address.phone",
                "tooltip": "address.phone.tooltip",
                "invalid": "address.phone.invalid"
            }
        }
    ],
    "request": {
        ...
    }
}
```

After we prepared the mapping, we may want to check in the browser console if it is accessible, and further investigate the entity attribute specifications:

```
  ⌞⌝  ⬚       Elements   Console   Sources   Network   Performance   Memory   »          ⋮   ×

  ▷  ⃠   top                      ▼  Filter            Default levels ▼  ✓ Group similar         ⚙

>  oui5lib.mapping.getPrimaryKey("address")
⟨  "id"
>  oui5lib.mapping.getEntityAttributeSpec("address", "lastname")
⟨  ▼ {name: "lastname", required: true, validate: Array(4), ui5: {…}, i18n: {…}, …}
      ▼ i18n:
          invalid: "address.lastName.invalid"
          label: "address.lastName"
          tooltip: "address.lastName.tooltip"
        ▶ __proto__: Object
      name: "lastname"
      required: true
      type: "string"
    ▶ ui5: {control: "sap.m.Input"}
    ▶ validate: (4) ["hasLetters", "minLength_3", "maxLength_20", "required"]
    ▶ __proto__: Object
```

The following example shows how compact the code to build the address form is when we use the FormController. It is another advantage to know that all the controls are constructed in the same way, which significantly reduces the potential for inconsistent behavior of form elements. Still, any customization of the generated controls remains easy.

Listing 17.2. Address form constructed with the FormController

```
const form = new sap.ui.layout.form.SimpleForm(this.createId("addressForm"), {
    editable: true,
    layout: "ResponsiveGridLayout",
    labelSpanS: 3, labelSpanM: 3, labelSpanL: 2
});

oController.addInput(form, "address", "firstname");

const nameInput = oController.addInput(form, "address", "lastname");
nameInput.attachChange(function(oEvent) { ❶
    oController.queryAddresses(oEvent);
});

oController.addInput(form, "address", "street");
oController.addInput(form, "address", "city");
oController.addInput(form, "address", "postcode");
oController.addSelect(form, "address", "countryCode");
oController.addInput(form, "address", "phone");
```

❶   Concerning addresses, we want to avoid duplicates. Therefore, after entering the last name, a request is sent to query existing addresses. If matching addresses are found, a dialog is opened displaying those addresses which are already in the system.

If the 'orderAddress' route is being requested, the view needs to be prepared. For this, we use the onInit function of the connected controller and attach the _onRouteMatched function to the pattern-

Matched event of the Route. We also need to provide the requested address data. These data will be requested asynchronously. This is why we have to wait for the related event. By now, it should have become a routine to subscribe to the 'loading ready' event to be notified of available data (see Listing 15.6, "Controller subscribing to 'loading ready' events" and Listing 16.7, "Initial order controller").

Listing 17.3. Order address controller

```
sap.ui.define([
    "oum/controller/OrderBaseController",
    "oum/do/orders",
    "oum/do/Order",
    "oum/do/addresses",
    "oum/do/Address",
    "oum/do/countries",
    "oum/lib/ui"
], function(oController, orders, Order, addresses, Address, countries, ui) {
    "use strict";

    const orderAddressController = oController.extend("oum.controller.orderAddress", {
        onInit: function() {
            const eventBus = sap.ui.getCore().getEventBus();
            eventBus.subscribe("loading", "ready", this._handleLoaded, this);

            this.getRouter().getRoute("orderAddress")
                .attachPatternMatched(this._onRouteMatched, this);
        }
    });
});
```

The 'orderAddress' route requires both an id and a type parameter. For a new order not yet saved the fake order ID is "-1", in which case we can move on to set the address model.

If the id parameter refers to an existing order to be edited, we construct the Order entity object, which either finds the data in the orders collection or requests them from the server.

```
_onRouteMatched: function(oEvent) {
    const messagesContainer = this.getView().byId("messagesContainer");
    ui.handleMessage(messagesContainer);                    Any message to show?

    const args = oEvent.getParameter("arguments");
    const orderId = args.id;
    const type = args.type;

    this.orderId = orderId;                                 Used by the setAddressModel function
    this.addressType = type;

    let order;
    if (orderId == "-1") {                                  A new order?
        this.setAddressModel();
    } else {
        order = new Order(orderId);                         Get Order entity object
        if (!order.isLoading()) {                           Are the order data already loaded?
            this.setAddressModel();
        }
    }
}
```

```
      this.setHeaderTitle(type);
},

setHeaderTitle: function(addressType) {
   const pageTitle = this.getView().byId("pageTitle");
   pageTitle.setText(
      oui5lib.util.getI18nText("address." + addressType + ".pageTitle"));
}
```

The handler function for the 'loading ready' event has to act upon the 'order' and the 'countries' data being available. The 'countries' work just like the 'statuses' of the order view.

```
_handleLoaded: function(channel, eventId, eventData) {
   if (typeof eventData === "object") {
      if (eventData.entity === "order" && eventData.id == this.orderId) {
         this.setAddressModel();
      }
   } else {
      if (eventData === "countries") {
         this.setCountriesModel();
      }
   }
},
setCountriesModel: function() {
   const countrySelect = this.getView().byId("address_countryCode");
   countrySelect.setModel(countries.getModel(), "countries");
}
```

The setAddressModel function first gets the Order entity object, from which it gets the Address entity object for the requested address type. If that address hasn't been assigned yet, a new one is constructed. At this point, we are ready to set the 'address' model for the form.

```
setAddressModel: function() {
   this.prepareEditedOrder(this.orderId);
   const order = this.getEditedOrder();
   if (!(order instanceof oum.do.Order)) {
      throw new TypeError("Need an oum.do.Order to edit");
   }

   let address;
   switch(this.addressType) {
   case "billing":
      address = order.getBillingAddress();
      break;
   case "shipping":
      address = order.getShippingAddress();
      break;
   }
   if (address === null) {
      this.info("new Address");
      address = new Address();
   }

   const form = this.getView().byId("addressForm");
   form.setModel(address.getModel(), "address");
}
```

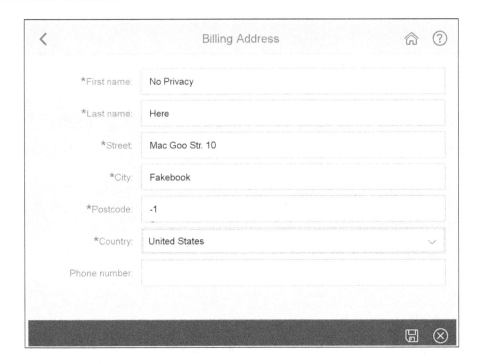

17.1. Search address dialog

There needs to be a way to find existing customers. This will help to avoid generating duplicates and save the user unnecessary input. Also, an existing customer may have preferences and be eligible for a discount, which could be carried along with the address data.

To achieve that, we have already attached a handler function to the lastname Input change event (see Listing 17.2, "Address form constructed with the FormController"). However, we will also need to add a button to the SimpleForm toolbar aggregation. Let us take care of that now.

```
form.setToolbar(
    new sap.m.Toolbar({
        content: [
            new sap.m.Button({
                type: "Emphasized",
                text: "{i18n>address.find}",
                tooltip: "{i18n>address.find.tooltip}",
                press: function() {
                    oController.openAddressDialog();
                }
            })
        ]
    })
);
```

The SelectDialog for addresses looks very similar to the one in Listing 16.11, "SelectProductDialog fragment". Check back there, if you are unsure how to write it, since we will take the liberty of omitting it here. The select address dialog works basically the same way as the product dialog we introduced in the previous chapter. Upon pressing the button the dialog is opened. The user inserts a search string and submits it. The search event handler function sends the request, and passes a callback function for the event of a successful response. The callback function takes the result and updates the model of the SelectDialog.

The user can cancel, which will close the dialog, or select one of the items, which will trigger the confirm event.

The difference to the previous example is that additionally to the button opening the dialog, we also want to use the dialog to show the user a list of addresses when he or she has filled in the lastname input field.

To summarize, we have two use cases for the dialog:

1. The first use case is about the user pressing the button to find an address. The dialog title text informs about finding an address. The query will return all addresses containing the given search string. There is no liveChange handler to avoid unnecessary data requests.

2. The second use case is triggered when the user leaves the last name input field. The dialog title text informs about already existing addresses having been found with the same last name as the one being filled in by the user. The addresses are popped up with an attached liveChange event handler filtering the matching addresses to conveniently find any fitting address, if it exists.

When the 'find address' button is pressed, the openAddressDialog function is called. To accommodate both use cases, we separate the issue of getting the dialog from opening it. And because the dialog might have been configured and used before to display addresses found for the lastname, we set the title, detach the filterAddresses function from the liveChange event, and clear the model data.

```
getAddressDialog: function() {
    if (typeof this.addressDialog === "undefined") {
        const selectAddressDialog = sap.ui.xmlfragment("oum.fragment.SelectAddressDialog", this);
        this.getView().addDependent(selectAddressDialog);

        selectAddressDialog.setModel(new sap.ui.model.json.JSONModel());
        this.addressDialog = selectAddressDialog;
    }
    return this.addressDialog;
},

openAddressDialog: function() {
    const addressDialog = this.getAddressDialog();

    addressDialog.bindProperty("title", "i18n>address.find");
    addressDialog.detachLiveChange(this.filterAddresses, this);
    addressDialog.getModel().setData([]);

    addressDialog.open();
}
```

The queryAddresses function is used both by the SelectDialog search and the Input change events. Luckily, both events return the input string with the same parameter named value. Only the matchType query parameter is different.

```
queryAddresses: function(oEvent) {
   const source = oEvent.getSource();

   let matchType = "Contains";
   if (source instanceof sap.m.SelectDialog) {
      this.getAddressDialog().setBusy(true);
   } else {
      matchType = "EQ";
   }
   const queryString = oEvent.getParameter("value");

   oui5lib.request.sendMappingRequest( ❶
      "address", "queryAddresses",
      {
         query: queryString,
         matchType: matchType
      },
      this.handleQueriedAddresses.bind(this)        Callback function for successful response
   );
}
```

❶   The request is configured in the address.json mapping file.

```
"queryAddresses": {
   "pathname": "queryAddresses",
   "method": "GET",
   "parameters": [
      {
         "name": "query",
         "required": true
      },{
         "name": "matchType"
      }
   ]
}
```

Following a successful response, the handleQueriedAddresses function is called. We know that the query originates from the SelectDialog when the busy property is true. Otherwise, it has arrived from the Input and we will only prepare and open the dialog if there are any matching addresses.

```
handleQueriedAddresses: function(responseObject, requestProps) {
   const addressDialog = this.getAddressDialog();

   if (responseObject.result) {
      const listBinding = addressDialog.getBinding("items");
      listBinding.filter([]);                            Clear any filters

      const addressData = responseObject.value;
      const model = addressDialog.getModel();
      model.setData(addressData);                        Update the model

      if (addressDialog.getBusy()) {
         addressDialog.setBusy(false);
         addressDialog.setNoDataText(
            oui5lib.util.getI18nText(
               "list.noMatchingData",
               [ requestProps.entity, requestProps.requestParameters.query ])
         );
```

```
         } else if (addressData instanceof Array && addressData.length > 0) {
            addressDialog.bindProperty("title", "i18n>addresses.found");
            addressDialog.attachLiveChange(this.filterAddresses, this);
            addressDialog.open();
         }
   } else {
      addressDialog.destroy();
      oui5lib.messages.showErrorMessage(
         oui5lib.util.getI18nText("query.result.error", [ requestProps.entity ]));
   }
}
```

When the user enters a `lastname` value and exits the input field, we interrupt the flow with a dialog popping up, in case there are addresses with an equal last name, offering the list of addresses. At this point, our only question is if one of the offered addresses is correct. To allow the user to quickly find a matching address, we filter the addresses on-the-fly, while he or she continues to input a string in the search field.

```
filterAddresses: function(oEvent) {
   const query = oEvent.getParameter("value");
   const listBinding = oEvent.getParameter("itemsBinding");
   const nameFilters = [
      new sap.ui.model.Filter("firstname", "Contains", query),
      new sap.ui.model.Filter("lastname", "Contains", query)
   ];
   listBinding.filter([
      new sap.ui.model.Filter({ filters: nameFilters, and: false })
   ]);
}
```

The `handleAddressSelected` function is called when the user selects an address in the dialog. It gets the address data of the selected item, adds them to the address collection and sets the related properties of the currently edited `Order` entity object. The order is marked as changed and the address model is updated.

```
handleAddressSelected: function(oEvent) {
   const selectedItem = oEvent.getParameter("selectedItem");
   const bindingContext = selectedItem.getBindingContext();
   const model = bindingContext.getModel();
   const addressData = model.getProperty(bindingContext.getPath());

   addresses.addData(addressData);
   const address = new Address(addressData.id);
   this.info("address selected: " + this.addressType + ":" + address.id);

   const order = this.getEditedOrder();
   order.setProperty(this.addressType + "AddressId", address.id);
   order.setProperty(this.addressType + "Name", address.getName());

   this.setOrderNotSaved(true);
   this.setAddressModel();
   this.resetRecordChanged();

   this.getAddressDialog().setNoDataText(null);
}
```

17.2. Validating and saving the address

We will leave the question open whether or not an existing address should be editable, as any changes may affect other orders already in the system. At this point of presenting our example application, we will simply move on to the question of saving the address. Pressing the 'Save' button triggers the submitRecord function.

```
submitRecord: function() {
   const form = this.getView().byId("addressForm");
   const addressData = form.getModel("address").getData();

   const addressSpecs = oui5lib.mapping.getEntityAttributeSpecs("address");
   const errors = oui5lib.validation.validateData(addressData, addressSpecs);
   if (errors.length > 0) {
      oui5lib.ui.handleValidationErrors(this.getView(), "address", errors);
      return;
   }

   ui.setBusy(true);
   this.saveAddress(addressData);
}
```

The code to validate the data is identical to the one in Listing 16.14, "Controller function to save an order". But the address form is different from the order overview form. Here, we have form elements to visualize the errors. This is what the oui5lib.ui.handleValidationErrors function is for.

Listing 17.4. Handle validation errors

```
function handleValidationErrors(view, modelName, errors, openMessageBox) {
   if (typeof openMessageBox !== "boolean") {
      openMessageBox = false;
   }
   let error, propertyName, control;
   for (let i = 0, s = errors.length; i < s; i++) {
      error = errors[i].split(":");
      propertyName = error[1];
      control = view.byId(modelName + "_" + propertyName);
      setControlValueState(control, false);
   }
   if (openMessageBox) {
      showValidationErrors(errors);
   }
}
oui5lib.ui.handleValidationErrors = handleValidationErrors;
```

The user can now tab through the elements, correct the wrong or missing entries and the related error state and the message will disappear.

If the address finally validates, the saveAddress function is called to send the request configured in the address mapping.

```
saveAddress: function(addressData) {
   oui5lib.request.sendMappingRequest(
      "address", "saveAddress",
      { "addressString": JSON.stringify(addressData) },
      this.addressSaved.bind(this)
   );
}
```

The callback function for the asynchronous saveAddress request has to add or update the address in the addresses collection. Depending upon the address type, it will then set the address ID to either the billingAddressId or shippingAddressId property of the Order entity object. We complete the data works updating the related address name with the help of the procAddresses function of the orders collection object (see Listing 12.10, "Function to add address names to orders").

After saving the address, we will leave the address view and navigate to the order overview. Before doing that, we set a message to be displayed on the order view to notify the user of successfully saving the address.

```
addressSaved: function(responseObject) {
    ui.setBusy(false);

    if (!responseObject.result) {
        oui5lib.messages.showErrorMessage(
            oui5lib.util.getI18nText("address.saved.error"));
        return;
    }

    const addressData = responseObject.value;
    const addressId = parseInt(addressData.id);
    addresses.addData(addressData);

    let propertyName;
    switch(this.addressType) {
    case "billing":
        propertyName = "billingAddressId";
        break;
    case "shipping":
        propertyName = "shippingAddressId";
        break;
    }

    const order = this.getEditedOrder();
    const orderData = order.getData();
    if (orderData[propertyName] !== addressId) {
        orderData[propertyName] = addressId;
    }
    orders.procAddresses(orderData);

    oum.message = {
        text: oui5lib.util.getI18nText("address.saved.success"),
        type: "Success"
    };
    this.getRouter().vNavTo("order", {
        id: order.id
    });
    this.resetView();
}
```

17.3. Reverting changes and resetting the view

To complete the controller, we have to implement the resetView and revertChanges functions, as required by Listing 16.16, "OrderBaseController function to handle unsaved changes".

The address may have been validated and controls marked with an error state. However, for the resetView function we need to clear all value states. As this is a recurring issue, the function is designed to work for both the sap.ui.layout.form.SimpleForm and the sap.ui.layout.form.Form and added to the oui5lib.ui namespace.

Listing 17.5. Reset value states of SimpleForm or Form

```
function resetValueStates(form) {
   if (typeof form.getContent === "function") {
      const content = form.getContent();
      content.forEach(function(control) {
         if (typeof control.setValueState === "function") {
            control.setValueState("None");
         }
      });
   } else if (typeof form.getFormContainers === "function") {
      const formContainers = form.getFormContainers();
      formContainers.forEach(function(formContainer) {
         const formElements = formContainer.getFormElements();
         formElements.forEach(function(formElement) {
            const formFields = formElement.getFields();
            formFields.forEach(function(formField) {
               if (typeof formField.setValueState === "function") {
                  formField.setValueState("None");
               }
            });
         });
      });
   }
}
```

With this function in place, resetting the view is fairly straightforward.

```
resetValueStates: function() {
   const addressForm = this.getView().byId("addressForm");
   oui5lib.ui.resetValueStates(addressForm);
},
resetView: function() {
   this.setEditedOrder(undefined);

   this.resetRecordChanged();
   this.resetValueStates();

   const addressForm = this.getView().byId("addressForm");
   addressForm.setModel(null, "address");
}
```

Since we took the precaution of working with cloned data (see Listing 16.6, "Common controller for order detail controllers to extend"), reverting any changes is even simpler. The setAddressModel will get the currently edited Order, which hasn't been modified, and the related Address from the address collection to set the 'address' model anew.

```
revertChanges: function() {
   this.resetRecordChanged();
   this.resetValueStates();

   this.setAddressModel();
}
```

17.4. Summary

With this chapter, we have come to the end of our example application.

Being already familiar with the code to construct the address view returning a `Page`, we constructed a `SimpleForm` and added form elements to it using the `FormController`.

To help the user find addresses already stored on the server-side, we provided a dialog to query addresses. We also used the dialog to interrupt the user if the given last name matched any existing addresses.

Again, we went through the flow of validating and saving the address. Finally, we did some house-cleaning, reverting any changes and resetting the view.

Chapter 18. Write user interface tests

Normally, we ought to write unit and integration tests while developing features. Yet, while developing the user interface parts, I have to continuously reload and look at the pages, until they finally meet the given expectations. At that point, I am usually happy to leave them behind. Admittedly, therefore, I am not the best teacher for user interface tests.

My attitude is quite different, however, when working with data, like implementing domain logic and posting data. Without test, I don't feel confident about my work, and that makes me nervous. Knowing this keeps me motivated to spend the time and energy to write tests and explore problems to increase my confidence level.

Having said that, I owe you, the reader, an introduction into OPA (One Page Acceptance) testing of UI5 applications.

The OPA framework speaks about arrangements, actions and assertions. It utilizes QUnit as test runner and also for the Assertions [https://api.qunitjs.com/assert/].

The OPA framework and the OPA5 extension give us an API to access the UI5 controls and drive the user interface. Using the sap/ui/test/opaQunit adapter, we get three objects to work with: Given (arrangements), When (actions) and Then (assertions).

18.1. One Page Acceptance testing

Let us begin with the basic test-runner code and a simple test sequence, navigating from the entry to the orders page, for which we verify a couple of assertions. We create a file test/oumTests.js.

Listing 18.1. Orders page

```
 1 jQuery.sap.require("sap.ui.thirdparty.qunit");
 2 jQuery.sap.require("sap.ui.qunit.qunit-css");
 3 jQuery.sap.require("sap.ui.qunit.qunit-junit");
 4 jQuery.sap.require("sap.ui.qunit.qunit-coverage");
 5
 6 QUnit.config.autostart = false;
 7
 8 sap.ui.require([
 9    "sap/ui/test/Opa5",
10    "sap/ui/test/opaQunit",
11    "oum/test/arrangements/Common"
12 ], function (Opa5, opaTest, Common) {
13
14    Opa5.extendConfig({
15       arrangements: new Common(),
16       autoWait: true,
17       timeout: 10,
18       pollingInterval: 200
19    });
20
21    sap.ui.require([
```

```
22          "oum/test/entry",
23          "oum/test/orders"
24      ], function() {
25          QUnit.module("Orders Page journey");
26          opaTest("Should test the orders view", function(Given, When, Then) {
27              Given.start_the_app();
28
29              When.on_the_entry_page.press_tile_to_List_of_Orders();
30              Then.on_the_orders_page
31                  .should_be_a_List_of_Orders()
32                  .should_be_no_queryForm()
33                  .should_be_a_button_to_show_the_queryForm();
34
35              When.on_the_orders_page.press_Show_Query_Form();
36              Then.on_the_orders_page
37                  .should_be_a_queryForm()
38                  .should_be_a_button_to_hide_the_queryForm()
39
40              When.on_the_orders_page.press_Hide_Query_Form();
41              Then.on_the_orders_page
42                  .should_be_no_queryForm()
43                  .and.iTeardownMyAppFrame();
44          });
45
46          QUnit.start();
47      });
48 });
```

If done right, reading the above test code should be self-explanatory. Nevertheless, let us take the time to go step by step. In line 11 we require the test/arrangements/Common.js resource, which is used to configure Opa arrangements (line 15). We provide only one common arrangement to start_the_app (line 27), which calls the Opa5 function iStartMyAppInAFrame.

```
sap.ui.define([
    "sap/ui/test/Opa5"
], function(Opa5) {

    const Common = Opa5.extend("oum.test.arrangement.Common", {
        start_the_app: function () {
            return this.iStartMyAppInAFrame("http://localhost:8801/index.html");
        }
    });

    return Common;
});
```

For each view, we create a corresponding test file with arrangements, actions and assertions. For this, Opa5 provides the createPageObjects function. The 'frame' code for each of the test files will always be similar, only with different requirements depending upon the actions and matchers being used.

For the entry page, we add two actions to Press the tiles titled "List of Orders" and "Create a new Order", in effect navigating to the related views.

```
sap.ui.define([
   "sap/ui/test/Opa5",
   "sap/ui/test/actions/Press",
   "sap/ui/test/matchers/Properties"
], function(Opa5, Press, Properties){

   const pressTile = function(headerText){
      return this.waitFor({
         controlType: "sap.m.GenericTile",
         matchers: new Properties({
            header: headerText
         }),
         actions: new Press(),
         errorMessage: "Didn't find GenericTile with headerText: " + headerText
      });
   };

   Opa5.createPageObjects({
      viewName: "oum.view.entry",
      on_the_entry_page: {
         actions: {
            press_tile_to_List_of_Orders: function () {
               return pressTile.call(this, "List of Orders");
            },
            press_tile_to_New_Order: function () {
               return pressTile.call(this, "Create a new Order");
            }
         }
      }
   });
});
```

The Opa5.waitFor function appends a command to the Opa test queue. It takes an object of options. Here is a list of the essential ones:

- controlType (string): Specify the type of control to match.
- visible (boolean): Exclude unrendered and invisible controls. Defaults to true
- matchers (array): Specify an array of matchers. Only controls will be collected, for which each of the matchers returns 'true'.
- success (function): Handler function to be called when at least one control meets all the given conditions.
- errorMessage (String): Will be handed to QUnit if no control could be found before timeout.
- actions (array): Will be executed for each of the matching controls.

For the 'orders' view, we have to implement the test functions (lines 30 to 42), starting with the assertions that there should_be_a_List_of_Orders, should_be_no_queryForm and should_be_a_button_to_show_the_queryForm, followed by the press_Show_Query_Form action, changing two of the previous assertions, that now there should_be_a_queryForm and should_be_a_button_to_hide_the_queryForm. Finally, we press_Hide_Query_Form and verify that there should_be_no_queryForm.

As usual, we don't want to repeat similar code.

We can recycle some code here: To match the button toggling the visibility of the query form, we can use the same properties. Depending upon the state of the button ("Show", "Hide"), the value of the text and icon properties will differ.

```
const getToggleQueryFormButtonProperties = function(text) {
   return {
      controlType: "sap.m.Button",
      matchers: new Properties({
         text: text + " Query Form",
         icon: "sap-icon://" + text.toLowerCase()
      })
   };
};
```

Having prepared the properties to match the button, we can check its presence with the expected text and icon with the following function:

```
const checkQueryFormButton = function(text){
   const buttonProperties = getToggleQueryFormButtonProperties(text);
   buttonProperties.success = function(buttons) {
      assert.equal(buttons.length, 1,
                  "Page should have exactly one Button to " + text + " the query form");
   };
   buttonProperties.errorMessage = "Missing the button to " + text + " the query form";
   return this.waitFor(buttonProperties);
};
```

The function to execute the Press action on the button is even shorter:

```
const toggleQueryForm = function(text) {
   const buttonProperties = getToggleQueryFormButtonProperties(text);
   buttonProperties.actions = new Press();
   return this.waitFor(buttonProperties);
};
```

After preparing the functions for the button, we can now move on to the function test for the presence and visibility of the query form.

```
const isQueryFormVisible = function(isVisible){
   return this.waitFor({
      controlType: "sap.ui.layout.form.Form",
      matchers: new Properties({                            Is the Form visible?
         visible: isVisible
      }),
      visible: false,
      success: function(forms) {
         const form = forms[0];
         assert.equal(form.getToolbar().getContent()[0].getText(),    Verify the toolbar title text
                     "Change Query Parameters",
                     "Query form visible? " + isVisible);
      },
      errorMessage: "Missing the query form"
   });
};
```

For the tests to be run, we have to create a page object with the required actions and assertions.

```
sap.ui.require([
    "sap/ui/test/Opa5",
    "sap/ui/test/actions/Press",
    "sap/ui/test/matchers/Properties"
], function (Opa5, Press, Properties) {
    ...
```
The above functions come in here
```
    Opa5.createPageObjects({
        viewName: "oum.view.orders",
        on_the_orders_page: {
            actions: {
                press_Show_Query_Form: function () {
                    return toggleQueryForm.call(this, "Show");
                },
                press_Hide_Query_Form: function () {
                    return toggleQueryForm.call(this, "Hide");
                }
            },
            assertions: {
                should_be_a_List_of_Orders: function() {
                    return this.waitFor({
                        controlType: "sap.m.List",
                        matchers: new Properties({
                            headerText: "List of Orders"
                        }),
                        success: function(lists) {
                            assert.ok(true);
                        },
                        errorMessage: "The List of Orders is missing"
                    });
                },
                should_be_a_button_to_show_the_queryForm: function() {
                    return checkQueryFormButton.call(this, "Show");
                },
                should_be_a_button_to_hide_the_queryForm: function() {
                    return checkQueryFormButton.call(this, "Hide");
                },
                should_be_no_queryForm: function() {
                    return isQueryFormVisible.call(this, false);
                },
                should_be_a_queryForm: function() {
                    return isQueryFormVisible.call(this, true);
                }
            }
        }
    });
});
```

Having implemented all the actions and assertions to make our first user interface test sequence, we only need the HTML page to run the test in a browser.

```
<!DOCTYPE HTML>
<html>
  <head>
    <meta http-equiv="content-type" content="text/html;charset=UTF-8"/>
    <title>OPA tests for OUM Example Component</title>

    <script id="sap-ui-bootstrap"
            src="resources/sap-ui-core.js"
            data-sap-ui-resourceroots='{
                "oum.test": "./test"
            }'>
    </script>

    <script src="test/oumTests.js"></script>
  </head>
  <body>
    <div id="qunit"></div>
    <div id="qunit-fixture"></div>
  </body>
</html>
```

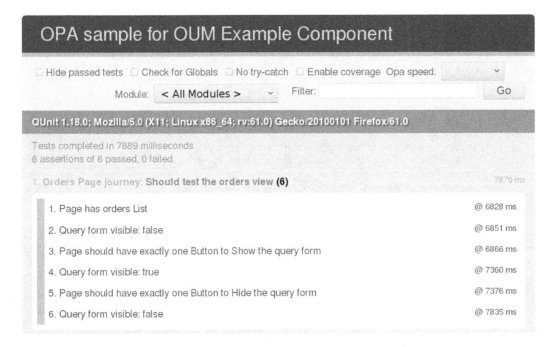

18.2. Matchers and Actions

To effectivly write tests, we need to learn how to unambiguously match controls. We find the available 'matchers' listed under namespace `sap.ui.test.matchers`. Again, this is only a selection. For the full list, refer to the OpenUI5 API.

- Properties
- PropertyStrictEquals
- AggregationEmpty

- AggregationFilled
- AggregationLengthEquals
- LabelFor

Let us look at examples matching controls and verifying assertions for the 'New Order' page.

If we come to the order view to create a new order, the line items table should be present, but without order lines.

```
should_be_one_empty_Ordered_Items_Table: function () {
    return this.waitFor({
        controlType: "sap.m.Table",
        matchers: [
            new Properties({
                headerText: "Ordered items:",
                mode: "Delete"
            }),
            new AggregationEmpty({
                name: "items"
            })
        ]
    });
}
```

For the orderNavigation view, we expect a list with three items, of which the last one should not be active.

```
should_be_the_orderSections_List: function () {
    return this.waitFor({
        controlType: "sap.m.List",
        matchers: [
            new Properties({
                mode: "SingleSelectMaster"
            }),
            new AggregationLengthEquals({
                name: "items",
                length: 3
            })
        ],
        success: function(lists) {
            assert.equal(lists.length, 1);

            const list = lists[0];
            assert.notOk(list.getItems()[2].isActive());
        }
    });
}
```

Besides the Press action, we can also use the EnterText action. To enter a new date into the start date field of the query orders form, we could write:

```
enter_a_startDate: function () {
   return this.waitFor({
      controlType: "sap.m.DatePicker",
      matchers: [
         new LabelFor({
            text: "From"
         })
      ],
      actions: new EnterText({
         text: "Oct 15, 2018"
      })
   });
}
```

18.3. Summary

This chapter introduced the One Page Acceptance testing framework shipped with UI5. We learned how to write user interface tests, using the OPA adapter for QUnit to describe the test scenario. Then, we implemented the tests with the help of OPA page objects providing functions grouped as arrangements, actions and assertions.

We concluded the chapter with a few more examples of how to use matchers and actions.

There is surely more to say about OPA-testing, which works quite nicely for matching and accessing UI5 objects. For further information, please take a look at the UI5 Developer Guide via topic Essentials > Testing > Integration Testing with One Page Acceptance Tests (OPA5).

Chapter 19. Automate development tasks with Grunt

For every project there are repetitive tasks which should be automated. Performing code analysis, running tests, generating documentation and building distribution packages are among the most common project tasks. In this chapter, we will only focus on some basic tasks every serious project needs.

There are some popular build and automation tools written in JavaScript. I use Grunt [https://gruntjs.com/] simply because I have got used to it. Other popular choices are Gulp [https://gulpjs.com/] or Brunch [http://brunch.io/].

19.1. Installing Grunt and Extensions

Grunt is available as a Node.js package/module. Like gem and bundler for Ruby, npm is the package management tool for Node.js.

To be able to use the **npm** (node package manager) command line tool, we need a package.json in the project root folder. For detailed information about the package.json file, please refer to the npm documentation (Working with package.json [https://docs.npmjs.com/getting-started/using-a-package.json]).

If not otherwise specified, npm installs packages into the node_modules subfolder. It also creates a file package-lock.json, where basic information about all installed packages and their dependencies are listed. Like the name suggests, it locks versions for the complete dependency tree. To avoid inconsistencies and surprises, add the package-lock.json to the versions control system.

npm is easy to use, but comes with a culture of continuously changing packages. Moreover, packages usually come with many dependencies. This leads to a situation, where our work depends upon hundreds of packages of different quality.

For developers just interested in using certain capabilities, we have to balance the need for timely bug fixes with the risk of importing bugs and breaking things on our side by updating the packages. We don't want our work to be unnecessarily disturbed by external dependencies. On the other hand, bug fixes need to be incorporated quickly. What can we do?

All Node.js packages are supposed to apply semantic versioning, where the version number has three parts:
1. Major version number
2. Minor version number
3. Patch version

We have to decide about our strategy to update the packages. If we don't specify a version number, npm will always take the latest release. On the other hand, we can also install a particular version and stick with it.

Listing 19.1. Install package grunt and add it as development dependency

```
npm install grunt --save-dev --save-exact grunt@1.0.3
```

Executing the command, npm will add the following entry into the `package.json`:

```
"devDependencies": {
    "grunt": "1.0.3"
}
```

If we want to allow npm to just install patches, we change the version string to `"~1.0.3"`. To have npm also install minor version upgrades, we specify `"^1.0.3"`, which is the default if we omit the `--save-exact` command line switch.

How we handle updates and upgrades depends upon the particular project we work on. The likelihood of elder versions not getting patched is high. Updating minor versions and upgrading to major versions requires constant attention and development. For a book, we better specify exact versions and upgrade only for another edition, if there will be one.

To use Grunt effectively, we have to choose among hundreds of so called plugins covering various tasks. The following grunt plugins are used for the examples of this chapter:

- grunt-available-tasks, version "0.6.3"
- grunt-contrib-clean, version "2.0.0"
- grunt-contrib-copy, version "1.0.0"
- grunt-contrib-compress, version "1.4.3"
- grunt-eslint, version "3.3.0"
- grunt-jsdoc, version "2.3.0"
- grunt-openui5, version "0.15.0"
- grunt-contrib-uglify-es, version "3.3.0"

19.2. Basic Grunt Setup

We use a `GruntRefs.json` file to define the paths to various files. This helps to keep the main grunt configuration file consistent while allowing us to flexibly organize the project folders.

```
{
    "webroot": "webapp",
    "controller": "webapp/controller",
    "fragment": "webapp/fragment",
    "view": "webapp/view",
    "lib": "webapp/lib",
    "i18n": "webapp/i18n",
    "css": "webapp/css",
    "img": "webapp/img",
    "oui5lib": "webapp/oui5lib",
    "domainObject": "webapp/domainObjects",
    "mapping": "webapp/domainObjects/mapping",
    "test": "webapp/test",
    "spec": "webapp/test/spec",
    "build": "build",
    "dist": "dist",
    "tmp": "build/tmp"
}
```

The following `Gruntfile.js` loads the above `GruntRefs.json` and all the tasks we are going to use. Initially, only the `availabletasks` task is configured and registered. Other tasks will be added throughout this chapter.

```
module.exports = function (grunt) {
   "use strict";

   grunt.initConfig({
      package: grunt.file.readJSON("package.json"),          Read package.json
      dirs: grunt.file.readJSON("GruntRef.json"),

      availabletasks: {
         tasks: {
            options: {
               groups: {
                  "Code quality": ["lint", "gendoc"],
                  "Build": ["dist"],
                  "Default": ["availabletasks"]
               },
               descriptions: {
                  "lint": "Run eslint for code analysis.",
                  "gendoc": "Generates html documentation.",
                  "dist": "Build distribution package.",
                  "availabletasks": "List available tasks."
               },
               hideUngrouped: true
            }
         }
      }
   });
   grunt.loadNpmTasks("grunt-available-tasks");
   grunt.loadNpmTasks("grunt-contrib-clean");
   grunt.loadNpmTasks("grunt-contrib-copy");
   grunt.loadNpmTasks("grunt-contrib-compress");
   grunt.loadNpmTasks("grunt-jsdoc");
   grunt.loadNpmTasks("grunt-eslint");
   grunt.loadNpmTasks("grunt-openui5");

   grunt.registerTask("default", ["availabletasks"]);        Register 'availabletasks' as default
};
```

If we run **grunt** from the command prompt, we just get a status message from the default task.

```
cahein@nobux:~/projects/book/Code-Devel$ grunt
Running "availabletasks:tasks" (availabletasks) task
```

Default
```
availabletasks    ->  List available tasks.
```

Build
```
dist              =>  Build distribution.
```

Code quality
```
gendoc            =>  Generates html documentation.
lint              =>  Run eslint for code analysis.
```

Done.

In the following sections we will see how each of the tasks is being configured and registered.

19.3. Linting

Automatically shecking code for errors and potential problems helps us to improve the quality of our code and saves time. This is often called 'linting'. My favorite JavaScript linting tool is eslint. It is highly configurable and therefore adaptable to particular project conventions. This is especially important because JavaScript lacks generally accepted code conventions. Additionally, the messages it generates are short and focused. Eslint is a generally useful node package and may be installed system-wide ('globally') with the following command:

```
npm install eslint -g
```

By default, eslint expects a configuration file named `.eslintrc.json`. For the book project, I use the following coding rules:

```
{
    "env": {
        "browser": true,
        "jquery": true,
        "es6": true
    },
    "extends": "eslint:recommended",
    "parserOptions": {
        "sourceType": "module"
    },
    "rules": {
        "no-extra-semi": 1,
        "no-inner-declarations": "error",
        "curly": "error",
        "no-eval": "error",
        "no-new-wrappers": "error",
        "no-array-constructor": "error",
        "no-mixed-spaces-and-tabs": "error",
        "linebreak-style": [ "error", "unix" ],
        "quotes": [ "error", "double" ],
        "semi": [ "error", "always" ],
        "indent": [
            "warn", 3, {
                "FunctionDeclaration": { "parameters": "first" },
                "FunctionExpression": { "parameters": "first" },
                "CallExpression": { "arguments": "first" },
                "ObjectExpression": "first"
            }
        ]
    },
    "globals": {                              Global variables
        "sap": true,
        "jQuery": true,
        "oum": true,
        "oui5lib": true
    }
}
```

With the configuration in place, we can easily run eslint from the command line: `eslint **/*.js` will lint all JavaScript files in the current directory and all subdirectories.

But we may also want to integrate linting with the build process. For this purpose, we need to configure a grunt task. The eslint configuration file is expected to be found in the project root folder along with the package.json, Gruntfile.js and GruntRefs.json.

Listing 19.2. Configure the eslint task in the Gruntfile

```
eslint: {
  options: {
    configFile: ".eslintrc.json"
  },
  target: [
    "<%= dirs.webroot %>/*.js",
    "<%= dirs.view %>/**/*.js",
    "<%= dirs.controller %>/**/*.js",
    "<%= dirs.fragment %>/**/*.js",
    "<%= dirs.lib %>/**/*.js",
    "<%= dirs.domainObject %>/*.js",
    "!<%= dirs.webroot %>/oui5lib.js",
    "!<%= dirs.oui5lib %>/**/*.js"
  ]
}
```

After registering the task with

```
grunt.registerTask("lint", ["eslint"]);
```

we can now run it with **grunt lint**.

```
cahein@nobux:~/projects/book/Code-Devel$ grunt lint
Running "eslint:target" (eslint) task

/home/cahein/projects/book/Code-Devel/webapp/view/help/index.view.js
  2:28  warning  'oController' is defined but never used  no-unused-vars

/home/cahein/projects/book/Code-Devel/webapp/view/help/intro.view.js
  6:28  warning  'oController' is defined but never used  no-unused-vars

/home/cahein/projects/book/Code-Devel/webapp/controller/entry.controller.js
  14:33  warning  'oEvent' is defined but never used  no-unused-vars

/home/cahein/projects/book/Code-Devel/webapp/domainObjects/addresses.js
  6:8  warning  'addresses' is assigned a value but never used  no-unused-vars

/home/cahein/projects/book/Code-Devel/webapp/domainObjects/products.js
  6:8  warning  'products' is assigned a value but never used  no-unused-vars

�x 5 problems (0 errors, 5 warnings)


Done.
```

While these warnings may be annoying, they won't stop the building process we are looking at next.

19.4. Building the distribution package

To optimize the loading process and to make sure all dependencies have been loaded before the Component is initialized, the Component-preload.js must be created.

To generate such a file, we will use the `grunt-openui5` Node.js package.

 Until version 0.14.0, grunt-openui5 used the `uglify-js` package to minify the code, which only supports ECMAScript 5. If you have to use a previous version, you can get around this limitation by not minifying/uglifying the code included in the `Component-preload.js` by setting the `compress` property to `false`

```
openui5_preload: {
    component: {
        options: {
            resources: {
                cwd: "<%= dirs.webroot %>",
                prefix: "oum",
                src: [
                    "Component.js",
                    "Router.js",
                    "controller/**",
                    "fragment/**",
                    "view/**",
                    "i18n/*.properties",
                    "lib/**",
                    "!**/*~"                      Exclude backup files
                ]
            },
            dest: "<%= dirs.build %>/webapp",
            compress: true
        },
        components: "oum"
    }
}
```

The related task is registered with

```
grunt.registerTask("generatePreload", "openui5_preload");
```

 Since it is only needed as part of the "dist" task, the "generatePreload" task is not called directly. We, therefore, haven't added it to the `availabletasks`.

Having prepared the task to generate the `Component-preload,js` file, we can implement the next step of our distibution package building procedure.

The following task copies all files required by the application into the `build` folder.

```
copy: {
    dist: {
        files: [
            {
                src: [
                    "<%= dirs.webroot %>/index.html",
                    "<%= dirs.webroot %>/Component.js",
                    "<%= dirs.webroot %>/Router.js",
                    "<%= dirs.webroot %>/*.json",
                    "<%= dirs.webroot %>/oui5lib.js",
                    "<%= dirs.oui5lib %>/**",
                    "<%= dirs.i18n %>/i18n*.properties",
                    "<%= dirs.controller %>/**/*.js",
```

```
                "<%= dirs.fragment %>/**/*.js",
                "<%= dirs.fragment %>/**/*.xml",
                "<%= dirs.view %>/**/*.js",
                "<%= dirs.view %>/**/*.xml",
                "<%= dirs.lib %>/**/*.js",
                "<%= dirs.mapping %>/*.json",
                "<%= dirs.domainObject %>/*.js",
                "!<%= dirs.webroot %>/**/*~"          Exclude backup files
            ],
            dest: "<%= dirs.build %>/"
        }
    ]
  }
}
```

 It is important to specify the src property in a way that prevents any garbage files to be include in our distribution. For example, the above configuration would include any webapp/*.json file instead of just the manifest.json, oui5lib.json, and config.json we need.

After generating the Component-preload.js and copying the all the other application files into the build folder, the next task will compress them all into a zip archive to be saved into the dist folder. A timestamp is appended to avoid overwriting previously generated archives.

```
compress: {
   build: {
      options: {
         archive: "<%= dirs.dist %>/<%= package.name %>-webapp." +
                  "<%= grunt.template.today('yyyymmdd-HHMMss') %>.zip",
         mode: "zip"
      },
      files: [{
         expand: true,
         cwd: "<%= dirs.build %>/",
         src: [ "<%= dirs.webroot %>/**/*" ],
         dest: "/"
      }]
   }
}
```

Now, it's time for some house-cleaning: to make sure that we don't keep old garbage files alive, the build folder gets cleaned before building a new distribution archive.

```
clean: {
   build: {
      src: [ "<%= dirs.build %>" ]
   }
}
```

Combining all the steps, the "dist" task is registered with

```
grunt.registerTask("dist", [
   "clean:build",
   "lint",
   "generatePreload",
   "copy:dist",
   "compress"
]);
```

Running **grunt dist** will create an archive in the `dist` folder, which can be distributed. The only required resource not included in the archive are the UI5 resources. These are expected to be found under `resources`. If they are located anywhere else, the `index.html` must be modified accordingly.

19.5. Documenting the code and generating HTML

JSDoc doesn't really like all the JavaScript constructs we have used. It generates documentation, but most functions appear under "Global". To properly get the objects grouped, and the functions properly assigned, we need to use certain JSDoc constructs.

19.5.1. Controllers

To group the controllers into a separate category, they are marked with the `module` tag. Surely, controllers are no modules, but we have only a limited number of categories to choose from.

For example, we would add the following tag to our 'entry' controller:

```
/**
 * Homepage of the application. It is a jump-pad with tiles to enter different sections.
 * Offers the ability to switch the language.
 * @module oum.controller.entry
 */
```

The functions need no further specification to be properly assigned to the object, which will appear as "entry" under the "Modules" category.

```
/**
 * Used as handler for tile press events. Will call the {@link oum.Router.vNavTo} function
 * to navigate to the route added as custom data property 'routeName' to the tile.
 * @param oEvent {sap.ui.base.Event} The event object.
 */
routeTo: function(oEvent) {
    ...
}
```

Some of our fragments may also benefit from getting some documentation.

```
/**
 * Use this fragment to get a 'Bar' with 'Save' and 'Cancel' buttons.
 * To work, it requires a controller implementing both a 'saveRecord' and 'cancel' function.
 * @module oum.fragment.CancelAndSaveBar
 */
```

19.5.2. Custom Namespaces

To group the `oum.lib` and `oum.do` namespaces, we simply use the `namespace` tag, which we have to add somewhere in the file.

```
/**
 * The eventHandlers namespace contains functions to handle events
 * published via sap.ui.core.EventBus.
 * @namespace oum.lib.eventHandlers
 */
```

This will allow JSDoc to group the `oum` namespaces under the "Namespaces" category of the generated documentation.

Unfortunately, to get the functions properly assigned to the namespace, we have to explicitly use the memberof tag. And if the function name is assigned to the namespace with a different name than the function name, it must be specified with the function tag.

```
/**
 * Use this function to subscribe to the 'xhr' events emitted from the
 * oui5lib.request namespace.
 * @function handleRequestFailure
 * @memberof oum.lib.eventHandlers
 * @param {string} channelId Is always 'xhr'.
 * @param {string} eventId Can be 'error', 'status', or 'timeout'.
 * @param {object} eventData Has keys 'entity', 'request', 'requestParameters', 'xhrObj'.
 */
function handleRequestFailure(channelId, eventId, eventData) {
    ...
}
```

19.5.3. Classes

The Router and Component are described as classes with the class tag:

```
/** @class oum.Router */
```

Again, the memberof tag is required to get the function documentation properly assigned.

```
/**
 * Navigate to the given route.
 * @memberof oum.Router
 * @param routeName {string} The route name to navigate to.
 * @param oParameters {object} Parameters as specified by the route pattern.
 * @param bReplace {boolean} Set 'true' to navigate without history entry.
 */
vNavTo: function(sName, routeParameters, bReplace) {
    ...
}
```

19.5.4. Interfaces

The OrderBaseController is not really anything of the above. It may be seen as some kind of interface. This is specified with the interface tag.

```
/**
 * Extends the oui5lib FormController with some common functions for the order detail views.
 * @interface oum.controller.OrderBaseController
 */
```

Sadly, the JSDoc generator needs the memberof tag again to correctly process the contained functions.

```
/**
 * Function to prepare the order entity object to be currently edited.
 * Use the {@link oum.controller.getEditedOrder} function to get the object.
 * @memberof oum.controller.OrderBaseController
 * @param {number} orderId The order ID.
 * @public
 */
prepareEditedOrder: function(orderId) {
    ...
}
```

19.5.5. Generating the documentation

Now, let's get back to the grunt tasks: The JSDoc task is configured to parse all JavaScript files in the web root folder and generate the documentation into the doc folder.

```
jsdoc: {
  dist: {
    src: [
      "<%= dirs.webroot %>/*.js",
      "<%= dirs.controller %>/**/*.js",
      "<%= dirs.fragment %>/**/*.js",
      "<%= dirs.lib %>/*.js",
      "<%= dirs.domainObject %>/**/*.js"
    ],
    dest: "doc"
  }
}
```

To clean up the doc folder before generating the documentation, we add an entry to the "clean" section of the configuration.

```
clean: {
  ...
  doc: {
    src: [ "doc" ]
  }
}
```

After registering the task

```
grunt.registerTask("gendoc", ["clean:doc", "jsdoc"]);
```

we can generate the documentation with **grunt gendoc**.

19.6. Summary

This chapter introduced the reader to the issue of automating the most important project-related tasks. After a few introductory words about the node package manager, we learned how to install grunt and grunt plugins.

After looking at general grunt configuration, our first real task concerned code quality. We had eslint check our code and print out its report. Running eslint without errors was made mandatory for the build task.

Implementing a build task required us to generate a `Component-preload.js`, copy all the files required for the application, and to zip them into an archive with a timestamp.

To complete this chapter, we saw how JSDoc can be used to document our code. The related task generates the code-embedded project documentation.

Appendix A. More interesting controls

We omitted to present a number of UI5 controls, which are quite useful. If you want to explore them, look at the Samples included in the OpenUI5 SDK. You will find the related code examples in the `test-resources/sap/m/demokit/sample` folder. Here is the list:

- `sap.m.Tree`: With this control, you can easily create a hierarchical tree structure from some JSON. Each level can be expanded and collapsed, and one or multiple nodes selected. The control even enables the user to re-order the nodes with drag-and-drop.

- `sap.ui.table.Table`: The control is designed to present and handle huge amounts of data while still remaining performant. We excluded this control in favor of the `sap.m.Table`, which is the 'responsive' table variant.

  A interesting subclass of the `sap.ui.table.Table` is the `sap.ui.table.TreeTable`, which can be used to present hierarchical data as a table.

- `sap.m.Menu`: If you need a hierarchical menu, use this control. It has a `title` and an `items` aggregation for an array of `sap.m.MenuItem` controls, which themselves have an `items` aggregation for multi-level menus.

- `sap.ui.unified.FileUploader`: The control provides a classical 'Browse' input field. It is a highly configurable and flexible control.

- `sap.m.UploadCollection`: If you need to handle collections of files, which can be grouped and sorted, with flexible upload and download capabilities, this is the control to use

- `sap.m.Wizard`: This is a very helpful control if you have to implement some multi-step process, like, for example, a complex configuration with choices leading onto different paths, or a usual online shop checkout.

- `sap.m.PlanningCalendar`: This control is designed to display colorized calendar entries (`sap.ui.unified.CalendarAppointment`) for a list of persons. It is a quite powerful control, especially when combined with a `sap.m.Popover` to show or edit appointment details. Appointments can even be moved by drag-and-drop.

- `sap.m.QuickView`: Consider this control, if you have to show detail information about an object. The information can be grouped and linked.

  The QuickView will display in a `sap.m.Popover` on large screens, usually placed right to the opening link, and as a full-screen dialog on mobile devices. It is is constructed with a number of special controls: QuickViewCard, QuickViewPage, QuickViewGroup and QuickViewGroupElement.

  Read more about how it is meant to be used: Fiori Guidelines: QuickView [https://experience.sap.com/fiori-design-web/quickview/].

- `sap.ui.layout.DynamicSideContent`: Sometimes we want to show additional content on the side of the main content. The additional content should not be critically important, because it will disappear out of view if the screen width becomes too narrow. This is the appropriate control to utilize the full space on wide screens.

• Feeds: To display feeds, you can combine the `sap.m.FeedInput` and `sap.m.FeedListItem` controls.

Index

Glossary

A

Aggregations

An aggregation is a special relation between two UI element types. It is used to define the parent-child relationship within the tree structure. The parent end of the aggregation has cardinality 0..1, while the child end may have 0..1 or 0..*. The element's API offers convenient and consistent methods to deal with aggregations (e.g. to get, set, or remove target elements). Examples are table rows and cells, or the content of a table cell.
—UI5 Documentation: Glossary

Associations

An association is a type of relation between two UI element types which is independent of the parent-child relationship within the tree structure. Directed outgoing associations to a target of cardinality 0..1 are supported. They represent a loose coupling only and are thus implemented by storing the target element instance's ID. The most prominent example is the association between a label and its field.
—UI5 Documentation: Glossary

Asynchronous Module Definition

To control asynchronous loading of JavaScript code, a Asynchronous Module Definition may be used. It describes modules and their dependencies. A loader like RequireJS will take care of asynchronously loading modules and handling their dependencies on the basis of the AMD.

C

Cross-Origin Resource Sharing

Cross-Origin Resource Sharing (CORS) is a mechanism that uses additional HTTP headers to tell a browser to let a web application running at one origin (domain) have permission to access selected resources from a server at a different origin. A web application makes a cross-origin HTTP request when it requests a resource that has a different origin (domain, protocol, and port) than its own origin.
—Mozilla Developer Documentation: CORS

For more information, visit the W3C Recommendation [https://www.w3.org/TR/cors/].

Cascading Style Sheets

CSS is based upon a W3C Specification defining a stylesheet language used to present HTML documents. The first Recommendation of specification was published in May 1998. CSS remained stable for many years, but was supplemented with specifications of media queries and selectors.

D

Document Object Model   The Document Object Model (DOM) is a programming API for
                                     HTML and XML documents. It defines the logical structure of
                                     documents and the way a document is accessed and manipulat-
                                     ed. In the DOM specification, the term "document" is used in
                                     the broad sense ...
                                                  —W3C Document Object Model Specification

I

IndexedDB   IndexedDB is a transactional database system, like an SQL-
                                     based RDBMS. However, unlike SQL-based RDBMSes, which
                                     use fixed-column tables, IndexedDB is a JavaScript-based ob-
                                     ject-oriented database. IndexedDB lets you store and retrieve
                                     objects that are indexed with a key; any objects supported by the
                                     structured clone algorithm can be stored. You need to specify
                                     the database schema, open a connection to your database, and
                                     then retrieve and update data within a series of transactions.
                                                  —Mozilla Developer Documentation: IndexedDB API

J

JavaScript Object Notation   JSON is a text syntax that facilitates structured data inter-
                                     change between all programming languages. JSON is a syntax
                                     of braces, brackets, colons, and commas that is useful in many
                                     contexts, profiles, and applications.
                                                  —ECMA JSON Data Interchange Standard

M

Web App Manifest   A web application manifest is a JSON file containing informa-
                                     tion about an application. It is a relatively new initiative and the
                                     specification is not stable yet. For more information, visit the
                                     W3C Working Draft: Web App Manifest [https://www.w3.org/
                                     TR/appmanifest/]

Model-View-Controller pattern   The MVC pattern is used to implement user interfaces. By sep-
                                     arating different aspects of development into Model, View and
                                     Controller parts, the code can be better organized and is easier
                                     to test, maintain and modify.

mime type   The Multipurpose Internet Mail Extensions (MIME) type is a
                                     standardized way to indicate the nature and format of a docu-
                                     ment. It is defined and standardized in IETF RFC 6838. The In-
                                     ternet Assigned Numbers Authority (IANA) is the official body
                                     responsible to keeping track of all official MIME types, and

you can find the most up-to-date and complete list at the Media Types page.

Browsers often use the MIME type (and not the file extension) to determine how it will process a document; it is therefore important that servers are set up correctly to attach the correct MIME type to the header of the response object.
—Mozilla Developer Documentation: Basics of HTTP MIME types

O

OASIS Open Data Protocol

OData is a OASIS Standard technically named "OASIS Open Data Protocol". The committee is presided by SAP and Microsoft with several other major companies involved. The current version is OData 4. It specifies a standard way of defining REST services and how to provide metadata about the defined entities and collections. It also includes specifications about parameters concerning paging, sorting, filtering and searching.

R

Responsive application

A responsive web application adapts to different devices. This is done by using style directives in combination with media queries. Depending upon the visible space of a device, the user interface displays differently.

X

eXtensible Markup Language

XML is a flexible markup language derived from the SGML (Standard Generalized Markup Language) standard, which is a way of defining markup languages via a DTD (Document Type Declaration). The most widely known markup language is HTML. XML is still quite popular as a data exchange format, although, nowadays, JSON has taken over as the primary data exchange format.

XML comes with further W3C specifications like XML Schema (validate documents), XSLT (transform documents), XPath/XPointer (address nodes within a document), XQuery (query documents), XLink (define relationships within and between documents) and XInclude (compose one document from multiple smaller documents). These specifications are widely supported by various programming languages.

In the early versions, HTML was a regular SGML-application with DTDs. With XML becoming ever more popular,

HTML4 was later turned into XHTML1. The current HTML5 and XHTML5 specifications have identical vocabulary, but follow different parsing rules.